BENTHAM, LAW AND MARRIAGE

Bentham, Law and Marriage:

A Utilitarian Code of Law in Historical Contexts

Mary Sokol

continuum

Continuum International Publishing Group
The Tower Building
11 York Road
London SE1 7NX

80 Maiden Lane
Suite 704
New York, NY 10038

www.continuumbooks.com

First published 2011

British Library Cataloguing-in-Publication Data
A catalogue record for this book is available from the British Library.

ISBN 978-1-4411-3293-2

Typeset by Newgen Imaging Systems Pvt Ltd, Chennai, India
Printed and bound by in Great Britain

With thanks to Jerry Sokol for 'mutuall society, helpe and comfourte'

Contents

Acknowledgements

Some years ago, when reading Bentham's manuscripts on property law in the Special Collections Library at University College, London, I came across a reference to something Bentham described as a 'marriage code'. I was intrigued but other commitments forced a delay before I could begin to search for this code among the manuscripts, by then temporarily housed on the Hampstead Road in a chilly disused warehouse filled with strange cranking noises from the automatic car wash next door. But the manuscripts, and the helpful archivists, were unchanged and my curiosity led me into ever greater excavations. This book, the first look at Bentham's writing on the law of marriage, is the result.

I owe much to others who have encouraged and helped me at every stage. These include William Twining who first interested me in Bentham, those who attended the Bentham Seminars at University College and the British Legal History Conference held at University College in 2005. I am also grateful to the organizers and participants at the London Legal History Seminars, where I read two parts of my work.

An earlier version of Chapter 2 below was published in the *Journal of Legal History* 30 (April 2009), and is revised here with permission. Comments from Neil Jones were particularly useful. Detailed comments from David Lieberman on the manuscript of this book were also very helpful. F. R. Rosen and Penelope Corfield were kind enough to read and comment on chapters. Philip Schofield, director of the Bentham Project at University College, London, where I am an honorary research fellow, helped with numerous queries, references and ideas. I am grateful to everyone at the Project, and especially Michael Quinn and Catherine Fuller. I am also grateful to J. H. Burns, Andrew Lewis, Pete Morris, Tim Hitchcock, Margaret Bird and Father James Elston who responded to requests for help. All errors, needless to say, are my own.

Emmanuelle de Champs, Jane Desmarais and Pete Coles undertook French translations for me. Many librarians, especially the archivist Gill Furlong at the University College London Special Collections Library, gave friendly assistance.

I am also grateful to Rita Boswell at the Westminster School Library and the librarians at the Bibliothèque Publique et Universitaire in Geneva, the Manuscript and Archive Division of the New York Public Library, and the British Library for their help. Lastly, I thank Jerry Sokol, without whose help this book could not have been written.

Abbreviations and Manuscript References

All references to English law reports use standard abbreviations.

Jeremy Bentham, *An Introduction to the Principles of Morals and Legislation*. Intro. F. Rosen. Oxford: Clarendon Press, 1996, from The Collected Works of Jeremy Bentham, is referred to as *IPML*.

Jeremy Bentham, *Traites de Legislation Civile et Penale*. Ed. Etienne Dumont. Paris, 1802 and Jeremy Bentham, *The Theory of Legislation*. Ed. C. K. Ogden, trans. from the French of Etienne Dumont by Richard Hildreth. New York: Kegan Paul Trench, Trubner and Co. Ltd., 1931, are referred to as the *Traites*.

Jeremy Bentham, *Works*. Ed. John Bowring. 11 vols. Edinburgh: William Tait, 1838–43, is referred to as 'Bowring'.

Bentham Manuscripts in University College Library Special Collections are referred to, for example, as UC xi 66, which means box 11, folio 66; the ancient form of Roman numerals (not the modern 'subtractive style') used in the Bentham collection for box numbers, for example, lxxxx for 90, have been retained.

1

Introduction: Contemporary Contexts

Bentham's writings on the law of marriage are firmly based on the principle of utility, the 'greatest happiness' principle, which recognizes that all human actions are motivated by a wish to avoid pain and gain pleasure. 'Nature has placed mankind under the governance of two sovereign masters, *pain* and *pleasure*. It is for them alone to point out what we ought to do, as well as to determine what we shall do. On the one hand the standard of right and wrong, on the other the chain of causes and effects, are fastened to their throne.'[1] An act is good, or not, according to its certain or probable consequences. Accordingly, Bentham made extensive examination of the various kinds of harm, or 'mischief', that can result from an act.[2]

Bentham's writings on marriage placed sexual pleasure as an important source of pleasure for mankind, and reflect a proposition that men and women, equally subject to pleasure and pain, are equal. Many of Bentham's specific proposals would have been controversial in his time, and indeed some, fixed-term marriages, for example, might be found surprising today.

Bentham responded to Enlightenment debates on the secularization of marriage, natural law, and distinctions between nature and culture. He drew on the writings of the *philosophes* of the French Enlightenment, and the English and Scottish political thinkers Locke, Hume and Paley.[3] But Bentham's writings on marriage were not intended to constitute a philosophical essay, but rather he proposed a framework for a utilitarian code of law. Here he made a practical application of the principle utility to the problems of reforming the law of marriage, or in his words gave the 'forme' of the law its 'matière'.[4] The conjunction between Bentham's ideas on marriage which responded to a wider European intellectual context, and his unique project for a utilitarian code of law, made his writings on marriage remarkable in eighteenth-century England, and in many ways they are remarkable still.

At first, Bentham planned to create a digest, or compendium, of law which would include a law of marriage,[5] but he soon embarked on a more ambitious plan to write a vast, all-encompassing series of utilitarian codes of law, and the regulation of marriage was to take its place within this scheme. He began work on marriage in 1780s, returning to these papers during the 1790s and again in the early nineteenth century. Very few of these manuscripts have been published. At the end of this Introduction there will be an extended discussion of their complex provenance.

The fraction of Bentham's manuscripts on marriage that were published in French in 1802 were translated into English later in the nineteenth century. Not only did they represent just a limited number of manuscripts, but also their editors chose to suppress Bentham's discussions of some subjects. As a result, 'recovering the historical Bentham' by reading Bentham's own manuscripts on love and marriage, rather than the published recensions, must be the basis of any comment on Bentham's law of marriage.[6]

Recovering the historical Bentham means understanding Bentham as a historical figure: a man who was born, lived and died in a certain period of history, who was subject to the trials and tribulations of his time, and who lived a private life too. From this viewpoint Bentham's work is not seen as timeless, *sub specie aeternitatis*, as it may be viewed by philosophers. Therefore, I must ask: what can be added to our understanding of Bentham's work on marriage by looking at Bentham himself as a historical figure? It has sometimes been said that Bentham personally knew little about English law, and even less about the realities of marriage; that he had only a limited experience of practising as a lawyer, and none at all of married life. In this introductory chapter I will address and correct such views by looking first at Bentham's legal education and then, briefly, at his several failed attempts to marry. Next, I will consider Bentham in his contemporary context by examining his work in relation to eighteenth-century literary treatments of marriage. Finally, I will describe the manuscript sources and explain their relation to Bentham's published work on marriage.

BENTHAM'S LEGAL EDUCATION

As a result of his father's careful planning, Bentham's legal education accorded with the most advanced ideas on the subject current in eighteenth-century England. His education, and particularly William Blackstone's part in it, was an important factor in determining what kind of a lawyer the young Bentham would become. In 1760, at the age of 12, he left Westminster School for Queen's College, Oxford. There, as an undergraduate in 1763 he attended Blackstone's celebrated lectures on the common law.

Blackstone aimed to present 'a broadly humane, liberal, and scientific' overview of the law rather than 'inchoate technicalities' and the 'mystic dark discordant lore' of traditional common law education.[7] Bentham's undergraduate notebook, containing his notes on Blackstone's lectures, is extant. But it contains notes only on the first ten lectures, and not on the later ones which would have included the law of husband and wife, under the heading of 'Private Rights'.[8] Yet it is likely that Bentham heard these, for he later told John Bowring that he had attended the lectures with two other students both of whom took copious notes, 'which I attempted to do, but could not continue it, as my thoughts were occupied in reflecting on what I heard'.[9]

William Blackstone, who was then a fellow of All Souls and a member of the Bar, began to give students a series of private lectures on the common law in 1753. This was significant because at that time the common law was not taught at the universities which offered instruction only in the civil law. In 1758, Blackstone was elected to the Vinerian Chair of Common Law at Oxford and his formerly private lectures continued as the Vinerian lectures on the common law. In 1765 to great acclaim he published these lectures as the *Commentaries on the Laws of England*.[10]

It is hard to exaggerate the success of that book; it has been claimed that Blackstone's *Commentaries* 'would become the most celebrated, widely circulated, and influential law book ever published in the English language'.[11] Blackstone's fame spread far beyond England. More editions of Blackstone's *Commentaries* were published in French than in English. It was translated into Chinese and Japanese,[12] Catherine the Great of Russia ordered a translation, and King George III is said to have much admired the book.[13] Blackstone's greatest and possibly most lasting influence was in the United States.[14] 'Blackstone', as reading matter suitable for educated people, was considered sufficiently important for an abridgement of the *Commentaries* made especially for the use of women to be published in 1822. This was written as a series of letters from a father to his daughter, the author writing that he did not want his daughter to be a 'learned pedant in petticoats', but rather a 'cheerful companion' and an 'accomplished woman'.[15] We know that Bentham owned a first edition of Blackstone's *Commentaries*, and some of Bentham's work has been said to echo Blackstone's phraseology and arrangement,[16] making Blackstone 'a pervasive factor in Bentham's early thought'.[17]

If Bentham had been an undergraduate at Queen's College since 1760, and if Blackstone had been giving his lectures on the common law since 1753, why did Bentham wait until 1763 to hear them? One answer may be that in 1760 he simply could not afford to pay the six-guinea fee that Blackstone charged students attending his private lectures. But it is not completely certain that Blackstone did in fact continue to charge students a fee after 1758, for once appointed as the first Vinerian professor of Common Law he was in receipt of a salary of £200 per annum. However it seems likely that he did.[18]

So perhaps Bentham simply could not afford to attend the lectures. Although his father, Jeremiah Bentham, was a successful attorney,[19] he was far from liberal in his provision for his son at Oxford. John Bowring, Bentham's literary executor, records Bentham's recollections of hard times and comments that 'the narrow allowance which Bentham got from his father did not allow him to live without incurring debt at Oxford; and miserable he was when he was obliged to confess the fact to his father.'[20]

Another possibility is that until Bentham had decided to become a lawyer, he saw no need to attend Blackstone's lectures. Surprisingly, it is not at all clear just when Bentham made this important decision. Bowring records that at the age of 20 Bentham first discovered that he might have a 'genius' – in the sense of a characteristic disposition; inclination; bent, turn or temper of mind – for legislation.[21] Bentham had asked himself: 'Have I a genius for anything? What can I produce? What of all earthly pursuits is the most important? Legislation was the answer Helvetius gave.'[22]

But by the age of 20 Bentham was already studying at the Inns of Court. So we have no record of what motivated his earlier decision to become a barrister. Most probably, his father, like many another eighteenth-century father, made that decision for him. In any event he recorded no dissent from his father's choice of career for him. But he did recall the mortification and misery caused by his father's manoeuvres to force him to cultivate the powerful friends who would assist him professionally.[23] Bowring records Bentham's memories of trying to attract the attention of Sir Thomas Sewell, Master of the Rolls, whose son had been a fellow pupil at Westminster School. Jeremiah Bentham had often boasted to his son that as students he and Sir Thomas had been close friends, and that Jeremiah had once helped the financially embarrassed Sir Thomas to paper his chambers. But then they had gone their separate ways, Sir Thomas to the Bar and Jeremiah to practise as an attorney. Despite Bentham's obedient attempts, Sir Thomas took no notice of him at all and 'issued no invitation.'[24]

If we assume that it was indeed Jeremiah Bentham's decision that his son should become a barrister, and who decided on the form of his legal education, then it seems that Bentham senior chose to make arrangements for that legal education exactly as Blackstone had instructed in his inaugural lecture after his appointment to the Vinerian Chair in 1758. In this lecture, which he called 'A

Discourse on the Study of Law', Blackstone described the dire consequences of defective legal education for the nation as a whole. This, he claimed, was because failures in legal education were an integral part of the larger problem of failures in the administration of legal institutions.[25] The radical solution that Blackstone proposed was that the common law should be taught in the universities.[26]

Blackstone's stringent criticism of contemporary legal education, together with his great achievement in lecturing on the common law at Oxford, quickly attracted public attention and acclaim. These efforts were an essential part of his plans to reform the common law.[27] His lectures on the common law were given at a time that has been described as 'the nadir of the eighteenth century administration and institutional life of the law'. David Lemmings in particular describes the decline in civil litigation which reached a low point in 1750 when the Courts of King's Bench and Common Pleas heard about one-sixth of the number of suits they had heard in 1650. At the same time the great and unprecedented increase in parliamentary legislation had made an incursion into the common law courts' traditional territory.

Lawyers were much blamed for court delays and for the expense of litigation. Much of the public criticism centred on the work of attorneys and the high fees they charged which were seen as contributing to the decline of the work of the courts.[28] Jeremiah Bentham was just such an attorney with great professional ambitions for his clever son, whom he saw as a future Lord Chancellor. It is apparent that Jeremiah was well aware that the route to judicial office began by becoming a barrister, but that a barrister's legal education was problematic. As we have noted, the universities did not teach the common law but only civil law, and the Inns of Court had long since ceased to provide education in the common law. Officially, in order to qualify as a barrister it was necessary only to attend an Inn of Court and to eat a certain number of dinners in hall, which was called 'eating commons'. Following this, after a certain number of years the student was called to the Bar and admitted. Eighteenth-century students who wanted to practise in the common law courts pursued a usually solitary course of practical instruction, making their own empirical study of the decisions and pleadings in the legal literature, and sitting in court and observing procedure.[29]

Most barristers no longer followed the earlier practice of first attending one of the Chancery Inns, which had by then become the preserve of the attorneys. Another custom, which ended in the 1750s, was to apprentice Bar students to attorneys in the early stages of their training, after which they would attend one of the four 'noble Inns' of Court.[30] Many lawyers, including Lord Hardwick, had taken this route to qualification, but it was much out of favour by the time Bentham began his own legal training.[31] Blackstone particularly criticized the apprenticeship of barristers to attorneys, which he said produced a merely mechanical understanding of law, with no knowledge of the principles on which practice is founded. 'In subservience to attorneys [the student] will find he has begun at the wrong end. If practice be the whole he is taught, practice must also be the whole he will ever know: if he be not instructed in the elements and first principles upon which the rule of practice is founded, the least variation from established precedents will totally distract and bewilder him.'[32]

So, in accordance with Blackstone's strictures, Jeremiah Bentham arranged for his son first to attend the university and then to seek admission at one of the Inns of Court, as Blackstone himself had done.[33] In 1763, Jeremiah Bentham took his son away from Oxford and back to London, where he was admitted to Lincoln's Inn. In Bentham's day, many gentleman undergraduates would leave university without a degree after only a few terms' residence, and aspiring lawyers who did go there stayed at university on average somewhat longer than other undergraduates.[34] After 1762 there was a greater incentive for lawyers to remain on at university and take degrees, because in that year the Inns of Court formally reduced the time required for call to the bar to five years, and gave university graduates a two-year dispensation.[35]

Bentham had not graduated in November 1763 when his father took him from Oxford to Lincoln's Inn. Once admitted to the Inn he began to keep commons, eating his set number of dinners, and as a result the time he needed to serve before qualification began to run. Then, because there was no residence requirement for membership of Lincoln's Inn, in December 1763 he left London and returned to Oxford. He graduated as a Bachelor of Arts the next year, in December 1764, and then as a Master of Arts in 1767. In 1769, at the age of 21, Bentham was called to the Bar.

So Bentham must have attended Blackstone's lectures at Oxford soon after his return from Lincoln's Inn. To facilitate just such arrangements as Jeremiah Bentham had made for his son, Blackstone gave his Vinerian lectures in the common law during the Law Vacations. This timetabling policy enabled serious students like Bentham to hear lectures in the common law at University, and also attend the courts at Westminster Hall during the Law Terms.[36] Bentham's father had arranged what was at the time undoubtedly the best possible legal education for his son – one that dovetailed a university and legal education yielding maximum benefit to his son with the least expense to himself. In this light, it seems likely that Jeremiah Bentham paid for Bentham's attendance at Blackstone's lectures in 1763, just as he paid for his son's reserved seat at Westminster Hall to hear Lord Mansfield in court in the same year, no doubt considering these outlays a worthwhile investment.[37]

BENTHAM'S MARRIAGE PROPOSALS

In 1931, C. K. Ogden suggested that in 1776 Bentham anonymously published *A Fragment on Government*, his critique of Blackstone's *Commentaries*,[38] because he wanted to marry a girl named Mary Dunkley and hoped to support himself and his wife from the proceeds of his writing.[39] Bentham was 26 years old when he met the seventeen-year-old Mary Dunkley, whom he addressed as Polly, in 1774. Polly was the orphaned daughter of Thomas Dunkley, a surgeon in Essex, who had died in 1767 leaving his five children to be brought up by a relative (his wife having predeceased him).[40] His death had left his children penniless and so Polly had no fortune of her own to bring to a marriage. Bentham's hopes of marriage, however, were thwarted by his father who was 'implacably hostile to their marrying', and who threatened to disinherit him if he did so.[41]

Jeremiah Bentham was a successful City attorney who had accumulated considerable wealth from a successful legal practice and from dealing in property. His wealth and social position enabled him to live in the West End of London, and to send his son Jeremy to Westminster School rather than Charterhouse. Jeremiah opposed his son's desired marriage on the grounds that it could bring him neither fortune nor social advantage.[42] His behaviour was not unusually avaricious for the age, although he was less indulgent than many other fathers who would give in to emotional appeals from their children.[43] Propertied men in the eighteenth century commonly arranged marriages for their children in accordance with dynastic and financial concerns. But using coercion or force to compel a child to marry was not considered acceptable, and neither was ignoring a child's own preference. However, as Bentham found out, financial pressure and the threat of to disinheritance gave his father a powerful weapon.[44] Bentham, deeply upset, wrote bitterly to his brother Samuel that, despite indications to the contrary, his father most probably did love him, or at least loved him 'next to his money'.[45]

It is an irony that in 1745 Bentham's father, Jeremiah Bentham, had completely disregarded his own parents' objections to his marriage to Alice Whitehorn, then a young widow without fortune.[46] Having opposed Bentham's own fortuneless marriage, Jeremiah criticized the marriage of one of Bentham's friends, the successful attorney Richard Clarke. According to Jeremiah, Clarke had chosen his wife for her fortune alone. Jeremiah pronounced this to be a mistake because although 'Fortune is absolutely necessary to the Comfort of Life in any Station . . . there shod. be something engaging as well as agreeable in the mind and manner' of a wife. Jeremiah hoped neither of his sons, when they married, would make 'so great a Sacrifice', otherwise a 'man must be a Stoic even With a Fortune to be able to make a good Husband'.[47] By 1774, Bentham was a barrister living in Chambers at Lincoln's Inn, but there is little evidence that he practised law. Instead he supported himself from his writing and from an allowance of £103 per annum settled on him by his father in 1766. This was made up in part from an inheritance from his mother's marriage settlement and in part from rental monies from property, which Jeremiah arranged to be paid to his son directly.[48] Bentham thought this income inadequate to support a family, but refused to abandon his wish to marry Polly. We can gauge the accuracy of his opinion by comparing it with Mary Wollstonecraft's conviction in 1773 that £300 per annum was 'a great fortune' and that 'a woman of any oeconomy may live very genteelly on £150 a year', or with Jane Austen's belief in the 1790s that an income of £300 per annum was 'sufficient to make Edward Ferrars comfortable as a bachelor but keep him too poor to marry'.[49]

Bentham decided to marry without his father's help. He planned to raise money by renting out his chambers in Lincoln's Inn and moving into his friend John Lind's house in Holborn, where Polly would join him. There he would support his wife from his writing.[50] Bentham's scheme followed the example of many impecunious eighteenth-century intellectuals who made a sometimes precarious living by writing.[51] In accordance with this plan Bentham did move house. He had already translated Voltaire's *The White Bull* into English anonymously in 1774, and he planned further similar work.[52] But what Bentham called his 'marriage Scheme'[53] came to nothing, and at some point in time he abandoned his hopes of marrying Polly. It used to be thought that his relationship with her ended sometime in 1776, but there is some evidence that Bentham continued to see her long afterwards.[54] All that is known for certain is that on 13 April 1790 Polly Dunkley, now aged 32, married one John Rudd at St Peter's Church in Colchester, Essex.

Whatever the truth about the length of Bentham's relationship with Polly, his father urged a reluctant but eventually compliant Bentham to attempt to make a financially beneficial and socially prestigious marriage instead. Jeremiah selected an heiress, Sarah Stratton of Ripley, as a suitable wife who would add to his son's fortune and smooth his path to becoming Lord Chancellor. In letters to his brother Samuel, to whom he had earlier revealed his anguish about Polly, Bentham described his father's instructions and his pursuit of Sarah. But despite his endeavours Sarah Stratton chose to marry someone else, and Bentham did not seem unduly heartbroken at his failure.[55]

His next recorded attempt at marriage took place 13 years later, in 1789, when he was 41 years of age. He had known Caroline Fox since 1781 when he had met her, then a girl of 13, at the house of her uncle, William Petty, second Earl of Shelburne and first Marquis of Lansdowne (1737–1805). Lord Lansdowne, who surrounded himself with a circle of intellectuals, had visited Bentham's chambers in Lincoln's Inn in 1781 in order to make his acquaintance, and for the next decade Bentham was a frequent visitor at Lansdowne's town house in Berkley Square, and at his country house at Bowood in Wiltshire.[56] In 1789, when Caroline was 21, Bentham gave serious thought to marriage, but Dinwiddy writes in 1792 'his attentions seem to have become unwelcome and relations were broken off'.[57]

A letter from Elizabeth Vernon to Lord Lansdowne dated 11 November 1790 may explain why Bentham's attentions became unwelcome.[58] Elizabeth Vernon, Lansdowne's 'sister' (as she called herself), wrote to him in great indignation that they, Elizabeth Vernon and Caroline Fox, were returning to him a packet of papers, written by Mr Bentham, forwarded to them by Lansdowne's secretary. Elizabeth expressed her 'surprise at his [Bentham's] writing in such a stile to us . . . You will perhaps think us too great prudes but I know you agree with us that women cannot be too delicate in their manners, conversation & ideas'.

It is impossible to discover its exact details, but the outlines of the affair are clear. The packet of papers sent to the young women included a sixteen-page 'Prospectus' titled *Establissement National pour faciliter les Mariages*, which was written in French and purported to have come from France.[59] This explained the damage that celibacy caused to individuals and the state. For example, celibacy depressed the growth in population needed to increase the prosperity of French agriculture, commerce and culture. The causes of celibacy differed between countries and climates, but its results were the same: many people had no option but to live a celibate life. Large numbers of men and women took religious orders in France, and large numbers were employed as domestic servants, all of whom were expected to remain celibate. Many parents prevented their sons and daughters from marrying because of lack of money, although mothers and fathers really wanted the best for their children and the sons and daughters themselves, in accordance with nature, all wanted to marry. The prospectus concluded by proposing a solution to the problem: to set up a bureau to facilitate marriages. People could register with the bureau for a fee, and then the bureau officials would examine the age, station in life, and fortunes of applicants and match them with suitable partners. In other words, the prospectus was a proposal to set up a national marriage agency.

It is most likely that it was Bentham's dedication, which was attached to the prospectus, rather than the prospectus itself that caused most offence to Caroline and Elizabeth. The dedication was to 'The Representatives of the Graces . . . submissively inscribed By One Who laments their Celibacy, Whilst he admires their virtues & their understanding, And Who is anxious that the advantages likely to arise, From the adoption of new Principles, in a neighbouring Country Should be for the benefit of Mankind communicated To the first part of the Creation in his own. Jeremiah Bentham.'[60]

In an arch, strangely humorous style, Bentham added a note laying claim to the authorship of the prospectus itself. He wrote that mention of his name 'would be superfluous since no English Authors excepting Mr. Bentham could be suspected of having devised the very extraordinary plan in Question, which is you will perceive supposed to proceed from a Citizen of France.' He was anxious to obtain the patronage of the 'Ladies who preside at Bowood', naming Miss Vernon and Miss Fox, for this project on marriage which was 'fully in the Sprit of the French Revolution', but that 'the diffidence, and amiable eccentricity of his Character' had led him to go through others. The project outlined in the prospectus would effectually eradicate the bashfulness of women which 'in these enlightened days has been discovered to be repugnant to Morals and Philosophy, and therefore a political evil of very considerable magnitude'.[61]

The dedication concluded by emphasizing that 'this Address' was a declaration of the author's 'Passion', and that a declaration less capable of offending 'the delicacy of a female ear . . . was never penned by any lover since the days of Ovid'. If Bentham really expected an encouraging reception of prospectus and his dedication, he was doomed to disappointment. Did he intend to address Lansdowne and other gentlemen in the Bowood circle rather than Elizabeth and Caroline? His reference to Ovid would support such a conjecture because Ovid's *Art of Love* and *Metamorphoses* concern seduction and promiscuity, a risky ploy if Bentham intended marriage. Whatever his intentions, for our purposes it is enough to see that sending the prospectus, and particularly its dedication to the young women, constituted a serious mistake on his part. Perhaps he acted as he did because he was *naive*, or perhaps his philosophical detachment may have led him too far away from the conventions of polite society, but whatever the reason the result was that his hopes of marriage to Caroline Fox came to an end.[62]

The former American Vice-President and political exile Aaron Burr's lively diaries provide the only evidence known so far of relationships with women that Bentham may have had outside marriage. The exiled Burr stayed with Bentham intermittently between 1808 and 1811, and his diaries give a fleeting glimpse of Bentham's relationship with a young Irishwoman, Amelia Curran who was an artist. Burr tells of Amelia's many visits, and of overhearing Bentham's offer to repair the little house in his garden for Amelia to live in. But then Burr censors the end of the story, so the outcome of Bentham's offer remains unknown.[63]

LITERARY CONTEXTS

In eighteenth-century England clandestine marriages, arranged and forced marriages, separation and divorce were frequent topics of novels, plays, polemical and legal literature and parliamentary debate.[64] The English Romantics, for instance, radically reassessed the relations between the sexes, expressing this in a variety of guises:[65] William Godwin's philosophical anarchism rejected marriage altogether,[66] his son-in-law, Percy Byshe Shelley, pursued utopian schemes for communal living,[67] and Samuel Taylor Coleridge promoted his 'Pantisocracy'.[68]

Bentham's own reading was not confined to legal texts. For instance, Bowring reported that after Bentham's death he found among his papers a reference to a chance reading in 1759 of an autobiography titled *An Apology*. This told the story of the life and times of the celebrated and twice-married courtesan Teresa Constantia Phillips.[69] In her book, 'the fair penitent', as Bentham put it, described being tossed from pillar to post between secular and church courts as she sought legal redress for her wrongs. Bentham was struck by her vivid exposure of the inadequacies of the law and legal processes.[70] Phillips's first marriage at the age of 15 had taken the form of a clandestine marriage of convenience to a bigamist, whom she paid to marry her in order to avoid her creditors.[71] Left destitute by her second husband, a Dutch merchant, she spent decades trying to prove that because her first marriage to the bigamist was invalid, her second must therefore be valid. In the meantime her Dutch merchant had remarried and if Phillips were to succeed his second marriage would be void and his children illegitimate.

Constantia Phillips undoubtedly wrote to make money; her book, published in 1748–9, caused a public sensation. Recent literary scholarship has recognized the place of Phillips and other 'scandalous memorists', in literary history.[72] In her story Bentham recognized the misery caused by the law's failure to regulate marriage, and as a result he made his vow to reform the law.[73] His interest in her story was not due to sympathy for her legal plight. Despite its 'kiss and tell' formula, she addressed many of the issues that formed part of the Enlightenment debate in England and France.[74] This debate raised questions about the nature, education and legal status of women, and about the purpose of marriage.[75]

Controversy about the law of marriage did not suddenly emerge in the eighteenth century. From the earliest times in European history to the present, the law of marriage, perhaps more than any other area of private law, has been the subject of extensive philosophical, religious and political discussion, and sometimes even deadly conflict. Notorious examples include Luther's controversial provisions for priestly marriage and Henry VIII's divorces. More recently, in the twentieth century, divorce law reform, and in the twenty- first-century same-sex marriage, have been fiercely debated. Similarly, in the eighteenth century the law of marriage and its outrageous scandals became a major topic of popular debate.

The most influential literary treatment of marriage in the eighteenth-century England was that found in *The Spirit of the Laws*, published in 1748 by Charles Louis de Secondat, Baron de La Bredè et de Montesquieu.[76] Translated into English in 1750, this quickly became so popular that Horace Walpole sat up all night to read it, David Hume read it and immediately wrote to Montesquieu, while Lord Chesterfield had read the book three times by 1752, copying out parts for his son's education.[77] Montesquieu explained his theory on the effect of climate on the character, laws and customs of nations,[78] and wrote of marriage customs, including polygamy and polyandry. Bentham frequently referred to Montesquieu's descriptions of the laws of other countries, but he rejected Montesquieu's climate theory altogether in favour of using the principle of utility instead as the basis for legislating on marriage.[79]

Treatments of marriage, and particularly of the unhappiness caused by arranged marriages, figured prominently in literature in both England and France. In France, the heroine of Jean-Jacques Rousseau's novel *Julie*, first published in 1761, has her marriage arranged by her father against her own wishes.[80] In England in his novel *Caleb Williams*, published in 1794, William Godwin describes the bullying squire Barnabus Tyrrel trying to force his orphaned cousin, Emily Melville, into an unwanted arranged marriage. His cruelty ends only with the wretched Emily's death.[81]

Samuel Richardson's immensely successful novel *Clarissa, or, The History of a Young Lady*, was published between 1747 and 1748.[82] This prodigiously lengthy book (some fifteen hundred pages in a modern edition) had influenced not only English writers but also Diderot as well as Rousseau in France, making it an immensely important European novel.[83] Richardson describes how Clarissa Harlowe's aspiring bourgeois family try to force her into a marriage with a wealthy man whom she hates. She runs away, but only to be imprisoned, drugged and raped by the wicked aristocratic Lovelace, and in the end she dies.

We know that Bentham read *Clarissa*,[84] but even if he had not done so he could not possibly have avoided hearing about it. The fame of *Clarissa*, and even more so of Richardson's earlier novel *Pamela*, was so great that Terry Eagleton describes them as functioning as badges of allegiance for women, becoming a 'code' for a whole cultural debate on marriage. Many women publicly displayed the books, and fashionable women painted scenes from *Pamela* on their fans.[85]

Henry Fielding, Richardson's great rival, hilariously spoofed Richardson's *Pamela* in his *Shamela* and then again in *Joseph Andrews*.[86] In 1780, Bentham's brother Samuel wrote to him from Russia mentioning Fielding's *Joseph Andrews* in terms that clearly indicate that Bentham had read it too. Samuel reported that he had heard that Catherine the Great read English and that her favourite book was *Joseph Andrews*. 'If she loves bawdy', wrote Samuel, 'there will be a little [of bawdy] no doubt in Codes and Punishments', alluding to Bentham's current projects.[87]

Bentham was familiar with other literary genres. Karen Offen writes of the 'veritable explosion . . . of books, periodicals, tracts, broadsides [pouring] forth from the presses'[88] in the eighteenth century. Growing literacy among women meant that they became an important audience, and for them novels dealing with marriage were especially popular. Conduct books were also widely read, and these usually didactic works were often aimed at women.[89] Indeed, Richardson had begun his literary career by writing conduct books.[90] Bentham read conduct books. He gave John Gregory's *A Fathers Legacy to His Daughters*[91] to Sarah Stratton during his courtship, wrapping it in white paper and hiding it in her harpsichord for her to find later. Perhaps he chose this particular book as a gift because Dr Gregory wrote feelingly and at length on the wisdom of allowing children to choose their own marriage partners. Sarah Stratton and her mother told Bentham they liked Dr Gregory's book and that they had been reading Lady Sarah Pennington's *An Unfortunate Mother's Advice to Her Absent Daughters*, and had recently visited that unfortunate lady.[92] Ironically, in 1790 Mary Wollstonecraft attacked Dr Gregory's book, along with Rousseau's *Emile*, because both contained strong arguments against educating women.[93]

Bentham was no doubt also familiar with a literary tradition referred to since the Middle Ages as the *querelle des femmes*: that is, the battle or dispute between the sexes, which found expression, for instance, in Chaucer's *Canterbury Tales*. This dispute had for its themes misogamy (the dislike of marriage) and misogyny (the hatred of women).[94] By the eighteenth century, assumptions about male superiority to women, whether derived from the laws of God, or from nature, were being questioned by many, including Bentham. In France, Madame d'Epinay, a friend of Diderot and Rousseau, published her *Les Conversations d'Emilie* in 1774, and in England in 1739 an anonymous writer calling herself 'Sophia' published *Woman Not Inferior to Man*.[95] Sophia argued that the difference between the sexes related only to propagation of the species, that there is no sex in the soul, and that all apparent differences between men and women come from education, exercise and experience of the world.[96] Because nothing granted legitimacy to men's assumption of superiority over women other than that which 'tyranny has created', men were unjust in excluding women from power and in denying them equality of esteem.[97] Sophia's book brought a reply from an anonymous 'Gentleman', who in *Man Superior to Woman* provokingly declared that anyone in their right senses would agree with Montaigne that a woman was 'learned enough' if she could tell her husband's shirt from his breeches.[98] Others in turn replied to this Gentleman's remarks, including Sophia. Even Dr John Gregory warned his daughter that an educated woman would be unattractive to men.[99] In the 1780s Bentham used language very similar to Sophia's to agree with her conclusions, which invites the conclusion that he too had read her book.[100]

THE MANUSCRIPT AND PUBLISHED SOURCES

The greater part of this study is based on Bentham's manuscript writings on marriage which are held in boxes at University College, London. These have been dated to the 1780s and 1790s by archivists, although there is one sheet dated to the mid-1770s. He returned to his work on marriage as late as 1828.[101]

Sometimes Bentham referred to a 'marriage code', which indicates an existence separate from either the civil or penal codes that he was preparing. I have not found a completed marriage code, but its outlines are quite clearly visible in fragmented form in many of the manuscripts. In these we find traces of a code of law with rules, punishments and attached 'expository' (i.e. explanatory) material. It may be that Bentham did not complete this work.

Much later, in 1828, Bentham explained his intentions. If a code has the law of contract for a subject-matter, he explained, then that code needs to be made public because obligations and rights in the code will only be 'effectual' (i.e. binding) to the extent that the person concerned knows about them.[102] Bentham's law of marriage was based on the law of contract, and therefore he instructed a legislator to ensure that a copy of the marriage code would be handed out to all men and women when they married.[103] A newly married husband and wife would then know with some certainty what were their respective rights and duties towards each other. This would be much more effective than a sermon preached in church, he remarked, possibly referring to the Elizabethan official *Homilie of the State of Marriage* that Parliament had ordered to be read aloud in church.[104] Parents should know about their duties towards their children, and thus a 'parental code' should be set out in the 'matrimonial code', but both codes should also be available separately.[105] Bentham complained that the 'want of a matrimonial code [was] a proof of the negligence of legislators'.[106]

It is not easy to unravel the story of these manuscripts and their relation to certain published versions of Bentham's civil and penal code. In 1789 he published *An Introduction to the Principles of Morals and Legislation*, which included many of the manuscripts on marriage, but excluded much more.[107] In 1802 Etienne Dumont, Bentham's friend and editor, collaborated with him to publish his *Traites de Legislation Civile et Penale* in Paris. This too included some parts of Bentham's law of marriage.[108]

There are evident differences of purpose between *IPML*, the *Traites* and the unpublished manuscripts. For example, as we shall see in Chapter 4, in a long footnote in *IPML* Bentham offered reasons for the subordination of married women.[109] In contrast, in the *Traites* and unpublished manuscripts Bentham set out in some detail the codified laws that actually applied to relations between men and women in marriage, but did not always give either explanation or reason for the laws.[110]

Dumont's version of Bentham on marriage should be treated cautiously, however, for Dumont omitted, deleted or amended Bentham's work as he saw fit. Thus Dumont belongs with Bentham's other early editors Francis Place and John Bowring, who also suppressed aspects of Bentham's work.[111] It is very likely too that Dumont did not have access to all of Bentham's extensive writings on marriage. He certainly did not have access to the manuscripts Bentham produced after 1802. Nevertheless, until the mid-nineteenth century, it was largely through Dumont's edition that Bentham's work was known.

The subsequent fate of *Traites* was to be translated into Russian in 1803, then into English by the American John Neale who published it in Boston in 1830. Bentham died in 1832 and in 1837 John Bowring, his literary executor, appointed an editor, only identified by the initials W. W., to translate the *Traites* into English for publication in an edition of Bentham's collected *Works.*[112] Finally, in 1864 another American lawyer, Robert Hildreth, translated Books One and Two of Dumont's *Traites* into English. In 1931 Charles Ogden reprinted Hildreth's 1864 work. Ogden did not consult Bentham's manuscripts or earlier publications.[113]

Thus much of Bentham's writing on marriage was not included in any published edition of his works. Conversely, sometimes I have been unable to find any manuscripts that correspond to the published work. In general I have found that Bentham's manuscripts are invariably more radical in content than the published editions.

Bentham's manuscripts on the civil code are less numerous than those on the penal code. The subject of marriage appears in both. The civil code manuscripts contain Bentham's plans for the formalities needed to make a valid marriage, the legal status of husbands and wives within their marriage, and inheritance of property. The penal code manuscripts contain various matters mostly set out under the heading of 'Offences Against Domestic Conditions'. These include desertion, divorce, adultery, fornication, incest, rape, wife-beating and many other matters relating to marriage.

A significant number of Bentham's autograph manuscripts on marriage are written in French, and some in Latin. Over the years, various theories have been advanced as to why Bentham wrote so often in French,[114] but in the 1780s his immediate purpose seems to have been a project to present his penal code to Catherine the Great of Russia, no doubt hoping she would implement it as part of her reforms.[115] For it is known that Bentham's brother Samuel had gone to Russia in 1779 to work on engineering projects and by 1783 was in the employment of the empress.[116] Bentham wrote to him in 1780 asking him to ensure that a letter was given to the sister of the Duke of Courland who knew the empress well and could be relied on to place the Code directly into her hands.[117] Other letters between the brothers follow the progress of this plan.[118]

Although Bentham travelled to Russia in 1785 and stayed until 1887, there is no evidence either that he met the Empress Catherine or that any part of his code was given to her.

Bentham's lifelong ambition was to draft a complete code of law that would be universally applicable to any state.[119] To this end, he continued to work on his penal and civil codes, including the law of marriage, until the last years of his life.

2

Sex and Utility

Bentham placed sexual love, which he described as physical desire, in the category of 'self-regarding' motives for human behaviour, along with 'pecuniary interest', love of power and self-preservation. The last encompasses the fear of pain, love of ease and love of life.[1] Therefore, in the course of drafting a utilitarian law of marriage he set out an explanation of the pleasures and pains of sexual love. His discussions led him far beyond the confines of legal marriage and into the realm of what would today be described as gender relations. These might be homosexual, heterosexual, monogamous, or otherwise, within or outside of marriage. Bentham's views on sex and the principle of utility are made particularly clear when he writes about wives, prostitutes and mistresses, and it was in this context that he made his radical suggestion for short-term marriages.

BENTHAM AND ENLIGHTENMENT DEBATES ON LOVE AND MARRIAGE

Bentham began by locating his law of marriage within the philosophical debate about whether physical or moral love was worth more. He did not name any particular philosopher, expecting recognition of his allusions by his classically educated eighteenth-century readers. In Plato's *Symposium*,[2] Socrates argues that ordinary mortals gain immortality either by physically begetting children or by spiritually begetting 'the progeny which is the nature of the soul to create and bring to birth'. Plato held that moral or spiritual love exceeds physical love in virtue, and that spiritual children surpass human children by being immortal as well as more beautiful.[3] But Bentham concluded that questions about the relative worth of physical or spiritual love were for an individual to decide for himself, and not a decision to be made by a legislator for 'the species in general'.[4] Later, in his property law writings, he explained again that 'to administer pleasure in a direct way belongs only to the individual himself – laws can only place the means within his reach'.[5] So, instead, Bentham said he intended to base his law of marriage on the principle of utility, which asserts that all actions are governed by a wish to avoid pain and gain pleasure.[6]

Bentham's simple assertion leaves open the question of how he intended the principle of utility to be applied by a decision-maker in any given case, a question that has long divided scholars. Was Bentham's utilitarianism a 'direct-act' utilitarianism leaving an adjudicator 'free to respond to the constantly varying demands of utility in particular cases'?[7] Or was it alternatively a 'rule-based' utilitarianism, where the principle of utility works through laws which have created the necessary 'framework within which each individual can pursue his own conception of well-being'?[8] While these debates cannot be addressed within the scope of this essay, it can be noted that when Bentham started writing on marriage in the 1780s he began by instructing his legislator first to establish and then regulate a law of marriage, so providing a framework of law often including expansive explanatory notes. His strategy indicates rule-based utilitarianism.

Applying his utilitarian idea of pleasures and pains to the law of marriage, Bentham explained: 'The pleasure derived from the union between the sexes is a pleasure: therefore, leaving aside the evils, if there can be such things, which derive from that source, here is why the legislator must do whatever is in his power so that its quantity in society be as high as possible. This pleasure is the greatest of all: the legislator's attentions must be in proportion to it.'[9]

Roy Porter has said that the naturalistic and hedonistic assumptions that underpinned much Enlightenment thought on sexuality asserted that 'nature had made men to follow pleasure, that sex was pleasurable, and that it was natural to follow one's sexual urges.'[10] David Hume, for example, considered that erotic attraction was a first and original principle in humans,[11] while in France the *philosophes* were much preoccupied by questions about moral and physical love, marriage and the family. Voltaire, Montesquieu, Diderot, and many others considered marriage as natural, beneficial to mankind and a civilizing institution,[12] although their views differed about the basis for men's authority over women and children, and about divorce.[13] The proper care of children, which was another Enlightenment preoccupation, would seem to demand long-lasting, possibly indissoluble, unions.

Bentham was aware of these debates and often addressed the ideas of French *philosophes* on marriage. He referred especially to Montesquieu's book, *The Spirit of the Laws* (1748),[14] in which as we have seen, Montesquieu described his theory that climate affected the character, laws and customs of nations.[15] His survey of marriage customs around the world controversially compared the laws of 'domestic servitude' – here meaning the servitude of women – with slavery.[16] Montesquieu's ideas became immensely influential, especially in England. But Bentham deliberately distinguished himself from Montesquieu, insisting that he would not look at comparative social and legal customs but only consult the principle of utility.[17]

MONOGAMY AND ENFORCING THE MARRIAGE CONTRACT

Bentham's ideal legislator had a twofold duty: first to enact a law of marriage, and then to enforce it. For Bentham the marriage contract was 'beyond comparison' the most important contract of any in law.[18] Enforcing a law of marriage was essential because to do so would be 'conducive to this design' – that is, to secure happiness by marriage.[19] For this reason, too, anything that would prevent increasing pleasure by marriage must be prima facie an evil.[20] Bentham instructed his ideal legislator that the objective must be 'clearly the same as with regard to all other pleasures: that as many persons as possible may enjoy as much of this sort of pleasure as possible' because all pleasure 'of this kind' is 'prima facie when considered by itself a good'.[21] Sometimes this would require specific legislation, but sometimes a legislator should do nothing at all because all coercive laws are painful and therefore an evil to be avoided.[22] Bentham did not offer an explanation of what he meant by 'enforcing' a marriage contract, but the context indicates that by enforcement he intended the regulation of marriage by his legislator. For example, in addition to freely given consent, Bentham required a minimum age for valid marriage.[23]

However, finding physical love to be a pleasure within a utilitarian scheme of marriage law does not necessarily exclude enjoyment of that very same pleasure outside the confines of a legal marriage, and Bentham was not slow to appreciate this. Between 1770 and the 1820s he wrote extensively on gender relations, including sexual relations between men and women outside marriage or for reasons other than procreation.[24] Bentham considered the harm that may result from enforcing a marriage contract 'is palpable enough',[25] because after enjoying 'the pleasure in question', as he phrased it, with one woman it almost always happened that a man realized he could enjoy it just as much with another. This was equally true for a woman, and therefore both were 'inconvenienced' by enforcing the sexual restraint demanded by a marriage contract. The paradox that marriage served to increase happiness while at the same time the sexual restraint required by marriage reduced happiness had been pointed out by others. For instance, the unhappily married Denis

Diderot considered lifelong commitment incompatible with man's natural inconstancy;[26] while Rousseau, describing the solitary existence of primitive man, declared: 'Once his appetite is satisfied, the man no longer has any need for a particular woman, nor the woman for a particular man.'[27] Admittedly it might be advantageous for the human race if men and women formed permanent unions, Rousseau commented, but it does not follow that nature so dictated.[28]

But Bentham disagreed, believing that the benefit for society of maintaining monogamous marriage far outweighed any pain caused by sexual restraint. He reasoned that the evils resulting from promiscuity, such as jealousy, conflict and child neglect, must have contributed to the institution of the marriage contract in the first place. To avoid such evils is why, once established, marriage contracts should then be enforced by the legislator.[29]

In order to illustrate the benefits of marriage Bentham wrote a fable about the origin of marriage, reminiscent of the foundational narratives of Thomas Hobbes, John Locke and Jean-Jacques Rousseau describing the origins of civil society.[30] Individuals too would benefit if marriage contracts were enforced. This was not because sexual relations were in themselves immoral, but because, as Bentham put it, 'intrigues . . . have a strong and almost unavoidable tendency to corrupt the heart'. While the love of pleasure 'corrupts no hearts',[31] the habits of treachery and dissimulation inevitably acquired by intrigues bring with them 'forever and more odious degrees of misery' for men, women and children.[32] Bentham possibly had in mind the example of his own brother Samuel, whose extramarital liaisons had resulted in the birth of three illegitimate daughters.[33]

It has been said that schemes to promote social harmony and happiness by means of laws are not 'in any sense peculiar to the Utilitarians' or, indeed, to the Enlightenment.[34] But eighteenth-century writers paid much attention to the role of marriage and the family in wider society. Montesquieu, for example, described marriage as a secular contract intended to benefit society,[35] and William Paley, writing in 1785, considered that the institution of marriage increased the 'peace of human society' because distributing the community into families made for better government.[36] Marriage, for Diderot, was 'a stupid and troublesome state', but nevertheless necessary as an institution to maintain the family and property.[37] Rousseau believed that when primitive man began to till the soil and build huts to live in, 'every family became a small society'.[38]

While Bentham held that registered secular contractual marriages were in accord with the principle of utility, in an apparent contradiction he said that marriage contracts should not be too strictly enforced. He wrote that the people of the country where the marriage contract was enforced with the least severity, France, were the happiest in Europe.[39] Greater still was the happiness in 'many of the new discovered Islands [where] there is no such thing as marriage'.[40] Here Bentham was most probably referring to Denis Diderot's *Supplement au Voyage de Bougainville*, published in 1783, which described Tahiti as a sexual utopia where no marital union was either permanent or exclusive.[41]

In contrast, Bentham wrote, while adultery is 'scarce ever heard of' among the Turks they do not give the appearance of being a 'happy people'. Similarly, in Scotland the 'Scotch [*sic*] however or such of them that stay at home' are far from appearing as cheerful as the English, despite the fact that in Scotland adultery is taken very seriously indeed. An individual might be induced to smile but it would be difficult to compel a whole people to look cheerful against their will.[42] Bentham brought this discussion to a sudden close remarking that external cheerfulness cannot really be a certain indicator of happiness in a people. Conclusions drawn from such evidence are weak, even if the strongest available.[43]

There is an odd contradiction between Bentham's insistence that his legislator should enforce marriage contracts and yet finding that people looked happier where adultery was not too severely punished. In part, this can be resolved by recalling Bentham's fable about the origin of contractual marriage. He thought that by far the greatest misery and unhappiness befell those who lived in a state of nature in totally unregulated unions.[44] But did Bentham's strong advocacy of monogamy mean that he intended his legislator not only to regulate marriage but also to force people to be monogamous by punishing them if they were not? A simple answer would have to be yes, if by forced monogamy it is understood that no other form of marriage was accepted as valid. Bentham, in common with many Enlightenment thinkers did consider and then reject incestuous marriages, polyandry, and polygamy.[45] In order to ensure compliance with his marriage code, he did provide various punishments for breaches. These relied primarily on publicly shaming the offender.[46]

Nevertheless, Bentham did not think his law-maker should legislate to enforce morals because to do so did not promote happiness. Instead the most effective check to promiscuity and immorality must be the 'censure of the world', not the 'artillery of the law'.[47] He thought some of the most cruel laws were those enforcing morality and gave as examples the laws passed to suppress idleness, to prevent usury,[48] or to punish homosexuality.[49] But, he went on to ask, would the world still censure a practice if the law did not?[50] Here Bentham addressed questions that have perplexed legislators throughout human history. How can private morals be publicly regulated? Should they be, and will public censure suffice to do so?[51] Optimistically, Bentham thought that the situation in England seemed to prove that public censure alone would suffice.[52]

THE PRINCIPLE OF UTILITY AND PROSTITUTION

While Bentham believed that the principle of utility demanded support for contractual marriage he recognized the prevalence of contemporary prostitution in all its guises. He considered prostitution in some length in 1773 and returned to the subject again in the late 1790s.

Bentham's language is that of the eighteenth century; he referred to 'gallants' (sexually predatory males),[53] 'courtesans', 'kept women' and 'public women'. The last were the numerous poor prostitutes who plied their trade on the streets.[54] In Bentham's time, prostitution and 'bastard-bearing' were among the sexual and public disorder offences subject to the jurisdiction of the church courts; church court punishments relied on publicly shaming the offender.[55] Parish authorities too, responsible for raising parish rates to maintain the poor, were anxious to reduce the cost of supporting illegitimate children and their mothers. The Act of Settlement of 1662, which Bentham condemned as unjust, allowed Justices of the Peace to return women to their parish of settlement, if, at some future date, they might become a financial liability to the parish they were currently living in by bearing an illegitimate child.[56] During the course of the eighteenth century the average age of marriage had 'dropped significantly' and the percentage of illegitimate children born increased threefold.[57] Bentham distinguished between the mischief of what he termed 'promiscuous venery', meaning prostitution of one form or another, and 'settled cohabitation without nuptials'. He described the latter as 'unpromiscuous venery'.[58] Bentham did not condone prostitution, but neither did he condemn the very poor women who plied the trade and who were often vulnerable to poverty because of low wages and irregular work. He was well aware that women, in particular single women, outnumbered men in parish lists of those in receipt of relief and in workhouses.[59]

Bentham described the evils of what he called 'promiscuous venery' as, first, the danger of disease, and secondly, the 'want of progeny' or else an uncertainty about the paternity of children. Should prostitution be 'discouraged', he asked, because of the dangers of disease?[60] Ignoring potential problems about establishing the paternity of illegitimate children, he addressed instead the harsh disabilities placed on bastards by the common law.[61] Bentham thought one partial solution to the unfortunate legal status of illegitimate children would be for the common law to follow the canon law and remove disabilities from them if their parents married subsequent to their birth.[62]

Another 'mischief' arising from prostitution was the possibility of child murder, or infanticide.[63] Bentham argued for decriminalization of this capital offence, which, he said, was 'totally distinct from murder' in motive and consequences.[64] He commented that he had never met with the intended killing of legitimate children, but always of bastard children.[65] These sad crimes were not the result of either avarice or hate but the 'inevitable impulse of self-preservation [of the mother] . . . at the expense of one being which does not feel the cost'.[66] Modern sensibilities might baulk at Bentham's quick dismissal of the feelings and rights of children, but he attributed his claim that infants do not feel pain to the authority of Dr Hunter's 'lectures'.[67] Despite all the punishments, said Bentham, infanticide was a frequently committed crime and constituted a case where the death penalty was a 'greater mischief than the crime' itself. He concluded that it should be the subject of new legislation.[68]

Some might say that taking away punishments for infanticide or prostitution would exonerate fornication, said Bentham, but if the offence itself cannot be stopped at the least harm done to others could be reduced. Putting up with 'evils' that are impractical to prevent is a difficult lesson for a legislator to learn,[69] but 'it is not to destroy the children who felt nothing that I contend for but to save the mother'. In order to save lives, he suggested legislating for a Foundling Hospital for unwanted children,[70] and proposed birth control measures as a means of reducing pauperism and the poor rates.[71]

As part of his plans for a Panopticon Poor House, in 1797–8 Bentham prepared notes on an 'Industry House'. This was a model for some 250 workhouses in England and Wales, to be managed by Bentham's National Charity Company, a joint-stock company.[72] To promote 'Domestic Morality' this Industry House would act as an 'Asylum for House Servants out of place',[73] and for 'Wives against bad Husbands'. Prostitutes would be catered for in 'a Magdalen for the low Prostitutes' and in an 'Asylum for exposed girls', which he also called a 'sotimion' (derived from the Greek, soteriology means a study of preservation or salvation). This would provide a refuge for unmarried pregnant women who would gain both concealment, and after the birth an asylum for their illegitimate children.[74] Robert Dingley's earlier call for the establishment of a refuge for 'Penitent Prostitutes' had been followed by the opening of the Magdalen Hospital in London in 1758.[75]

Evidently holding much the same opinion in 1797 as he had in 1773, Bentham lamented the difficulty of putting an end to prostitution by coercive measures, even if indeed coercion was 'desirable'.[76] With any other offence, the only question a legislator had to address was how to suppress it, but with prostitution the question was to what degree it ought to be suppressed.[77] In 1780 Bentham suggested that the 'moral sanction' against prostitution might in fact be 'the universal cause of the evil of the offence', and queried the need to reinforce the moral with an additional political sanction.[78] Should prostitution be practised openly and without control, he asked in 1797, or should it be completely suppressed? Rejecting both propositions, Bentham complained that 'there rages on this subject an appetite for contradiction: an appetite almost universal, and where it prevails insatiable'.[79] Even if it could be proved that by repealing all repressive laws against prostitution the number of prostitutes could be reduced to half, or even a quarter, he doubted that this would be acceptable to public opinion. 'Yet dram drinking, a practice much more pernicious, is tolerated and protected. There is nothing obscene in dram drinking: it is only poisonous, nothing worse.'[80]

Bentham saw prostitution as an economic problem, arguing that if poor women were able to find work they would have an alternative to prostituting themselves. He pointed out that women suffered particular disadvantages in finding suitable occupations above the level of an ordinary labourer. The problem was exacerbated because men carried out many occupations that might be supposed best suited to women: for example, keeping fashionable shops, selling children's toys, or making women's shoes, stays or dresses. Men 'even perform the office of midwife'.[81] Proposing a form of positive discrimination, Bentham suggested legislating to exclude men from certain occupations.[82]

COHABITATION, COURTESANS AND SHORT-TERM MARRIAGES

In 1773, Bentham suggested either 'settled cohabitation without nuptials', or else temporary marriages, as an alternative to prostitution. Importantly, such arrangements would also have the advantage of providing an alternative to lifelong marriage, a significant consideration because divorce was not easily available in England,[83] while overt sexual relationships without marriage were considered socially unacceptable.[84] Some of Bentham's arguments in favour of divorce were published by Dumont and are well known,[85] but a far greater number of his manuscripts on the subject remain unpublished and unknown. In these Bentham provided details of grounds for divorce for a number of matrimonial offences. But Bentham's controversial suggestion for temporary or short-term marriage contracts would render it unnecessary to terminate a relationship by divorce, because such marriages would end at the date agreed.

In 1790, Bentham returned to this subject, writing on it extensively.[86] Here, as a partial solution to the problem of prostitution, Bentham advocated a form of legally recognized cohabitation, reminiscent of modern European debates on 'registered partnerships'.[87] While the principle of utility dictated that the happiness of the greatest number was to be found in long-lasting marriages, there might still be others for whom shorter marriages would be more suitable.[88] The young, for example, might benefit, or those otherwise unable to enter lifelong relationships. Bentham asked: 'For those whose fortunes allow it, is there a simpler and a nicer way to preserve health, to guard against the inconvenient appetite for variety, to preserve the calm of passions, to protect the studies from distraction?'[89] While youth is satisfied with just a night-time companion, he continued, 'a more delicate taste, in a more mature age, shall require a mistress . . . [whom] one would come to . . . when one feels the need for a companion of all moments. The first relationship shall be between bodies. The second shall add the union of souls.'[90]

In 1797, Bentham repeated his suggestions for short-term marriages. 'Permanent connections are suitable to some situations in life: transient, to others. This the legislator sees, because no man can help seeing, but thinks it not decent to acknowledge.' Fully aware that the subject was controversial, Bentham added a marginal note to himself: 'Memorandum, To evade this subject rather than grapple with it. Prostitutes and loose women are wives for short terms . . . freely performed and but once the act stamps infamy: perforce and habitually it confers honour.'[91]

Bentham also discussed 'kept women' and courtesans, both of whom provided eighteenth-century alternatives, for men of sufficient means, to either marriage or prostitution. Like 'public women', courtesans earned their living by accepting payment in exchange for sexual favours. But, unlike prostitutes, eighteenth-century courtesans were often fashionable celebrities, famous for their beauty and wit as well as notorious for their liaisons. For example, the actress Mary Robinson, known as 'Perdita', who was a former pupil at the worthy Hannah More's school in Bristol, was the mistress of George, Prince of Wales, and later became a successful writer.[92]

When Bentham referred to 'kept women' he meant mistresses financially supported by men who were often described as their 'protectors'. They were not necessarily fashionable courtesans, although they could be. Bentham held that kept women unjustly shared the scorn, hatred and contempt attached to 'public women'. Public women were forever on the verge of complete poverty, and kept women shared their shame because it appeared that they too could just as easily become degraded.[93] 'However', wrote Bentham, 'the longer one such woman has lived with the same man, the further away she moves from the degraded condition.'[94] Although not specifically named by Bentham, an example was the courtesan Elizabeth Armistead who moved in aristocratic Whig circles. She lived for many years with Charles James Fox before they finally married in 1795.[95]

The relationship between an eighteenth-century kept woman, or mistress, and her protector was not at all comparable with most twenty-first-century cohabitation. The kept woman quite probably did not live in the same household as her protector and their relationship may not have been exclusive.[96] Rather, keeping one or more mistresses was a status symbol for wealthy men who often entered into written financial agreements for their mistresses' support.[97]

Fiction provides the famous example of Richardson's Pamela, a young servant-girl, whose master attempts to persuade her to sign a lengthy document settling property on her in return for her cohabiting with him as his mistress.[98] When Pamela demurs she is roundly castigated by the other household servants for failing to take advantage of her good fortune.[99] History provides many other examples, including Perdita, who spent many years trying to enforce her financial agreement with the Prince of Wales.

Bentham's fixed-term relationships would give mistresses some respectability, together with some of the legal rights (e.g. to financial support) attached to a lifelong marriage. Bentham argued that logic surely dictated that 'If the service of love were not supposed to be a dishonour in itself, why should it become one when it receives a reward? . . . it is forbidden to sell oneself for a quarter of an hour, but allowed to sell oneself for life'.[100] As we have seen, he held that the most effective check to promiscuity was public censure,[101] and he recognized that women suffered a greater burden of public condemnation and persecution for entering into irregular sexual relationships than did men. But, he asked, 'if the law of public opinion is unfair and tyrannical, should the law of the state express that unfairness?'[102] In any event, the laws that proscribe temporary relationships on the pretext of preserving morals do not succeed in preventing them. Therefore, these laws are to be blamed for causing moral corruption. The cause of the corruption was not the courtesans, 'that unhappy class of women who draw a revenue from their charms',[103] whom Bentham held to be mostly unfortunate innocents. Why should a contract of marriage for one day be forbidden, but be allowed if it was to last forever? 'Theft, damages, homicide, do all truly pernicious actions become good when they are repeated?', he asked, 'No – if what is called bawdiness was a wrong, then marriage would be a crime.'[104]

Bentham's sympathetic views on courtesans and mistresses were not shared by others. William Paley, for instance, argued that promiscuous concubinage was a danger because it discouraged marriage. Paley claimed 'the male part of the species will not undertake the encumbrance, expense, and restraint of married life, if they can gratify their passions at a cheaper price; and they will undertake anything, rather than not gratify them.'[105] Paley therefore disapproved of 'kept mistresses', as he called them.[106] Paley criticized people who claimed that marriage was a ceremony of human, and not divine invention and if a man and a woman promised to be faithful to one another without ceremony this made no difference in the sight of God. But, he said, if concubinage was really the same as marriage, then why did the parties not marry? 'If a man choose to have it in his power to dismiss the woman at his pleasure, or retain her in a state of humiliation or dependence inconsistent with the rights which marriage would confer on her, it is not the same thing' as a marriage.[107]

Paley believed that concubinage adversely affected the children of the relationship; and argued too, that if a marriage rite was a mere form then so were bonds, wills and conveyances – yet these forms made a great difference to the rights and obligations of people concerned.[108] It is likely that he was addressing here the arguments of those who sought to repeal Lord Hardwicke's Marriage Act of 1753, which had ended consensual marriages and regulated English marriages by requiring the calling of banns, marriage ceremonies and registration.

In fact, men of sufficient wealth frequently made contracts for the financial support of a mistress, assuring her maintenance during his life or after his death. These contracts, Bentham pointed out, were 'politically discouraged' because the courts would find them invalid if cohabitation was the consideration for the contract.[109] Looking at some eighteenth-century Chancery cases gives an historical context for Bentham's proposal for temporary marriage contracts. There is, in fact, some indication that in the second half of the century evidence of past cohabitation did not inevitably lead the court to regard a contract for the support of a mistress as void for immoral purposes – that is, for prostitution. For instance, in *Earl of Chesterfield v. Jannsen* (1751) the court distinguished between a 'common prostitute' and a 'mistress who is true to one person'. In the latter circumstance the court did not relieve the contract because 'she may be presumed to be imposed upon, as well as imposing upon'.[110] In 1778 Lord Mansfield, in a case referred from Chancery for the opinion of King's Bench, upheld a bond for a protector's former mistress on the basis that a promise to marry was good consideration for the bond.[111] Here a protector had arranged for his long-term mistress to marry someone else, promising the couple financial support.

However, cases involving agreements made prior to cohabitation were much more likely to be held void for immoral purposes.[112] If the agreement was in a deed, consideration was not an issue, but the deed might still be found void for immoral purposes. The law regarding such matters was not settled until the mid-nineteenth century when the court decided that past cohabitation was *not* good consideration and therefore such claims failed thereafter.[113]

It has been pointed out that, in practice, these eighteenth-century cases all have in common arrangements for temporary cohabitation, with the man providing financial support for a woman who was socially his inferior.[114] But this was not at all the sort of domestic arrangement that Bentham had in mind. He was not concerned with piecemeal reform of the law, but intended rather that his plans for short-term marriages should form part of a codified utilitarian law of marriage. Therefore, his plans connect more with eighteenth-century European philosophical debates on marriage and the family than with contemporary English legal practice.

INFLUENCES ON BENTHAM

It is interesting to speculate as to which out of several possible intellectual threads prompted Bentham's radical thinking on the law of marriage. For instance, did he look to supposed ancient traditions of consensual marriages, or ancient customary laws, for his temporary marriages?[115]

Bentham was certainly opposed to moves to repeal Lord Hardwicke's Marriage Act of 1753, and so did not support claims made in Parliament by

Charles James Fox that Lord Hardwicke's Act had adversely affected the poor by making invalid the popular clandestine, or irregular forms of marriage which previously had made a valid marriage.[116] Neither was he likely to have been persuaded by Thomas Pennant's reports of Scottish marriages entered into for 'a year and a day', performed at annual fairs. These marriages, according the second volume of Pennant's *A Tour in Scotland* (1790), were then either renewed or abandoned at the following year's fair.[117]

Rather than supposed ancient customary traditions of English consensual marriage or Scottish temporary marriages by handfasting, it is far more probable that Bentham had read with interest Diderot's description of marriage in Tahiti as 'the agreement to occupy the same cabin and to sleep in the same bed, so long as we find this agreeable',[118] especially as he made reference, as we have seen above, to customs in 'newly discovered islands'.[119]

Bentham followed events in contemporary France closely.[120] Some of the post-1789 revolutionary reforms were short-lived and reversed by the Napoleonic Code in 1804, but canon law was permanently abolished and marriage became a secular contract. Married women were given a right to share equally in family property, and by 1792 divorce by mutual agreement became possible.[121] We might wonder if he knew about the former courtesan and playwright Olympe de Gouges, or had read her 1791 pamphlet, *Les Droits de la femme* (published one year earlier than Mary Wollstonecraft's *Vindication of the Rights of Woman*). de Gouges' pamphlet included a deed for temporary marriage that reads: 'We, X and Y, of our own free will join ourselves for the term of our natural lives and the duration of our mutual love . . . '.[122] Unfortunately, de Gouges fell foul of the Jacobins and went to the guillotine in 1793, notorious in her death as in her life.

Bentham's law of marriage was strongly secular. Religion had nothing to do with a contract of marriage made by a man and a woman.[123] While it is clear that the canon law of marriage did not provide him with his idea for short-term marriage nevertheless it can be argued that his marriage law owed much to canon law. For example, incest did not become a secular crime until 1908[124] but Bentham wrote extensively on this canon law offence. His language, as when he wrote of the 'evil fame of chastity',[125] and the instructions he gave to his legislator to punish 'the "rare" offence of incest' as the English church courts did (by ignominious punishment or a fine) rather than by death as in France,[126] all indicate his familiarity with the jurisdiction and work of the church courts. On occasion he even proposed adopting canon law, as noted above in relation to illegitimacy.[127] Bentham assumed that the church would continue to conduct the administrative business of recording births, deaths and marriages, even if the last were secular. The records would be made by a priest or by a church officer. He also thought that a church was a suitable place for marriages to take place because it would offer a safeguard against underage or forced marriages because if a priest suspected such a situation he could question the parties privately.[128]

EQUALITY BETWEEN MEN AND WOMEN

Finally, we might ask whether Bentham's fixed-term marriage proposal was a hypocritical gesture, only legitimizing the agreements already commonly made by wealthy men for the upkeep of their mistresses? Was this any more than legal concubinage? He made no mention of how agreement was to be reached on the length of a short-term marriage, or on how it was to be terminated. Certainly, Bentham's conception of temporary marriage had an expectation of monogamous fidelity, for he did not condone promiscuity in either short-term or lifelong marriages, and he did not restrict his discussion of the evil effects of promiscuity to lifelong marriage. Neither did Bentham make any suggestion that short-term marriages were inferior and would not merit the same considerations on termination as lifelong marriages ended by divorce. So the same provisions for the maintenance of children and wives, and for division of property, would apply to a short-term marriage, unless the contract itself provided otherwise.

To answer the question of whether or not Bentham intended more than legitimating concubinage requires a brief survey of his views on equality between men and women. I do not refer here to the nineteenth-century ideas about the political or legal equality of the sexes associated with John Stuart Mill, but to notions of equality in nature. Do Bentham's writings on marriage justify claims that he was a 'proto-feminist'?[129]

By the eighteenth century, ideas about marriage and the relations of men and women within marriage had changed. Earlier claims that families represented a microcosm of the commonwealth and that women must necessarily be subject to the rule of men, just as a king rules his subjects,[130] had given way to an understanding that the relationship between men and women in marriage was contractual. Man's authority over woman was no longer considered to be derived from divine law. When the model of the hierarchical ordering of men above women, analogous to the ordering of kings above subjects, gave way to a contractual theory, then logic should have dictated the equality of men and women. Indeed just this was argued by Samuel Pufendorf 1632–94, a

Protestant German jurist, philosopher and precursor to the Enlightenment. He claimed that natural law dictated an original equality between men and women which was then modified by state and civil society, and concluded that neither divine law nor superior strength gave males sovereignty over females.[131] By the eighteenth century some, including William Paley, agreed, considering that 'nature . . . left the sexes of the human species nearly equal in their faculties, and perfectly so in respect of their rights'.[132] Yet others disagreed. For example, Jean-Jacques Rousseau firmly believed that women were made specially to please men, and should be educated accordingly.[133]

The paradox that, although nature might give men and women equal faculties, women were not treated as equal in law, was deftly disposed of by William Blackstone. Blackstone acknowledged that the common law may appear to disadvantage women by imposing various legal disabilities on married women under coverture, but then justified these same disabilities because 'even [these] . . . are for the most part intended for her protection and benefit. So great a favourite is the female sex of the laws of England.'[134] Blackstone, who evidently read and admired Pufendorf, stopped short of arguing for equality, although neither did he cite greater male physical strength as a justification for inequality.

To resolve questions about relations between men and women, Bentham did not refer to the law of nature but to the principle of utility. Notably, when he said that the pleasure derived from the union of the sexes was a pleasure, possibly the greatest pleasure, he made no distinction between men and women. Therefore, his legislator's task was to ensure that as many people as possible, regardless of gender, would benefit. For the logical basis of his notion of sexual union as a universal source of human pleasure, Bentham's principle of utility, premised 'an original equality of all members of the human race, based on their common psychological structure', as Lea Campos Boralevi has aptly expressed it.[135] It is certainly true that he clearly made a connection between utility and equality between men and women in his later writings. For example, in 1830 he made clear that the principle of utility dictated that when the legislator made laws for inheritance the rule should be one of equality between men and women.[136] However, Bentham's recognition of equality between men and women received its clearest exposition in his earlier writings on marriage, and in particular in his comments on fixed-term marriages. He asked why, given that physical love was a pleasure and devoid of moral sanction, sexual shame in temporary marriages should attach to the woman and not the man. He also wrote: 'The scorn that chastity deserves, let us not extend it to modesty. Nothing is more different than those two qualities, though weak eyes are bound to confuse them.'[137] Diderot, too, had undertaken such a discussion on chastity and absolute continence in *D'Alembert's Dream*, which he wrote in 1769. This was not published until 1782, but Bentham may have known of it because it was widely circulated in manuscript form.[138]

Contrasting the harsh attitudes of his own time with those of ancient Greece and Rome, Bentham decided that the problem was that 'the demon of asceticism has chosen to establish his capital' in the regulation of sexual relations. But, he added, 'I write on legislation, and not on history'.[139] Thus, his proposals for legally contracted fixed-term marriages were part of his utilitarian reform of the law of marriage. He sought to banish the demon of asceticism with a reformed law of marriage which would look to the greatest happiness of both men and women.

3

Making a Marriage

THE REGULATION OF MARRIAGE AND LORD HARDWICKE'S ACT

When Bentham began his work some 25 years or more had passed since Parliament had enacted The Clandestine Marriages Act (1753), popularly known as Lord Hardwicke's Act.[1] This had regulated the formation of marriage in England by statute by requiring compliance with certain formalities, including the entry of the marriage into a register kept by the parish priest. Marriages were to be solemnized in a local parish church within prescribed seasons and hours, according to the form set out in the marriage service in the *Book of Common Prayer*, and after banns had been called on three successive Sundays. Alternatively a bishop's licence or special licence would dispense with the need for banns, but parental consent was needed instead for those under 21. Bentham accepted the provisions of the Act, making little reference to legislation which after all was neither new nor innovatory by the time he began his work on marriage formation.

Even before the Act an eighteenth-century marriage was most unlikely to be contracted by means of supposedly traditional marriage customs and practices, such as handfasting or troth-plight.[2] Instead before 1753 an 'irregular', or unsolemnized marriage could be contracted by exchange of promises in the present tense, *per verba de praesenti*, or by a promise of future marriage, *per verba de futuro*. Both canon and common law had accepted such marriages as valid, albeit defective because they failed to meet canon law requirements.[3]

Recent scholarship claims that both before and after Lord Hardwicke's Act most English people went to considerable lengths to make certain that their marriages conformed with the requirements of the 1549 Act of Uniformity (2 & 3 Edw. VI c. 1), and its successors, so as to ensure that they were valid. These Acts made the *Book of Common Prayer* the only legal form of worship and provided the English church with a form of ceremony, 'The Forme of Solemnization of Matrimonie' in the vernacular. Marriages were to be solemnized in a parish church after due publicity by the calling of banns or by bishop's licence.[4] The church's teaching on the need for banns and solemnization had been generally successful, and few marriages took place without church solemnization.[5] For if a marriage were later discovered not to be valid, the risk was that any children would be illegitimate and would lose rights of succession to property. Thus in 1771, in order to comply with statute, the Dissenter Thomas Paine married twice in one day, first in a Nonconformist chapel at Lewes in Sussex, and then at the nearby Anglican church.[6]

In the years just before Lord Hardwicke's Act, much public criticism was made about clandestine marriages taking place in 'lawless' churches called 'peculiars'. Peculiars existed outside of the jurisdiction and control of the bishop, and claimed their own rights to issue marriage licences and to conduct marriage ceremonies.[7] Some prison chapels, notoriously that at the Fleet Prison, also claimed the status of lawless churches and carried on a profitable trade in 'clandestine marriages'.[8] Such marriages were termed 'clandestine' because of some defect in the formalities as, for example, a failure to call banns. Before the Act they were nonetheless valid.[9] As we have seen, it was the tale of one particular clandestine marriage that drew Bentham's attention to the need to reform the law.[10]

Lord Hardwicke's Act made most of the canon law requirements for forming a marriage statutory,[11] and so brought to an end the public scandals of runaway elopements and clandestine marriages. If the Act's requirements for publicity, registration and solemnization were not met, the marriage would be void.[12]

Despite Bentham's own acceptance of the need for the statutory regulation of marriage formation, Lord Hardwicke's Act was not universally popular. Even two decades after it had become law, the mandatory formalities required by the Act met with much parliamentary and popular opposition.[13] One difficulty was that by specifying the use of the marriage service in the *Book of Common Prayer* the Act had imposed Anglican marriage ceremonies on everyone, including Dissenters[14] and Catholics (although it specifically excluded Quakers and Jews) which made the Act difficult to enforce.[15] Complaints were made to the effect that the Act added yet another statute to an already excessive number of new Acts of Parliament,[16] and let Parliament take on an unwarranted regulation of private life.[17] Fears were voiced too that the Act would lead to a fall in the numbers of marriages and that this in turn would result in an unwanted fall in population.[18] Thus, Blackstone worried that putting restraints on marriage might inhibit lower class population growth.[19] The anonymous author of a 1753 pamphlet, calling himself 'Bystander', quoted Hume to argue that the 'only End of Marriage, with which the Publick has any concern, is that of the Propagation of the Species', and that England, like every other modern state, should act to promote, and not to prevent, 'the Propagation of the Species'.[20]

When Lord Hardwicke's bill was first debated in Parliament, alarming predictions were made that the Act would leave women more vulnerable to seduction, because promises to marry *per verba de praesenti* or *per verba de futuro* could no longer be enforced by the church courts.[21] Blackstone feared that by prohibiting all suits in church courts to compel marriage for promises exchanged *per verba de praesenti*, and by abolishing pre-contract, the Act would, in effect, encourage unscrupulous gallants in their seduction of women.[22] In the 1780s Bentham was sufficiently concerned about the seduction of women to list it as an offence in his penal code. He defined seduction as 'where a man by false promises of marriage attains carnal knowledge of an unmarried woman who is of good fame of chastity'.[23]

It is true that women were disadvantaged in finding paid employment and that marriage brought financial support, but it has been claimed that in the event Lord Hardwicke's Act did not bring about such dire consequences for women.[24] Nevertheless, bills to repeal the Act were repeatedly brought before Parliament. The Act was especially criticized for imposing a mandatory financial burden on the marriages of the poor. Charles James Fox took up Blackstone's claim that the Act discriminated against the poor, particularly soldiers and sailors, who could not always comply with residence requirements and could not afford to pay for solemnization in church.[25]

Bentham did not write in support of any of the bills to amend the 1753 Act, and so, by implication, he supported the retention of its crucial section that rendered void any marriage which did not comply with the Act.[26] Indeed, Bentham's support for the regulation of marriage formation went further, for he supported moves to extend the Act to Scotland. He complained that the law in Scotland was far too accommodating because it allowed impatient English minors to 'relieve themselves by an off-hand marriage at a village on the Scotch frontier, called Gretna Green'.[27]

SECULAR MARRIAGE

Bentham intended his law of marriage to be secular. So, in his code, forming a marriage would depend on the law of contract and not on church solemnization.

Generally he made very few references to canon law or to the role of the church courts over marriage formation, although this was increasingly discussed in the years before the Ecclesiastical Commission was appointed in 1832.[28] His silence here may be because he wanted to avoid confrontation and controversy; after all, in the 1780s he expected to publish his civil and penal codes, and hoped too that the penal code would be enacted by some benevolent despot, perhaps Catherine the Great of Russia, if not by the English Parliament. Alternatively, rather than ignoring the role of the church courts, perhaps he intended to reserve his comments on church court reform for a separate work on the Church of England, which he did in fact begin before 1800.[29]

By 1830 Bentham was much less circumspect: 'why is it' he asked, 'that religion should be thought to have anything more to do with the contract by the execution of which the species is preserved' than a contract for, say food and drink?[30] His irate, somewhat scurrilous, remarks concluded by referring to the tradition of saying grace before some meals but not others, a custom for which he could find no rational basis.[31] But, whatever his opinions, until their jurisdiction over marriage ended in 1857,[32] the English church courts retained their jurisdiction over marriage, and the church claimed a special interest in marriage.

Nevertheless, Bentham's plans for secular marriage would not necessarily have alienated all his readers, for between 1600 and 1800 religious and secular traditions on marriage law coexisted in Europe. Arguably, a secular, contractual theory of marriage was in many respects perfectly compatible with reformed Protestant theories on the nature of marriage. For during the course of the sixteenth century, European Reformation Protestant reformers had rejected the Catholic doctrine of the sacramental nature of marriage, and the leading Protestant reformers all saw marriage as a civil contract.[33]

In particular, the teaching of the Church of Rome is that marriage is a sacrament – that is, the outward sign of inward grace. As a consequence, when husband and wife contract before God an indissoluble bond is created between them.[34] By contrast, in Protestant England the *Book of Common Prayer* of the Church of England (1549 and 1559) described marriage as an 'honourable estate'.[35]

As we have seen, the German philosopher Samuel Pufendorf (1632–94) considered marriage to be contractual and not sacramental.[36] Pufendorf's work became widely available when it was translated into French in the eighteenth century, and was known to many who wrote on marriage, including the travel writer and historian Thomas Salmon, and William Blackstone. Salmon's anonymously published *Critical Essay Concerning Marriage* (1724), and then Blackstone's *Commentaries on the Laws of England* (1765), both describe marriage as a secular contract, and both cite Pufendorf.[37] Salmon, Bentham and Paley all made comparisons between marriage contracts and contracts for services, particularly in order to argue for a law of divorce.[38] We know that Bentham read Blackstone,[39] and it is likely that he read Salmon on the law of marriage too.

Salmon and Blackstone, said to be Tory in their political sympathies, were nevertheless influenced by Enlightenment thought.[40] For Blackstone, although natural law was dictated by God himself, the common law treated a contract of marriage as it did any other. It became valid if the parties were willing and able to contract, and then did so contract in the required form.[41] Salmon also likened a marriage contract to any other contract where the parties meet to conclude their agreement and then 'Writings are ordered to testify the Agreement, and there is the Solemnisation of signing and sealing etc.' in order to prevent fraud.[42] Among Bentham's own contemporaries, William Paley confessed that he was quite unable to find anything in a marriage contract that distinguished it from other contracts.[43]

Blackstone's opinions reflected his Protestant belief that there was no necessity for priestly intervention between God and man, but his purpose here was to accommodate canon law into the English system of common law which he presented in the *Commentaries*.[44] He achieved this by suggesting a hierarchy of law, with canon law being inferior in status to common law.[45] Bentham, however, was not concerned with hierarchies of law, or with multiple legal jurisdictions. Although he too understood marriage contracts as secular, his purpose was to produce a new unified and codified law of marriage based on the principle of utility.

Bentham's secularism also reflected his Enlightenment interest in non-European cultures, a perspective that in turn allowed a new vantage point for the scrutiny of existing English customs. Bentham and his contemporaries knew well that marriage was not considered a religious event in some other countries, for eighteenth-century Englishmen and women read reports of voyages to the South Seas,[46] and many also read Montesquieu's popular books with their descriptions of laws and customs of other cultures.[47] For Montesquieu marriage was a secular contract designed to benefit society.[48]

Salmon likewise concluded his book on marriage with a very lengthy appendix which described marriage customs in different cultures and ages,[49] including ancient Rome where marriages were contracted by civil ceremony.

History also revealed English precedents for secular marriages. In Anglo-Saxon England civil and church marriages coexisted for a time, while during the Interregnum, between 1653 to 1657, civil marriage ceremonies had been mandatory, following a Commonwealth Statute of 1653 which made void all marriages except those made by civil magistrates.

Blackstone blamed the Catholic Church for the introduction of religious ceremony into marriage. He claimed that marriage had been 'totally' civil until papal intervention in the Middle Ages. Thereafter, during the English 'grand rebellion', marriages could only take place in a civil ceremony before a Justice of the Peace. After the Restoration these civil marriages were accepted as valid (by statute), which proved that a second, religious, ceremony was thought unnecessary.[50] But Bentham made no mention either of Rome's interference or of Commonwealth statutes, although his education would have made him familiar with Roman law, and it is safe to assume that he was familiar too with the history of the English Civil War and the Commonwealth.

Bentham died in 1832, and some years later civil marriage ceremonies were reintroduced by the Marriage Act of 1836, which followed the recommendations of a Royal Commission on the establishment of an office of Registrar General of Births, Deaths and Marriages.[51] Some claim to see Bentham's influence at work here, because the Commission's findings reflect his ideas. It is true that one of the Commissioners was his friend and literary executor, John Bowring, and this might well explain Bentham's influence.[52]

BENTHAM'S MARRIAGE CONTRACT

In the 1780s, in manuscripts headed 'Project Matière. Private Law. Marriage Questions', probably used by Dumont for his edition, Bentham posed a particular question concerning what terms and conditions a marriage contract should contain, 'whether the marriage contract is for two seconds' or longer.[53] He concluded that this was difficult to know, because men and women usually forgot to give any thought to such matters in advance of their marriage. While this forgetfulness might be quite 'normal', it did not accord with the greatest happiness principle. Much unhappiness would result if the conditions of a marriage subsequently failed to meet the expectations of wife or husband. Remarkably, Bentham's solution was to propose a model marriage contract, a part of his 'marriage code'. It was a copy of this marriage code that the legislator was to give to every couple on their marriage, so that they would know about their respective rights and obligations towards each other.

Bentham's model contract set out some terms and conditions which he intended would be implied by law into every marriage contract, while others were left to the parties themselves to agree on in order to meet their own particular needs. This arrangement would be 'a precious recipe for this contract, as for so many others!' he concluded.[54]

The first term of his model contract was the subordination of a wife to her husband's authority, which meant that during their marriage administrative decisions were for the man alone.[55] The second term required husbands and wives to make reciprocal promises to be faithful to each other.[56] The third term addressed property rights: all property was to be held in common by husband and wife during their marriage, although this was necessarily modified by the basic law that subordinated one to the other.[57] Lastly, the duration of the marriage was to be for an indefinite term, rather than for life as the Prayer Book marriage service demanded.[58] Except for this last term it is not possible to be certain which of Bentham's terms and conditions were capable of amendment and which were not. This may be because some of the 1780s manuscripts are incomplete or missing. However, his overall aim is clear: he wished to reconcile private interests with public needs. His model contract was therefore a 'simple et unique moyen pour mettre d'accord ces deux eternels rivaux, gouvernment et liberté', giving 'all that the parties may wish'.[59]

The second term of the model marriage contract, requiring the prospective husband and wife to give reciprocal promises to be faithful, also appears to be incapable of amendment. Although the promises of fidelity that each gave were to be identical, the reasons Bentham gave for extracting the promises were not. These reasons are likely to represent popular sentiments rather than his own opinion. In particular, the wife would promise not to grant her favours to any other man because, as Bentham put it, what is paid for at a high price will not be sold to another for nothing. Emphasizing the significance conventionally attached to female chastity, he stated that the 'treasures of love' lose their value once they have been used, so that the pleasure one receives loses its value in proportion to the number of other hands that receive it.[60] There would seem to be a contradiction between Bentham's insistence on mutual fidelity in his marriage contract, and the admiration he expressed for the indulgence of extramarital sexual pleasure for husbands and wives among the French aristocracy of the *ancien régime*.[61] But, as we shall see in Chapter 6, Bentham thought that while infidelity brought with it (usually) only transitory pleasure, it also brought great harm. It generally brought harm to husbands, wives, lovers and children, and great danger too of harm to the whole community.[62]

Applying a utilitarian analysis, Bentham explained that the foundation of a union between a man and a woman was pleasure, this being the great 'cement' that binds together all their other interests. If this pleasure were to weaken then all other interests within a marriage would be adversely affected. For instance, if a husband were less valuable to a wife 'in this quality', then she would be less motivated to behave well towards him in her accessory roles as servant, steward, nursemaid, companion, and so on. In addition, the more a wife multiplies her infidelities, the greater will be her husband's danger of finding himself raising the children of other men, which is a burden that does not elicit the sentiment of paternity. In fact, Bentham concluded, the sources of life itself will have been poisoned.[63]

In his turn, the husband promises to be faithful to his wife during their marriage and not to seek pleasure in the arms of another woman.[64] However, Bentham believed that a man's infidelity does not weaken the interests he shares in common with his wife, because the right to exercise administrative power within the marriage is always more favourable to him than to her.[65]

He then turned his attention to the children that may possibly result from an extramarital union. He thought that the dangers relating to the obligation to raise the children of others would be less onerous in the case where it is the wife who takes on this role. It is interesting to note that Bentham expressed these opinions before the birth of his brother Samuel's illegitimate daughters, one of whom, Elizabeth Gordon, was brought up with Samuel's legitimate children.[66]

Bentham incorporated the existing rules of canon law into his marriage code, holding that children produced by a wife during their marriage will be deemed to be legitimate, whereas the children born to another woman will not be deemed to be the husband's unless the affair was with an unmarried woman. In this latter case, the woman will take a share in the expense of raising the children, but the man will bear the burden too.

Finally, of all the motives men have for stipulating fidelity in a marriage only the last, that the sources of life itself have been poisoned, and the third, that the pleasure one receives loses its value in proportion to the number of other hands that receive it, have equal weight for both men and women.[67]

A further term in Bentham's model marriage contract addresses the duration of the marriage. He asked 'For how long?', and replied, for the time the parties find appropriate: lifelong marriage may not be possible, suitable or desirable. Therefore, as we saw in Chapter 1 in connection with his proposal for short-term marriages, and will see in Chapter 7 on divorce, Bentham's solution was to leave the parties themselves to decide on the duration of their marriage.[68]

AT WHAT AGE?

Bentham was concerned to ensure that marrying couples should have reached marriageable age, which (without parental consent) was 21, and that they were not being forced to marry by parents or anyone else. In 'ordinary cases' – presumably by this he meant marriage by banns rather than by special licence – marriage should be celebrated only in a specified place, such as a church, and only at certain hours. Then, if the bride or groom appeared to be too young, the officiating priest or officer should question them privately.[69]

Bentham's laws ensuring the freedom of marriage belonged to the civil code, while laws regarding marriage forced by the use of unlawful threats of physical or other injury belonged to the penal code. Duress had long been a *diramentary impediment* to marriage in canon law, and if proven, a church court would grant a divorce *a vincula* and annul the marriage. Despite its presence in the penal code, Bentham provided no punishment for forced marriage but instead declared that the marriage would be held void. This, he wrote, would have the effect of taking away the inducement for committing the crime in the first place. He added that if a forced marriage had been consummated, the offence should be punished as rape, because a marriage ceremony could not operate to justify or excuse this offence.[70]

Bentham particularly deplored marriages forced on young people by their parents.[71] Enlightenment arguments in favour of freedom of choice of a marriage partner were much in evidence in philosophical writings and popular literature at the time.[72] One English writer explained that an immediate cause of unhappy marriages was the way in which young people were married off by their parents who took more interest taken in the money changing hands than in whether the young people were matched in 'Ages, Tempers, and Constitutions'.[73]

Bentham thought such forced marriages to be so iniquitous that no penalty should be incurred by the unhappy couple should they later commit adultery. 'Where there is no happiness at first, there is no happiness to be disturbed. There can be no happiness lost where there is no happiness to lose. It is the contracting the engagement that is the misfortune, not the violation of it. If the parties are not permitted to consult their own happiness/make themselves happy/in their first choice, it is high time they should consult it in a second.'[74] When the marriage is 'a marriage not between persons but between families or estates, let the families or the estates (if it be so remain united) but let the persons be set free/at liberty'.[75]

Bentham likewise argued that blame for adultery vanishes altogether in those unhappy countries where the custom is for young people to be married off by their parents, or by someone even less concerned for their happiness, without any regard for their own inclinations.[76] Perhaps his vehemence was because he recalled his own unhappiness in 1776 when his hopes of marrying Polly Dunkley had failed in the face of his father's objections.[77] He was also no doubt familiar with the famous case referred to as 'Sir G. D. and Mrs. Forester', in which two young people whose child marriage had been arranged for them by their parents in order to further dynastic interests, petitioned Parliament to dissolve the marriage. Rejecting counsel's arguments on the contractual nature of marriage, Parliament had refused their joint petition.[78]

Bentham also criticized Lord Hardwicke's Act for failing to ensure that young people freely consented to their marriage. He wrote that the formalities necessary for making a marriage ought to have two objectives: first, to establish the willing consent of both parties to their marriage, and second, to establish a record of the marriage for future reference. The existing law, he wrote, paid insufficient attention to the question of free consent, and insufficient attention also to preventing the officials entrusted with enforcing the required formalities from abusing their power for 'any sinister end'.[79]

In fact in the 1780s much criticism of the Act claimed that it mainly benefited aristocratic patriarchs who sought to control their children's lives. Both Henry Fox and his son Charles James Fox were particularly critical of that part of the Act,[80] and another observer complained that rather than preventing political 'evil' to the state, the Act was really about private interest or 'the Pride of Family', which sought to prevent marriages deemed unworthy because of a lack of fortune.[81] Blackstone too was concerned about the Act's extension of parental control over marriage, and he complained that it had followed what he called 'the French example', because following the Act underage marriage without parental consent was void. He pointed out that Roman law had been less harsh. Although marriage was forbidden without parental consent, yet it was at the same time less rigorous 'with regard to other restraints'. He explained that if a father failed to provide his daughter with a husband by the time she reached 25 'and she afterwards made a slip in her conduct, he was not allowed to disinherit her on that account'.[82]

In France, where as Blackstone noted, sons did not reach their majority until the age of 30, a father had greater authority than in England. A disobedient son or daughter could be imprisoned by means of a *lettre de cachet* in order to prevent an unsuitable match. The encyclopaedist Denis Diderot met with this fate when he defied his father, but managed to escape to marry as he wished. Sadly, his marriage is reported to have brought him much unhappiness.[83]

Earlier, in 1724, Salmon too had criticized those English parents who, by withholding money, prevented their children from marrying, and so compelled them 'to be wicked'. How, he asked, can a father possibly know who would be the best match for a child? 'Will a Father pretend to know which Lover is like to make the most agreeable Companion for his Daughters? Nor can it be properly be called a Marriage, where there is not a Union of Souls as well as Bodies.'[84] Salmon, using John Milton's language, wrote that the 'worst of all punishments [was] deemed the tying a living Body to a dead Carcass', but even that was not as bad as a marriage forced on a son or daughter by a father.[85] Such marriages should 'be declared null from the beginning'.[86]

Aristocratic or propertied families in England in the eighteenth century often saw the marriages of their children as opportunities to further family interests, and as, Bentham well knew, financial pressure could be brought to bear on a son or a daughter who resisted a parent's wishes.

An important part of the pre-marriage negotiations concerned marriage settlements. These set out the arrangements made for the payment of a marriage portion (or dowry) to be brought to the marriage by the bride. The bride's family would then negotiate for payment of dower, or more usually a jointure, for the wife, to provide her support should she be widowed. A jointure was a life estate in property, which often took the form of an annuity based on a rent-charge on the property. Unlike common law dower, which it replaced, jointures were not regulated by law but negotiated and arranged by private contract.[87]

It was usual practice for the cost of a jointure to be met by the marriage portion property that a bride brought with her on marriage. By the eighteenth century draft agreements set out in precedent books used by lawyers presupposed a ratio of ten to one between portion and jointure in aristocratic families, a steep rise in cost that has been seen as an indication of the decline in the bargaining power of women.[88]

While Bentham deplored marriages forced on young people by their parents, he made stringent criticism too of the notion that overwhelming romantic passion was the only suitable motivation for marriage. He held rather that romantic love was a childish foolishness, and that a belief in the perfection of a loved one, or in everlasting love, was a 'delusion'. Maybe such foolishness was forgivable in 'two naive children blinded by passion', but it was unforgivable that the 'wise old men of the law' acted as if they too believed in everlasting love.[89]

PROHIBITED MARRIAGES

Bentham approached the problem of prohibited marriages by drafting a Table of Prohibited Alliances to prevent marriages between people related by blood (consanguinity) or by marriage (affinity). The table also set out the 'evil', meaning harm, to both individuals and the community, that would otherwise be the result,[90] and provided many punishments for those who offended against the prohibitions.

When he drafted his table, affinity was defined as a pre-existing relationship between the parties created by a former marriage or by carnal relationship outside marriage. Affinity extended to the first, second and third cousins of a spouse or of any person with whom one had had sexual relations. Affinity was also created by 'spiritual' connections with godparents and their relations. In contrast, consanguinity was a blood relationship between the parties within the prohibited four degrees. The complex laws about consanguinity had been reduced by the Marriage Act (1540) which set out simplified prohibited degrees based on the Book of Leviticus. These Henrician revisions to the law still remain in place, together with the 1907 amendment which allows marriage to the dead wife's sister.[91]

Incest, which was punished by the church courts as a sin, did not become a secular crime in England until 1908.[92] Strangely, to modern sensibilities, Bentham did not regard incest, which he defined as voluntary carnal knowledge between those who are prohibited from marrying by reason of their relationship,[93] as either a common or a major concern. He believed that most often 'natural avoidance' would operate to make it unlikely,[94] and compared the English law favourably with that of France, where incest between lineal blood relatives could be punished by death.[95] In contrast, the English ecclesiastical courts punished incest by exhibiting the offender 'with circumstances of ignominy in a Church or with such a fine as a person could be got to pay'.[96] Although the punishment in England was so much less severe, Bentham believed incest was probably rare in both countries.[97]

In Dumont's *Traites* Bentham is reported as remarking that what one age or country found acceptable another regarded as criminal. 'Every people pretend to in this respect what they call the law of nature' and look on anything that does not accord with the matrimonial laws of their own country with horror.[98] But I have not found this comment in the manuscript sources. Instead, applying a psychological analysis, Bentham writes that the great abhorrence people felt for incest is the result of the physical horror they felt at the thought of committing it themselves.[99]

In 1785 William Paley wrote of incest as 'abhorrent' and 'forbidden by the law of nature'.[100]

However, Bentham applied the principle of utility rather than the law of nature or of scripture, to determine whether incest was right or wrong. To accomplish this it was necessary to decide whether any danger of harm arose from incest which would then justify legislation making it a criminal offence. Despite its rarity he held that it was clear that 'evil' (i.e. harm) did result from committing this crime, which justified in turn the 'evil' (meaning the pain caused by loss of pleasure) of legislating to punish it.[101]

Certain unions should therefore be forbidden, such as those between siblings. Bentham believed such unions were anyway very rare, a factor which in itself reduced the 'evil' by forbidding it. Lot's daughters, he wrote, only gave themselves the trouble of sleeping with their father to save the human race from extinction.[102] His reason for forbidding unions between children and parents, or grandparents, or uncles, was the primary harm, or evil, that such unions brought to 'the weaker party'. Inevitably, children were disadvantaged.[103] He listed other 'inconveniences', or evils, as (1) evil of rivalry, (2) evil to health, (3) looseness of discipline, (4) danger of future well-being prevented by a link that cannot be other than temporary. By this last 'evil' Bentham meant that a child's future marriage was prevented by a relationship that could not itself last long, such as an with older parent or grandparent.[104]

In addition to public shaming, Bentham proposed specific punishments for various forms of incest. He proposed banishment for life for a man who committed incest with a daughter or other female relative in his descending line, or in the descending line of his brother or sister. The victim was to be financially compensated and the offender's wife permitted to remarry and to dispose of his property as if he were dead. A female transgressor received the same punishment but was not banished. A brother and sister under the age of 19 or 20 who committed incest were to be whipped at the discretion of the judge, but if the brother were over that age he was to be treated in the same manner as a transgressive father.[105]

Predictably, Bentham dismissed the idea that spiritual affinity was an offence at all, arguing that it was falsely deemed incestuous. 'In some countries they punish under the name of incest the having carnal knowledge of one's Godfather or Godchild. It were as well to punish in the same manner all intercourse between the sexes on pretence that we are all brothers and sisters in Christ.'[106]

'HOW MANY PEOPLE?': POLYGAMY AND POLYANDRY

Bentham asked 'How many people' should be in a marriage, and his question initiated a lengthy discussion of polygamy and polyandry. Much of this was suppressed in the redacted versions published by both Dumont and Bowring. Bentham defined polygamy as an offence whereby one person marries another during the continuation of a previous marriage; this would make the later marriage void. His comments accorded with the understanding of bigamy which had been an offence in common law since 1604.[107] He had little to say on polyandry, but found polygamy unacceptable because it was typically an aggravated species of fraud used to gain the person, and sometimes the fortune, of a deluded woman. It was composed of two other crimes, defraudment and seduction, but did not fit perfectly with either because the disgrace brought on a woman by polygamy is not as great as the disgrace of seduction. A woman married polygamously has been unfortunate but not culpable. However, he concluded that this may not help her much, because 'popular prejudice is seldom perfectly equitable to misfortune'.[108]

Bentham addressed many of his remarks to the writings of Montesquieu, especially to Book 14 of *The Spirit of the Laws* (1748) where Montesquieu surveyed the variety of forms of government, and the social, historical and geographical circumstances of various peoples at various times.[109] He concluded that 'the law permitting only one wife' had more relation to the physical aspect of the climate of Europe than that of Asia.[110] Enlightenment interest in comparative cultures prompted many eighteenth-century writers to make comparisons with laws and customs of other countries. For example, in 1799 Hannah More, in a book on women's education, wrote generally of the customs in countries newly discovered by circumnavigators; she was especially disapproving of the conditions of women's lives in Arabia.[111] William Paley in 1785 similarly condemned the abasement of one half of the human race in countries where polygamy was practised.[112] But Bentham departed from Montesquieu's comparative, culturally relativistic approach by arguing that it was necessary only to consult the principle of utility and not to look at other customs.[113]

Bentham's proposed punishments for the offence of multiple marriage relied mostly on public shaming. For example, a married man who committed polygamy with an unmarried woman should be ignominiously punished by being forced to wear the 'Polygamists yoke'. There is no description of this device. In addition, the offender would lose all marital rights, and was to be indelibly marked in the neck with the 'Polygamists chain', which again is not described. The offender's first wife was to have the right to 'have him put away', an act that would repudiate the marriage. If she did so, then the second wife had the choice of either marrying the polygamist or repudiating the marriage, and so on. The offender was to pay maintenance for any children and to return any property to the second woman, and also to pay her a sum in compensation which would be doubled if she were a virgin. There should be a legal presumption that the woman was in fact a virgin, unless it were satisfactorily proved she was either a widow, or else of 'evil fame'.[114] Public notices, expiring on a fixed date, should be given to alert any other woman who might be eligible for compensation. Certain defences were allowed, such as knowledge on the part of the second wife, desertion ab initio by the former wife, or subsequent desertion, in which cases the man was to be punished as an adulterer. Other 'excuses' – that is, defences – were ignorance of the law, innocence of intention, intoxication and deference to authority (presumably meaning compulsion).

A single woman who married a married man was also to be punished by the 'Polygamists yoke' and treated as an adulterer too because this offence was 'an aggravated species of adultery'.[115] Similarly, a single man who committed polygamy with a married woman was to be punished as an adulterer.[116]

Bentham worried about the disclosure of the marital status of foreigners who came to live in England. They might already be married, and so their subsequent marriages in England would be bigamous or polygamous, and therefore void. Accordingly, when foreigners arrived in England they should 'be obliged to declare whether they are married or single: and if single whether Bachelors or Spinsters, Widowers or Widows'.[117] Registers of these declarations would be kept and would be produced before any foreigner was allowed to marry. The declarations should contain some details of parentage and last abode so that a check could be made if necessary. A false declaration would be punished as perjury. If the foreigner had previously been married in their own country, they must produce their spouse's death certificate before being allowed to marry in England. 'At the moment', Bentham pointed out, 'these important enquiries are left to the prudence of individuals.'[118] He suggested that if a foreigner did marry bigamously then the man should be punished by 'forfeiture of such and such marital rights', but he did not explain what these were. Foreign men, and women too, who married bigamously were also to be punished with a fine.[119]

4

The Subordination of Women

THE DOCTRINE OF COVERTURE

Until its last ghostly presence was finally laid to rest in 1981,[1] the common law doctrine of coverture governed the legal relationship between husband and wife during marriage. Under this doctrine an unmarried woman, called a feme sole, was transformed by marriage into a feme covert, and she was thereby subject to far-reaching legal disabilities, particularly with respect to her ability to own real and personal property.

Until the late nineteenth century a wife's real property (land) vested in her husband for the duration of the marriage: she could neither alienate (sell or give) nor devise (leave by will) her land without her husband's consent. In contrast, all her personal property (including money, furniture, jewellery) vested in her husband absolutely and it was his to dispose of as he saw fit.[2] In addition, until the twentieth-century reforms, a married woman was unable to sue or to be sued in her own name, and neither could she enter into contracts in her own name.[3]

Now, but not necessarily in Bentham's time, the best-known definition is William Blackstone's:

> By marriage, the husband and wife are one person in law: that is, the very being or legal existence of the woman is suspended during the marriage, or at least is incorporated and consolidated into that of her husband: under whose wing, protection, and *cover*, she performs everything; and is therefore called in our law-French a *feme-covert*.[4]

In the 1780s, Bentham made no mention at all of Blackstone's definition of coverture – perhaps surprisingly in view of the fact that Bentham as a student at Oxford attended Blackstone's lectures on the common law, and must therefore have heard it from Blackstone himself. Of course, Blackstone's now-famous definition embodied a legal fiction, that of 'unity of person',[5] and as such Bentham rejected it, describing it in 1827 as 'grim gribber' (the unreformed law) nonsense.[6]

Bentham's omission was certainly not because he was unaware of the doctrine of coverture. As an eighteenth-century gentleman and lawyer, Bentham was well versed in the legal niceties of his class. He knew all about marriage agreements, dower, jointure, trusts, and about the legal disabilities imposed on married women. When he read Constantia Phillips's memoirs he no doubt noticed that Phillips admitted that the purpose of her first, faulty, marriage had been to use the doctrine of coverture to her own advantage. That is, at the age of 15 she had paid a bigamist to marry her in order to escape her debts, because once married she was under her husband's *cover* and her debts became his instead. Phillips's purported husband then conveniently disappeared, leaving her creditors to bear the loss.[7]

Bentham also had close personal acquaintance with the workings of coverture. As a young man, he knew that it was his inheritance of monies from his late mother's marriage settlement that enabled him to lead an independent life. In 1777 he and his brother Samuel tried to help the Wise family, who were close relations of the Davies family with whom Samuel Bentham lodged at Chatham during his naval apprenticeship. Robert Wise had borrowed money from his mother-in-law on the understanding that the Wise family house in Battle and other property were security for the loan. But Robert failed to execute the mortgage deed in favour of his mother-in-law and instead granted an equitable mortgage of the family home to two other creditors by depositing the title deeds with them.[8] Bentham and his brother strove to protect the house for Robert's wife Sarah, who was subject to coverture and therefore unable to hold property herself (although her widowed mother could do so). Bentham spent much time and effort but in the end failed to uncover the whole truth about Robert Wise's financial and legal dealings, or to persuade him to execute a new deed.[9] He complained to Samuel:

> I am sick to death of this whole business as you may well believe. It forces me partly to rummage up or partly to learn *de novo* such a quantity of that villainous grim gribber, which I hoped by leaving off business [presumably the practice of law] I had gotten rid of. It is a great load on my weak shoulders, added to what I have got already. Yes indeed am I heartily sick of it. But when I think of 9 children and two women whom together with at least one of their husbands we both love and with whom you are so inextricably connected, I am still more sick at the thoughts of giving it up. *Allons donc*, I see I must draw at last the deeds for W. to execute: and then

> shall I have to whip, spur, cut slash to make him execute them and do the other etcs.[10]

In the event Robert Wise deserted his wife and children in November 1777,[11] and Sarah committed suicide.[12]

As a trained lawyer, Bentham was well aware that married women's property rights had a significance beyond the disabilities imposed on them by coverture. In particular he knew that a widow's common law right to dower had a profound effect on property law, particularly conveyancing. Dower rights were extensive. Calculated as a life estate in one-third of all her deceased husband's lands, even those he had sold or alienated before his death, the widow's dower rights continued even if she remarried.[13] Dower rights were sometimes understood as a corollary to a wife's inability to hold land in her own name during her marriage.

Admittedly, by the late eighteenth century, dower had more or less disappeared because dower could be barred by an agreement made before marriage for payment of a jointure to a widow instead.[14] Yet until the Dower Act (1833) allowed a husband to bar dower at will, dower continued to cause problems in conveying land.[15] Conveyancers drafted deeds putting land into trust to prevent dower arising in the first place, and prospective purchasers were forced to undertake lengthy searches of previous title deeds (sometimes looking back a hundred years) to ensure they acquired a good unencumbered title to land. Much legal expertise was applied to property law and marriage. For example, in 1816 the lawyer Peregrine Bingham devoted 100 out of a total of 205 pages of legal treatise on coverture to a careful description of a wife's separate estate, a widow's right to dower (and how to bar it), jointures and marriage settlements.[16]

By the late eighteenth century, dower rights were seen as inhibiting the growth of a free market in land. Bentham supported a right to private property and, late in his life, in 1826, approved the benefits of a free market in land.[17] His 'disappointment preventative principle', a branch of the greatest happiness principle, was particularly adapted to land law,[18] but on the other hand Bentham certainly did not agree that private property rights meant a complete freedom of testation for property owners in which widow's rights had no place. 'Property and the law are born together and die together', he remarked.[19] In about 1790 Bentham prepared a code for a law of succession set out in 15 articles together with explanation and comment. The code applied on both intestate and testate succession, and made no distinction between real or personal property. Importantly, he restricted the testator's 'temptation of acting the part of the tyrant'.[20] Here he praised existing the French law of the *legitime*, and the 'orphan's share' found in the customs of London. It was just not acceptable that parents should have the power to starve a child by failing to provide for it. Bentham's code set out a statutory regime for inheritance, with generous provision for children and, particularly, a surviving spouse, anticipating the reforms eventually made by the Administration of Estates Act 1925.[21]

Complaints about the ill effects of dower on conveyancing were still being voiced in 1829, when the Real Property Commissioners presented their *First Report* to which Bentham had been invited to contribute.[22] In fact all the law that Bentham described as 'villainous grim gribber' made conveyancing lawyers wealthy, property law complex,[23] and a widow's rights increasingly precarious.

THE SUBORDINATION OF WOMEN IN MARRIAGE

The doctrine of coverture assumed an unequal legal relationship between men and women in which married women were subordinate to men, and therefore coverture's effect was not confined to the problems of legal practice. Inevitably, the doctrine raised political and moral questions concerning the nature of marriage and the status of women.

Since the seventeenth century the evident legal inequality between men and women in marriage had been much commented on by religious, moral and political writers on marriage. These texts often relied on scriptural authority to explain and justify a wife's subordination to her husband.[24] Coverture, sometimes called 'unity of person', was frequently closely identified with the church's teaching that on marriage husband and wife became 'one flesh'.[25] But in reality different considerations were being addressed: the church's teaching addressed the nature and purpose of marriage (the founding of a new family – husband and wife must leave mother and father and cleave to one another), whereas the common law doctrine of coverture described the content of the legal relations between husband and wife. It is most likely that the origins of the doctrine can be found in the treatment of women as inferiors in the more primitive society of earlier times.[26]

In Protestant England the *Book of Common Prayer* of the Church of England (1549 and 1559) described marriage as an 'honourable estate'.[27] At the start of the ceremony marriage was declared to be for purposes of procreation, for avoiding sin and lastly (innovatively) for 'mutuall society, helpe and coumforte'. It was this last purpose that led to marriages contracted by the Prayer Book service being known as 'companionate marriage'.[28] Husbands and wives were to be partners in their marriage. In the eighteenth century this companionate thesis of marriage was reflected in Dr Gregory's conduct book on marriage where he wrote that he considered women not as drudges or slaves of men's pleasure, but as their companions and equals.[29]

In the seventeenth century the institution of marriage was often described in political terms as a microcosm of an ordered commonwealth, with the man as the head and governor of his household exercising authority over his wife, children and servants, just as the king ruled his subjects. A man 'must govern his wife', wrote the Puritan preacher William Whately in 1619; 'Nature hath framed the lineaments of his body to superiority, and set the print of government in his very face', and God's authority was invested in his person.[30]

By the time Blackstone published his definition of coverture in the *Commentaries* in 1765,[31] the legal relationship between men and women was more likely to be described as contractual rather than hierarchical, but this change should not be unduly emphasized. Relations within marriage continued to be described variously as companionate, hierarchical or contractual.[32] All three models continued to exist side by side despite their evident incompatibility.[33] The writings of John Milton and William Blackstone have been used to argue that despite a new emphasis on domestic relations as contractual, even the most radical writers on marriage automatically assumed that the husband had authority within a family.[34] Blackstone, for example, saw marriage as a contract. This implies a certain equality between the contracting parties, and yet at the same time Blackstone asserted that a man had (hierarchical) legal authority over his wife. Other writers advised husbands to 'rule in love' – that is, to be patriarchal yet companionate.[35]

Blackstone recognized his own inconsistency in accepting women's equality in nature and yet imposing legal disabilities on married women. He attempted a reconciliation: the authority men possessed over women was not God-given but founded in nature and modified by civil society.[36]

Tim Stretton explains that Blackstone grounded his definition of coverture on the fiction of unity of person, but that prior to the eighteenth century this was not the main source of the law governing the relations between husbands and wives. Instead, a wife's subordination to her husband was described as the power – meaning physical and legal authority – that a husband exercised over her. For example, according to Bracton a wife was 'under the rod' of her husband. Indeed, Stretton holds that Blackstone's unique achievement in the *Commentaries* was to fuse together an understanding of the common law doctrine of coverture with that of the fiction of 'unity of person'.[37]

Bentham's mode of rejecting Blackstone's formulation of the doctrine of coverture was to ignore it completely and to substitute his own regime for legal relations between husbands and wives. Although he did not say so explicitly, he might have retorted, as he did elsewhere: 'in Blackstone every abuse had its varnish or its apology'.[38]

Bentham was not alone in ignoring Blackstone's definition of coverture: other contemporary moralists writing on marriage made no mention of it either. William Paley, for example, stressed equality between men and women, but made no mention of the doctrine of coverture.[39] Some, like Mary Wollstonecraft and Hannah More, found the poor education of women, particularly in fashionable boarding schools and seminaries, and not the largely economic operation of the doctrine of coverture, to be the most significant factor in the subjection of women. Neither made any mention of coverture.[40] Many legal writers referred to a husband's physical strength as the defining factor in legal relations between husband and wife, rejecting Blackstone's notion that common law disabilities were somehow designed to protect and benefit wives. For example, in 1818 Peregrine Bingham considered that a married woman was subject to even greater disabilities than an infant, because while the disabilities attached to infancy were designed to protect them, those attached to coverture 'are the simple consequence of that sole authority which the law has recognized in the husband, subject to judicial interference whenever he transgresses its proper limits'.[41] Perhaps, then, some present-day understandings of the effects of the doctrine are oversimplified, relying too heavily on Blackstone's definition and tending to overlook its bizarre nature and uneven application in the eighteenth century.

In any event the legal fiction that husband and wife were one person, and that the husband was the head, was never applied consistently. For one thing, as a common law doctrine it was simply ignored in some other jurisdictions. The church courts and local courts 'unlike the courts of common law . . . did not observe the doctrine of coverture',[42] and the central equity courts, the Courts of Requests and Chancery, allowed married women rights of audience.[43] Also, in practice, as Margot Finn writes, there was a 'disjuncture between legal theory and social practice' evident in married women's debt and credit relations;[44] Finn argues that in relation to these coverture existed in a state of 'suspended animation', for many women could live quite unaffected by it until some event brought it sharply into consideration.[45]

BENTHAM'S NEW LEGAL REGIME

Bentham believed the principle of utility demanded reform of the common law doctrine of coverture. His solution was a new legal regime for relations within marriage, based on the law of trusts and the principle of utility. As we have seen, this principle accepted an equality in nature between men and women.[46] Yet, when we turn to Bentham's published work on marriage, we discover with some surprise that he confirmed a patriarchal hierarchy of sorts, for in other contexts Bentham proposed equality between men and women.[47]

A brief explanation of publishing history, as far as it is known, is necessary at this stage. In 1970, H. L. A. Hart repeated Bentham's own explanation that he had completed and printed *An Introduction to the Principles of Morals and Legislation* by 1780, but did not publish it until 1789.[48] He published a second, corrected edition in 1823, and then in 1838, after his death, a third edition was published by his literary executor John Bowring.[49] Bowring inserted into this third edition some passages from Etienne Dumont's edition of the *Traites de Legislation Civile et Penale*, published in 1802, while Dumont had in turn incorporated the first six chapters of *IPML* into the *Traites*. As a result of these cross borrowings it is hard to establish dates for the composition of the manuscripts on marriage on which the several editions relied. If *IPML* was already printed by 1780 then it must have been written in the 1770s. An additional difficulty is that Dumont did not publish all of Bentham's writings on marriage. Indeed quite difficult is to discover which papers Bentham gave him access to, and then what became of them later. Bentham believed that Dumont retained some of his papers in Geneva and after Dumont died in 1829 he wrote to his nephew asking for their return.[50]

I will turn first to Bentham's explanation of a wife's subordination in *IPML* and the *Traites*, and will conclude with a consideration of his unpublished manuscripts. In *IPML* Bentham explains that in domestic relations where two people live together the superior role could be given either to one or to both. If to both, then disputes could only be settled by physical force ('laying aside generosity and good breeding which are the tardy and uncertain fruits of long-established laws').[51] In domestic relations between parents and children, authority is given to parents to protect children from harm, but this does not apply between man and wife. So the only real reason for giving authority to the husband is to avoid competition between the two partners, and to forestall the need to adjudicate disputes between them. Looking around, a legislator will see that wherever men and women live together the man possessed the power in the relationship, and so the legislator should 'place legal power in the same hands as physical power' – those of the man.[52] Bentham then adds a last comment: 'so much for *reasons*: add to which, in point of *motives*, that legislators seem all to have been of the male sex, down to the days of Catherine'.[53] Bentham gives two examples of the kind of petty dispute that could never be resolved without resort to a judge if husband and wife had equal authority: quarrels about roast or boiled meat, and about the colour of a child's clothing.[54] We can conjecture that Bentham intended a husband's authority to extend beyond household management to include weighty decisions about, for example, the allocation family finances.

By contrast, in the *Traites* Bentham describes a wife subjected to the will of her husband, with a right of appeal to a court, because if authority were given to wives instead of husbands then a man's greater physical strength would result in inevitable discord. Control of the affairs of the family should rest with the man alone because men are more likely than their wives to have some experience of life, steadiness of mind and greater aptitude for affairs and are therefore more suitable to a superior role in marriage.[55]

A lengthy search through the Bentham manuscripts at University College, London, and the Dumont collection in the Bibliothèque Publique et Universitaire in Geneva has not uncovered any manuscripts corresponding exactly to the *Traites*. So can these remarks be attributed to Bentham or do they serve as an example of Dumont's editorial interjections? And what of Bentham's explanations in *IPML*, which suggest that Dumont did follow Bentham's instructions? Bentham's unpublished manuscripts provide some answers.

First, it becomes apparent that he addressed the question of legal relations in marriage between husband and wife at two distinct dates: first briefly in the 1780s, and then again at greater length in the late 1820s. In the 1780s, in manuscripts probably used by Dumont, we find Bentham's marriage code. The first condition reflects that given by the *Traites*. A wife 'shall be subject to the laws of the husband: unless there is a recourse to the courts'. But then Bentham continues 'as master of the woman regarding his own interests, he will be her guardian regarding her interests'.[56] This is of interest for two reasons: first, here Bentham again apparently confirms the status quo of coverture by his support for male legal superiority within marriage (albeit subject to the important right for wives to apply to court in the event of a dispute); secondly, Bentham makes no use of either the common law doctrine of coverture or Blackstone's formulation of it. Instead, he makes a husband his wife's master and also her guardian.

Much later, between 1823 and 1827, Bentham produced a second much lengthier set of unpublished manuscripts on the legal relationship between husband and wife. Once again he assigns authority within marriage to the husband, and once again gives as his reason the need for peace and accord. But here Bentham greatly expanded his explanation of the function of the law of equity and trusts in marriage.

Bentham wanted a unified, codified system of law and recommended the 'waters of Lethe . . . for the oblivion of statute law and common law'. Nothing at all should remain of the *Statute of Uses*,[57] he declared, but then went on to recognize that there was nevertheless a need for trusts to operate as a legal device.

At the time trusts existed as an equitable creation, but Bentham understood a trust as a concept, or a 'relative idea', and explained that his object was to establish a legal regime of rights and obligations that would enable 'the severance of the benefit on the one hand from the right and power on the other'.[58] Briefly, the modern law of trusts presupposes three parties: a settlor, whom Bentham referred to as a 'trustor', who transfers property to a trustee who holds that property for the benefit of a beneficiary whom Bentham called a 'benefitee'. Thus the trustee retains legal ownership of the property, but in equity the beneficiary is the owner.[59] For Bentham, creating a trust for an individual allowed a power in the hands of one person (the trustee) to be severed, or 'split' between that appointed trustee, and the beneficiary of that trust.[60] Because in a trust the power and the benefit of that power are vested in different people this legal device brings benefit to individuals,[61] and clear good to society in general by allowing for more complex relations between people than was otherwise possible in the common law system.[62] Thus, in a marriage a husband (who had authority and therefore the power) can be placed in the role of trustee for his wife, the beneficiary of the trust. In the margin of the manuscript Bentham summed up the position tersely: these implied trusts separated power from a corresponding benefit 'so as to promote the welfare of the individual subject'.[63]

In 'an original state of things', by which Bentham meant the early English common law system, any distinction between powers and correspondent obligations was comparatively unknown.[64] Even now 'in no existing system of law' were equitable and common law systems and remedies available simultaneously to litigants. Here Bentham anticipates the Common Law Procedure Act of 1854 and the subsequent nineteenth-century legislation which, in effect, assimilated the work of the previously separate equity and common law courts.[65] In 1827 assimilation was still in the future, and Bentham complained that trusts were not part of an 'all comprehensive' scheme, even though trusts law pervaded every part of the field of law. But in his new regime trusts and equitable remedies would all be assimilated into Bentham's code.

Penal law too, declared Bentham, had its place in the law of trusts, and in 1827 he went on to explain why in the lists he drew up of 'offences against domestic conditions'.[66] On sheets headed 'Penal and Civil Code Offences Against Trust' Bentham listed several possible private relationships, or 'domestic conditions': husband and wife, parent and children, guardian and ward.[67] Earlier, in 1823, in a manuscript written in the hand of an amanuensis, Bentham had given examples of the benefits and burdens attached to various domestic conditions in life. The benefits included wealth, power and reputation, while the burdens included perpetual servitude or forced celibacy. At the end of the page Bentham himself added a note: domestic conditions are most commonly beneficial, but can 'become burdensome with respect to a certain person . . . husbandship, wifeship, *fathership*, *sonship*, guardianship and wardship'. Bentham, who had a strained relationship with his father, added an emphasis to fathership and sonship.[68]

All these domestic conditions were subject to trusts, which could be created in one of two ways: an express trust, if drawn up in a deed; or a trust implied by law. In the existing law of equity, writes Bentham, only the relations between guardian and ward were subject to an express trust, and therefore all other domestic conditions were subject to an implied trust.[69] Here Bentham's manuscripts depart from his published work. In *IPML* not all domestic relations are subject to trusts law. The power that a master was able to exercise over his servant was instead 'beneficial', whereas in relations between guardian and ward a power, 'coupled with a trust', made that power 'a fiduciary one'.[70]

Any one domestic relationship could be subject to more than one trust regime. For example, Bentham's marriage code gives a husband authority over his wife and therefore the legal relationship between them is the trust implied between master and servant. If that same husband is expressly charged with an obligation to confer a benefit of any sort on his wife, or to have regard to her welfare, then for that purpose the relation between them is that of guardian and ward.[71] Eighteenth-century marriage settlements most usually imposed two express obligations on a husband: to provide a wife with an annual sum of money for her own use, and after her husband dies to provide her with a jointure for her maintenance. Therefore, in each one of Bentham's 'domestic conditions' the husband/father/master could become a trustee/master/ward, and a wife/child/servant the servant/beneficiary/ward, and so on.

BENTHAM AND THE SUBORDINATION OF MARRIED WOMEN

It is now possible to return to the vexed question raised above about Bentham's advocacy of the subordination of women during marriage. It appears that Bentham, like Blackstone, accepted that men and women were equal in nature. Yet, again like Blackstone, Bentham superimposed legal inequality on married women. Was there really any difference between them?

Blackstone rested his claim for gender equality on Pufendorf's arguments that natural law was understood to suppose an original equality in faculties between men and women, but that natural law was then modified by the laws of state and civil society in favour of men, and women were subordinate within marriage for their protection and for their own good.[72]

Bentham rested his claim for equality not on nature but the principle of utility, the greatest happiness principle. As we saw in Chapter 2, when he said that the pleasure derived from the union of the sexes was a pleasure, possibly the greatest pleasure, Bentham did not distinguish between men and women. As a result the principle of utility must premise 'an original equality of all members of the human race', based on their common psychological structure.[73] But then, as we have seen, within a marriage Bentham deemed a wife's subordination necessary, not for her protection, but to ensure peace and accord in a family by putting an end to competition for authority between husband and wife.[74]

Here Bentham's views reflect those of John Locke, who reasoned that although the absolute sovereignty of a husband over his wife was not necessary either to marriage or to the state, equality between men and women in marriage was not possible because disputes between husband and wife could not be settled by simple majority. Therefore in the event of disagreement 'the last Determination, i.e. the Rule' must rest with the man as the abler and stronger because otherwise disputes could never be resolved.[75]

In 1818, Peregine Bingham too relied on Locke to justify the evident injustices of coverture by finding 'an absolute necessity for the preservation of the peace, that where two or more persons are destined to pass their lives together, one should be endued . . . with pre-eminence' to prevent or bring to an end all contestation.[76] Why should the man be given pre-eminence? 'Simply because he is the stronger. In his hands the power allotted him at once supports itself without external interference'. If a wife had legal authority over a husband, it could only be maintained with outside assistance. Those who 'from some ill-defined notion of justice or generosity' extend absolute authority to women do them no favours.[77] But it is not the object of sound legislation to reduce to a state of 'passive slavery that sex which, from its weakness and softness, stands most in need of legal protection', so a husband's 'necessary prerogative' is limited, and redress always available.[78]

Bentham's views also reflect the distaste of enlightened eighteenth-century opinion for the subordination of married women which was attributed to outdated feudal laws. In that outmoded scheme, the dominance of one person over another was the 'defining feature of society' and applied to relations within marriage.[79] By the mid-eighteenth century, aspirations for companionate marriage, expectations of mutual love and the ideology of contract challenged an older concept of relations in marriage based on status.[80] The idea that marriage was governed by laws from a feudal past became less acceptable.[81] Although in practice the common law rules of coverture changed very little between the sixteenth and eighteenth centuries, Tim Stretton has shown that the justifications cited for those rules 'underwent a subtle but significant transformation'.[82] Prior to the eighteenth century the application of the fiction of unity of person between husband and wife in marriage was mainly restricted to property law, in particular to the shares that a married couple held in interests in land. A wife's legal subjection to her husband was variously described as her living 'under the rod' or *sub virga*, as his legal power over her derived from the feudal customs of landholding and inheritance in a military state.[83]

After 1765, in the *Commentaries* Blackstone employed the doctrine of 'unity of person' to downplay older justifications for rules affecting married women because the implicit suggestion of feudal subjection in a 'dark and primitive past' was no longer acceptable to him in marriage, any more than in the larger society.[84] Bentham reflected a similar strong eighteenth-century distaste for what he saw as a barbaric feudal past. He strenuously condemned the inappropriate use of feudal laws particularly in relation to the laws of property and inheritance. For example, he describes primogeniture (inheritance by the eldest male) as 'political economy and barbarous feudal law' that is no longer needed.[85] The only possible reason to retain such laws was political: primogeniture and coparceny (whereby if there is no male heir then any females take shares in an inheritance equally) remained acceptable only because men possessed political power. Accordingly, the rule that prevailed was that of the greatest happiness of men, the stronger of the two sexes, over that of women, the weaker of the two sexes.[86]

Bentham may well have rejected the laws of a feudal past and endorsed Locke's arguments, but by subordinating married women he contradicted claims he made elsewhere for legal equality between men and women. For example, in Bentham's model marriage contract during marriage husband and wife enjoy their property in common.[87] In 1790 when he drafted a codified law of succession, Article 1 proclaimed that both sexes were to inherit equally, and that in legal documents the use of the term 'male' should be understood as including 'female'.[88] Then, on her husband's death a wife would inherit all the property she had enjoyed in common with her husband during their marriage.[89]

Bentham went further and proposed what we might term a form of reverse discrimination: if the greatest happiness principle is used as a measure of the true worth of a rule of law, then female should take precedence over male interests because 'as between male and female, in regard to strength, the less the care taken by nature the greater should be that taken by law'.[90] He reasoned that females had more wants – presumably the care of children – and fewer means of meeting them because they were disadvantaged in finding employment. Also, it was harder for females both to acquire property and to make the most of what property they did have. 'The stronger sex . . . has run away with all the preferences', Bentham explained, 'Enquire for the justification reason, you will find none: ask for the historical reason, the efficient cause, you will find it in the difference in point of force.'[91]

It is evident that Bentham was a strong proponent of women's equality. Could it be that he was subconsciously so imbued with the near-universal customary hierarchical male dominance within marriage that the contradictions between the equality that he demanded and yet at the same time denied in marriage did not puzzle him? It is certainly true that he was sufficiently an eighteenth-century gentleman wholeheartedly to endorse hierarchical relations in general. Status mattered to him. For example, he wrote that servants owed a duty of obedience to their masters, and should act with 'the same humility and deference to every gentleman as to his own master, in everything that is not incompatible with his duty to his master'.[92] A gentleman was justified in giving a menial servant or day-labourer who affronted him 'moderate chastisement' on the spot. A blow from a gentleman to a servant does not dishonour the servant but a blow from a servant to a gentleman dishonours the gentleman.[93]

If it seems too far fetched a thesis to suggest that Bentham was unconsciously imbued with the prejudices of his time, then consider that in 1985, in an introduction to Mary Wollstonecraft's *Rights of Woman* the editor thought it 'strange to us to see how Rousseau, whom we are taught to regard as the father of the Revolution, was taken to pieces by Mary Wollstonecraft.'[94] Two decades or so later Mary Wollstonecraft's complaints about Jean-Jacques Rousseau do not seem strange. Rousseau, after all, believed women are unequal to men.[95] Bentham himself gave no indication that he was aware of any inconsistency between the principle of utility and the subordination of women in marriage. On the contrary, in *IPML* he writes that 'in point of utility' it was not expedient to give men and women equality within marriage.[96]

Alternatively, by subordinating married women to their husbands authority was Bentham giving precedence to political considerations? In the civil code Bentham set out four principles, security, equality, abundance and subsistence, which together are subordinate to the greatest happiness principle.[97] He stresses the importance of the principle of security, sometimes called the non-disappointment or disappointment preventing principle, because this principle looks to the future, and is concerned with establishing and maintaining stable patterns of behaviour on which individual expectations can be based.[98] So perhaps one could argue that he aimed at a gradual transition to a new order in domestic relations, rather than the disruption caused by a sudden reassignment of power relations within marriage – particularly since it is claimed that by the 1820s earlier eighteenth-century optimism about equality between men and women had ended because contract ideology was thought to be 'socially intolerable'.[99]

Miriam Williford suggests that such considerations lay behind Bentham's exclusion of women from participation in government. Williford points out that by the early nineteenth century Bentham recognized no reason for not advocating female suffrage, but in the *Constitutional Code* 1827 writings explained that he could not do so 'because the prepossession against their [women's] admission is at present too general, and too intense, to afford any chance in favour of a proposal for their admission'.[100]

By the 1820s, could Bentham have been just as pessimistic about the acceptability of legal equality between men and women in marriage? He was certainly pessimistic that those in power – men – would find his new codified laws of succession acceptable: 'For England, I give and bequeath these measures as a legacy to the next Elizabeth; For Russia for the next Catherine. In a democracy, though in all other accounts the only form of government admissible by the greatest happiness principle, I see little chance for it.'[101] However, a careful reading of the conditions of Bentham's marriage code reveals that in its provisions Bentham dismantled key components of common law coverture. For example, a denial of legal personality to a married woman was a significant part of coverture, but Bentham largely restores this legal personality to married women. During a marriage a wife would be 'subject to the laws of a husband' he writes, and administration would be the responsibility of the man alone as a 'natural and almost necessary consequence of his authority'. But then this authority would be qualified because it would be made subject to a wife's right of recourse to the courts.[102]

Equity and the Court of Chancery allowed married women to circumvent the common law imposition of lack of legal personality for certain limited purposes,[103] but married women had no general right of access to equity or common law courts.[104] In contrast, Bentham's code adds to, or supplies for the first time rights of access to all courts. His code presupposes a unified system of law and equity and does not employ the fiction of 'unity of person', or any restriction based on feudal notions of status, to deny married women access to any court for any purpose whatsoever, including questioning the proper exercise by her husband of his right to the authority to make administrative decisions in their marriage. Bentham's marriage code also provides that in certain situations men should instead be subordinated to their wives' authority, and the general rule or condition should not apply. 'In reality' he concluded 'there are sometimes exceptional circumstances, in which case it is a matter of establishing another general law'.[105]

In conclusion, according to Bentham's code, within any marriage, the location of administrative authority with the husband would remain of great significance for a married woman and for society at large, whatever the extent of that authority and even with a right of appeal to a court to question its proper exercise. But in her relations with the outside world that same woman would no longer be under the disabilities of common law coverture. Bentham's marriage code dismantles coverture to allow a married woman to sue and to be sued, to enter into contracts, to hold real and personal property in her own name (including retaining her own earnings). Bentham's code on the law of succession allows women to inherit equally with men. Lastly, Bentham's marriage code allows married women to act as guardians to their own children.

THE CHILDREN OF THE FAMILY

Bentham felt much sympathy for children, and feelingly wrote of the plight of young people forced into unhappy marriages by their parents, or infants torn from their mother's arms when parents separated, divorced or died. This is reflected in Bentham's marriage code in its description of the legal relations between mother, father and children all living together during marriage and infancy.

In the eighteenth century a child's legal relationship to his or her parents was premised on strict patriarchal rules. A father had a 'sacred right' over his children which extended beyond the grave because he was considered to have a right to appoint guardians which would override a mother's interest.[106] A wife who left her husband knew that she must also leave her children, and that her husband could prohibit her access to them. For instance, in 1784 Mary Wollstonecraft helped her sister Eliza Bishop run away from her unhappy marriage, and letters between the sisters reveal Eliza's sorrow at leaving behind the child she would not see again.[107]

Where very young children were taken away from their mother, she would meet with little success if she made an application to Chancery for habeas corpus or wardship.[108] Even in cases of extreme cruelty or ill-treatment towards a mother it was thought that Chancery could not intervene unless the children had property to be administered. Only extreme depravity was considered sufficient to justify the denial of a father's rights to his children. In June 1827 Lord Eldon decided a case, *Wellesley v. Beaufort*, which attracted publicity because it questioned a father's automatic right to custody over his children.[109] Eldon reported that he would 'sooner forfeit' his life than return the children to their father. The decision was said to have caused 'considerable anxiety' to the public. Pamphlets and open letters, including several from the aggrieved father, debated the issues raised.[110] The father in question, Wellesley, sought Bentham's support for his cause by sending him his publications, but Bentham, evidently not impressed, failed to reply.

In this historical context, Bentham chose to base his new codified regime for relations between parents and children not on the rules of patriarchy but on equity and trusts law. The relation between a child and its parents was another 'domestic condition'. Here the relationship between father and child was one of master and servant: the child owed a duty of obedience to his father, who had authority over him. This relationship was governed by an implied trust unless some clear duty was imposed on a father.[111]

This much was clear, reported Bentham, but if the relations between mother, father and child were looked at in detail they would reveal 'considerable complexity, of which correspondent perplexity is among the results'.[112] The mother and child were fellow servants to the husband/father. Under an express trust the father/husband is under a fiduciary obligation to have regard to the welfare of 'wife/mother and under age child who are fellow wards'.[113]

Bentham next looked at the relations between a mother and child if her husband should die. What were the mother's rights with respect to her children? At the time, a father had the right to appoint anyone he chose, either inter vivos or by will, to act as his child's guardian, and that guardian then took precedence over the child's mother. Did this still apply in the domestic conditions set out in Bentham's code? Bentham replied that the answer provided by the greatest happiness principle must be an emphatic 'no', because, in general, a mother values her child far more than any other human being would, and similarly has a far greater regard for her child's welfare.[114] Therefore, according to the greatest happiness principle a widowed mother should be the mistress and guardian to the child. Bentham recognized that his code thus provided a strong contrast with the general practice of most political institutions where instead the practice was 'almost universally the reverse'. This was the same in both English and French law and the cause was 'the universal tyranny of the male over female'.[115]

Bentham pointed out that an objection frequently advanced to allowing a widowed mother to act as the child's guardian was that a mother would not have sufficient 'aptitude', meaning ability, for such a task, while a lack of appropriate aptitude for the job of bringing up children was not so improbable 'on the male side'. But Bentham believed that if the 'moral branch' of aptitude for rearing children was taken into account, then superiority weighed heavily in favour of mothers. 'There is the natural instinct of the biped feathered race and the quadruped race . . . and in intellectual aptitude no decided difference.'[116] He conceded that it may be true that males have greater 'active aptitude', meaning experience in worldly matters, but in bringing up children moral aptitude was more important.

Of course, some particular mother may indeed be unsuited to the task. If so, then the remedy was to allow an application to be made to a court where, if proved necessary, a judge could make an order for an alternative provision for the child. Therefore, if a concerned father believed that his wife was unfit to be his child's guardian, then he should apply to the court for an order allowing the appointment of a better alternative. If a mother appeared unfit after a father's death, then any other person on proof of her unfitness could apply to the court for such an order.[117]

TRUSTS LAW AND BENTHAM'S EQUITY DISPATCH COURT

Despite his dislike for a legal system where law and equity were separate, Bentham recognized the historical and contemporary importance of equity and the Court of Chancery to married women subject to coverture. In certain circumstances, the court would treat a wife under coverture as a feme sole.[118] For example, in principle a court of equity could compel performance of a marriage agreement,[119] or protect a wife's pin-money (an annual sum for her own personal use) and her paraphernalia (clothing, jewellery and personal effects) against her husband's creditors.[120]

There were limits to what property could be protected by the Court of Chancery. Equity would set aside a contract made before marriage if the wife-to-be had intended to deceive or cheat her husband out of some of her property, or if it were in derogation of the marriage.[121] In contrast a contract made by a previously married woman intended to benefit the children of her first marriage was held to be valid against her fortune hunting abusive second husband.[122] But in general the rules developed by equity were 'idiosyncratic', with much confusion about, for example, the nature and purpose of pin-money: was it a gift or an enforceable contractual agreement between husband and wife?[123] Staves comments that reluctance to expose private family behaviour was one reason for the refusal to enforce spouses' obligations in a coherent way.[124] In his concern to respond to such matters Bentham made much reference to Miss Campbell's expectation of pin-money when he reviewed the marriage settlement in James Humphreys' book in the Westminster Review in 1826.[125]

The doctrine of coverture had its greatest impact on the lives of wealthy and aristocratic women whose marriages were likely to have been arranged by their families, who might have given priority to family advancement rather than other considerations.[126] In 1816, one writer went so far as to claim that 'the middling People are certainly more happy in the married State than Persons of a more elevated Dignity', where 'Portions and Jointures' take precedence over compatibility of age, health and temperament.[127] In fact, Joanne Bailey's investigations have led her to conclude that 'in general a large disparity between spouses' contributions to marriage was fairly uncommon'.[128] Unlike those of the aristocracy, the marriage settlements of gentry, merchant and yeoman families provided a widow with a cash sum or with bonds secured by a double penalty. These typically matched the value of the portion she had brought to the marriage. As a result, the cost of jointures for these gentry and merchant families did not rise dramatically as it did among the aristocracy who instead used the bride's marriage portion to purchase expensive land in order to provide her with an annuity on widowhood.[129]

During the eighteenth century the business of Chancery grew 'exponentially', greatly in excess of its resources leading to complaints about protracted delays in cases.[130] Complaints centred around the complexity of the procedure, which led to an inordinately lengthy and expensive process. There were also complaints about payments which had to be made to office-holders in the Court, who did nothing in return: for example, the famous Six Clerks who had long since ceased to perform their original function of acting as attorneys. As Bentham put it, they had 'long ascended into Epicurean heaven, the region of sinecures: the masters are jogging on the road to it'.[131]

In 1825, Bentham took note both of the delays in equity business and also of the importance of the courts of equity to married women, when he drafted a *Proposal* for a bill to be presented to Parliament, for a new court of equity, which he named the Equity Dispatch Court. This was in response to the Chancery Commission, appointed in February 1824 by Robert Peel, the Home Secretary, to investigate causes of delay in the Court of Chancery.[132] The commissioners were also asked to consider the possibility of removing some part of the Court of Chancery's business to another competent court or tribunal.

The commissioners alleged public misconception about delays, blamed dilatory solicitors, and complained about the increased burden placed on the court by the bankruptcy laws.[133] Also, there had been a 'vast increase in personal property' which included a rise in traded shares in joint-stock companies. This, together with the difficulty in obtaining justice under the common law against executors, trustees, agents or partners in trade, had put an increased burden on the court. Because large numbers of women were the beneficial owners of annuities, insurance and trust property (passive property yielding an income without risk), many cases in the Court of Chancery concerned women and property ownership. The commissioners made no comment about this, although others did so. James Humphreys, for one, wrote of the 'harsh law' that gave a wife's personal property to her husband during marriage, which 'cries feelingly for correction'.[134] This custom had originated when people had few personal possessions, but made little sense in 1826.

It was against this background that Bentham worked on the Equity Dispatch Court bill from approximately 1825. His Equity Dispatch Court writings fall into two parts: a *Proposal* for the new court; and a draft bill for the new court. The *Proposal* was published separately as a pamphlet in 1825, addressed to both men and women: 'Jeremy Bentham to the honest and afflicted among Equity Suitors, fellow countrymen and fellow countrywomen'.[135] Bentham asked existing court users for their support for a parliamentary bill for a new Court of Chancery which he promised to draft and present to Parliament. This *Proposal* was distributed to supporters and dissatisfied litigants in the Court of Chancery and included a petition for signature.

Bentham's proposed Equity Dispatch Court was a prototype for a whole new tier of local courts which he termed 'local judicatories', likening them to the system of courts that had existed in Anglo-Saxon England, and which would be geographically limited in the cases they could hear. However, because a new multiple court system would be exorbitantly expensive to establish throughout the entire country, he proposed an initial inexpensive three-year experiment for a single court, using summary procedure, to replace the existing Court of Chancery.

Eventually, in 1846, a system of local courts was set up.[136] Although Bentham is sometimes credited with influencing this establishment of local courts, they were not the Equity Dispatch Courts he had planned in the 1820s.[137]

5

'Offences against domestic conditions'

Bentham described a number of wrongs committed by wives or husbands against each other as 'offences against domestic condition'. 'Domestic conditions' were the legal relationships existing between husband and wife, parent and child, guardian and ward, and master and servant,[1] all of which were based on the law of trusts. As a result, Bentham's offences against domestic conditions might well have been considered as civil wrongs, or breaches of trust.[2] But, unlike eighteenth century, and indeed most modern, family law, Bentham chose to classify such offences as criminal and listed them under his heading 'Penal Code or Pannomium', by which he meant a complete body of laws universally applicable.[3] Penal law too had a place in the law of trusts.[4]

Despite this clear statement about the criminal nature of these offences, Bentham did not provide any further details.

For example, he did not say how these crimes were to be prosecuted, or whether he intended to retain the distinctions between heinous felonies and misdemeanours or lesser wrongs?[5]

Unfortunately there are no answers to these questions which Bentham no doubt intended to address in a yet unwritten procedural code to be attached to his penal code, a part of his 'Pannomium', or complete body of laws.[6] It is worth remembering that at the time Bentham was writing a criminal Bar had not long existed, rules of evidence were still few, and although prisoners on trial for a felony were usually granted legal representation they had no legal right to it until 1836. The archaic practice of pleading benefit of clergy as mitigation was still in use, and it was not abolished until 1827. Undertaking the reform of existing legal procedure and process was therefore an enormous task.[7]

Bentham wrote on offences against the particular domestic condition of husband and wife briefly in the 1780s, and then again at greater length between 1818 and 1827. In this later work, he gave more detail about the number of offences, together with definitions, expository comments and appropriate punishments. Despite the gap of 30 or so years between the earlier and the later writings, he remained remarkably consistent. He wrote little in the 1780s, so the main difference lies in the far greater volume of material completed when he returned to the penal code in the early nineteenth century. This presents a puzzle because his work on the penal code was published in 1789 as *IPML* which must have been based on manuscripts completed by the 1780s.[8] If *IPML* is compared with the unpublished manuscripts, the difference becomes apparent: in *IPML* only a general theoretical outline of a domestic condition appears and most offences are listed without explanation. For example, offences against the condition of a husband are contained in a brief two pages, while those against the condition of a wife are summed up in just one paragraph.[9] In contrast, in the unpublished manuscripts many more details of offences are given, often set out in a finished state as if prepared for publication and set out as a code of law. Therefore, the main purpose of this chapter is to discuss the offences against domestic condition in Bentham's unpublished manuscripts, and thereby add to our understanding of Bentham's penal code in *IPML*.

In the unpublished manuscripts the offences against the domestic condition of husband and wife include adultery, wife-beating, and the confinement and harbouring of wives. Several offences address particular eighteenth-century concerns and scandals. Because Bentham wrote so extensively on adultery this will form the subject of the next chapter. The other offences against domestic conditions, together with the punishments Bentham provided, are discussed here.

BENTHAM'S PUNISHMENTS FOR OFFENCES AGAINST DOMESTIC CONDITIONS

Bentham abhorred all physical violence against any living being, whether man, woman, child or animal. He regarded the last as sentient beings which should not be treated cruelly because 'the question is not, Can they *reason*? nor, Can they *talk*? but, Can they *suffer*?' His strong reactions to individual human suffering are well documented: for example, his recollection of his distress on hearing the screams of soldiers being flogged when he was living at Queen's Square, Westminster, near a military barracks.[10]

It does not follow from this that Bentham objected to the punishment of wrongdoers, including corporal punishment. But his theory of punishment was grounded on the principle of utility. According to this, the object of all laws ought to be to augment the total happiness of the community, and to exclude anything that takes away from that happiness. Bentham recognized that all punishment, including physical punishment, undoubtedly caused unhappiness. Therefore, it was appropriate to punish people only in order to prevent a greater wrong,[11] and the punishment should be commensurate with the crime that occasioned it.[12] No man or woman should suffer disproportionate or unnecessary violence as punishment for wrongdoing – and here Bentham made particular reference to the example of the 'horrible punishment . . . of burning alive'.[13]

In the 1790s, Bentham put his ideas on punishment to practical use when writing on prison reform. He set out three guiding principles for prison punishments. The first of these was a rule of lenity, which demanded that the ordinary condition of prisoners should not involve physical suffering or danger to life or health.[14] In 1827 he listed the 'characteristic' punishments suitable for punishing petty offences; these included public shaming and the use of 'sedative instruments', such as a gag or strait-jacket. An odd example of the former is the punishment for using 'vituperative' language, which was to place 'a parrots head over the delinquents'.[15] Bentham's purpose was to deter wrongdoers with a punishment analogous to the offence, and each punishment had to be adjusted to the particular offence committed.[16] So punishment for a 'blow' inflicted on another was to tie the offender's hand up to a beam.[17]

Bentham's penal code writings, including those on punishments, deserve greater investigation, but are considered here only in the context of the domestic condition of husband and wife. In these family law writings, punishments, like those for petty offences, mostly rely on fining and rituals of public shaming, which can be described almost as secularized church court punishments. He supplied many specific punishments for particular offences, for example, those for incest or polygamy.[18]

Generally, Bentham's punishments for offenders owe much to the importance attached in eighteenth-century England to a man's (and woman's) personal reputation. For instance, a good reputation guaranteed financial probity in the community. Therefore, great damage could be done to reputation by punishments that relied on shaming and public humiliation, as the church court punishments had done. For example, offenders would be ordered to stand for a certain amount of time, on a specified number of Sundays, in the market square or at the back of their parish church, clothed in a penitential white sheet, holding a white wand, and labelled with a description of their offence for all to see.[19] By 1780 all these church court punishments were likely to be commuted to payment of a fine, but public naming and shaming did still take place.[20]

If the use of humiliating punishments had declined in the church courts, this was not equally true of the criminal courts. Although by the mid-eighteenth century Justices of the Peace no longer punished adultery and fornication by public whipping, or placing in the stocks, some other offences were still publicly punished. Public whipping, mainly for theft, continued to take place either at the back of a cart or at a post outside the court until the 1780s. Thereafter, most whippings, but by no means all, took place in private, in a prison or house of correction.[21] Public executions still took place for the perpetrators of notorious crimes, and although the use of the public pillory for fraud and perjury had declined by 1760, it was not abolished until 1837. All these public punishments involved physical pain, and damaged the reputation of the offender, and were also intended to act as a deterrent to onlookers. The crowds who attended such public spectacles were not always passive bystanders, for they could play an active role by hurling insults or missiles at those in the pillory.[22]

Bentham's family law writings also make great use of a punishment described as 'presence banishment'. This, Bentham explained was a form of corporeal punishment. Here the offender was ordered not to approach the victim, and could be banished from a fixed place, or from certain named localities. Alternatively presence banishment could be 'migratory', and in this case the offender was banished from any place at the wrongee's (i.e. the victim) option.[23] Bentham explained that presence banishment was suitable as a punishment for physical insult or menace, lascivious insult, seduction or adultery.[24] Rather than owing something to church court punishments, these presence banishment orders look curiously modern, resembling present-day equitable injunctions used to control the abusive behaviour of private individuals, and also the antisocial behaviour orders sought by police and local authority officers.

WIFE-BEATING

Bentham condemned personal violence inflicted by one person against another, most particularly wife-beating. He declared, in the 1780s that 'none but a coward attacks a woman'.[25] Quite possibly he recalled the notorious case brought in 1757 by the Countess Ferrers against her husband, Earl Ferrers, a homicidal maniac who subjected his wife (and his servants) to fearful violence. The Countess Ferrers was helped by her brothers to go to court, and articles of the peace were granted against the Earl in 1757. One year later he was brought before Lord Mansfield again and had to find security for £5,000. But nothing deterred Earl Ferrers from his violent behaviour, and he was executed at Tyburn two years later for the murder of his steward.[26] For Bentham such attacks on a wife by her husband as those suffered by the Countess Ferrers were crimes, defined as offences against domestic condition in the penal code. Because he believed domestic violence to be particularly offensive the offender should receive 'extra-punishment', a 'characteristic' penance more or less public at the court's discretion.[27]

Despite Bentham's condemnation, wife-beating was not an uncommon occurrence in his day and was not defined as a crime unless it led to death, in which case it was murder, a capital felony.[28] Yet it is hard to establish any legal basis in England for a husband's right to inflict a violent assault on his wife. In 1608 a famous argument had taken place in Oxford between William Heale and William Gouger. Gouger gave a public lecture, called an 'Act', upholding a husband's right to beat his wife, while Heale's published reply denied the existence of any such right and instead upheld the Protestant Reformation theory of 'companionate marriage'.[29] Heale referred to the official *Homilie of the State of Matrimonie* (1582) which had been ordered to be read aloud in churches and which declared that beating a wife brought shame on a husband.[30]

It has proved difficult to verify supposedly ancient customary Welsh laws that specified the number of strokes a husband was allowed to apply to his wife (three), or to verify the customary English rules about the thickness of the stick he could use (the 'rule of thumb'). Similar claims about ancient Irish customary law have likewise proved elusive. Maeve Dogget found her search for an English Carolingian statute enacting a husband's right to beat his wife equally fruitless.[31]

But if wife-beating had no statutory authority, and if customary rules are hard to verify, it was nevertheless understood to be part of the common law. Wife-beating was explained in legal texts to be part of the exercise of a man's patriarchal authority. For example, William Lambarde in *Eirenarcha*, a manual for the use of Justices of the Peace, claimed that a man, in his role as parent, husband or master, had both a civil and a natural right to exercise authority over subordinates, and that included beating them, which Lambarde referred to as 'chastisement'.[32]

The common law right of a man to beat his wife was subject to legal control designed to prevent an excessive abuse of his patriarchal authority,[33] but the courts interpreted claims of cruelty strictly, demanding proof of abuse sufficient to endanger life or well-being.[34] Abused wives had several means of legal redress available to them. First, they could complain to the church courts, although such an action was usually intended to form part of an action for divorce *a mensa et thoro*. Next, a wife could apply to a Justice of the Peace and to the Court of King's Bench in person. In 1818 Peregrine Bingham advised this method for a wife whose husband beats or threatens to beat her 'outrageously, or otherwise use her ill'.[35] Lastly, an abused wife could apply to the Court of Chancery for a writ of *supplicavit*, a remedy that Bingham considered by far the most efficacious because the wife was granted the writ (after swearing to her grievance in person) without having to confront her husband directly, which she otherwise would have to do before the Justices of the Peace. The sheriff would then confine the husband until he entered security for his good behaviour 'in a large sum' for himself and two sureties.[36]

Given that wife-beating was a legally condoned legal exercise of a husband's authority, and that legal remedies to restrain abuse existed, what was the consensus of opinion on the rights and wrongs of wife-beating in the 1780s? Domestic violence has been much investigated by historians, and it is claimed that its existence provides 'evidence about the exercise of power' within a household.[37] Joanne Bailey surveyed modern studies of attitudes towards wife-beating (whether in the form of investigations into records of litigation, advice literature or novels) and discovered that historians present two alternative views. The first concludes that wife-beating was widely understood to be the inevitable and accepted patriarchal response to a wife's shortcomings and disobedience.[38] This belief in a husband's right to beat his wife in order to correct her behaviour continued throughout the eighteenth century in England, and indeed much later. With some astonishment the present writer discovered that it still existed in the popular imagination in the late twentieth century.[39]

The alternative view presented by historical studies concludes that wife-beating was considered to be unmanly and abnormal behaviour, and was subject to legal, social and cultural control.[40] It is certainly true that a complex set of informal checks on domestic violence existed in addition to the formal legal interventions that were provided by the church courts, Justices of the Peace and Courts of King's Bench and Chancery. For example, parish constables, in their role as community peacekeepers, would deal with domestic violence, as would Justices of the Peace who could act outside of Quarter Sessions. Local parish officers administering the poor laws also intervened when enforcing the settlement and vagrancy laws.[41]

Informally, a local community often expressed disapproval of wife-beating that exceeded common notions of appropriate behaviour. Neighbours, church wardens, parish priests and local dignitaries intervened in a variety of ways, including by means of shaming rituals known as rough music, or *charivari*. Martin Ingram claims that the term 'rough music' did not become current until the early eighteenth century.[42]

Cultural disapproval of domestic violence appears in legal texts and in conduct books. Most of these accepted that the exercise of a husband's legitimate authority over his wife included the right to chastise her, but urged moderation. 'God send Gentlewomen better sport, or better companie' commented the anonymous author of *The Lawes Resolutions of Womens Rights*, first published in 1632.[43] In 1732 the author of *The Treatise of Feme Coverts, or the Ladies Law* claimed that although a husband 'shall neither do nor procure to be done to her, any Bodily Damage', this does not exclude violence that 'appertains to the Office of a Husband, and for lawful Correction. She has no right of action at common law'.[44] The Puritan preacher William Whately was more direct in condemning domestic violence; he advised men to govern their households well and not to strike their wives, because bitterness 'works hatred' and 'They will hate whom they fear.'[45]

By the late eighteenth century wife-beating was generally no longer considered to be an acceptable exercise of patriarchal authority. This is not to say that it did not take place, and many of Bentham's contemporaries continued to uphold the practice. But changes in the understanding of the human body, together with the rise of a culture of sensibility, meant that women were increasingly portrayed as 'the gentler sex', physically weaker and more passive than men. As a result wife-beating was no longer regarded as good law, but as Blackstone remarked wryly, 'the lower orders of people, who were always fond of the old common law, still claim and exert their antient privilege' of wife-beating.[46]

The spread of Enlightenment ideas contributed greatly to a change in thinking about the relations between men and women. In France the *philosophes* had equated the power of a husband over his wife with the tyranny and despotism of the monarchy over the people, and with slavery too.[47] The revolutionary period of family law reform in France in the 1780s arose directly from the writings of the *philosophes* who argued for egalitarian relations within the family, and for the freedom to choose a marriage partner instead of arranged marriages.[48] Bentham had followed events in France closely, and his family law writings reflected his Enlightenment ideas. No doubt Bentham, as an Enlightenment thinker, considered wife-beating just as barbaric as burning alive for petty treason, and as outdated a feudal practice as primogeniture, both of which he criticized strongly. Therefore, he made wife-beating a crime in his penal code.[49]

Blackstone approached the same subject by making it clear that a husband's sovereignty over his wife was limited. He wrote: 'The husband also (by the old law) might give his wife moderate correction. For, as he is to answer for her misbehaviour, the law thought it reasonable to instruct him with this power of restraining her, by domestic chastisement.'[50] But Blackstone doubted that this was correct in common law, relying on Coke and on Hale in *Lord Leigh's Case* (1674).[51]

Bentham's many references to the circumstances of particular cases show that he followed English case law and was therefore aware of the 'uncertainty' in the common law about the legal basis for the right to beat a wife. He probably knew of the numbers of women seeking help from Justices of the Peace,[52] and, like Blackstone, he certainly knew that domestic violence contributed to the ills suffered by the wives and children of the poor, and accordingly suggested means to assist victims. He roundly condemned using bodily or mental force against a wife as morally offensive and also as an offence against justice.[53]

Did Bentham's penal code add anything to enlightened eighteenth-century opinion on wife-beating? It certainly ignored all justifications for wife-beating based on ancient common law patriarchal rights. Instead, in 1818 Bentham listed several offences against domestic conditions, including one named 'Wrongful detrection of Husbandship'.[54] The *Oxford English Dictionary* defines to 'detrect' as to decline, refuse, detract from or depreciate, and Bentham explained that this offence occurred when a husband did some 'unlawful act', such as inflicting bodily force on his wife. Wrongful detrection extended to a husband's inflicting 'mental force' on his wife, and to all unlawful actions against her, whether positive or negative. For example, a husband was guilty of this offence if he failed to do some act in order to avoid becoming subject to an obligation to his wife, by which Bentham meant failing to maintain her.[55]

Another offence in the penal code may well have been intended as an alternative means of addressing wife-beating, although it is less clearly aimed at physical beating. In 1818, Bentham described the crime of matrimonial oppression as the oppression of a wife by her husband by means of the power conferred by the marriage contract. Here he defined oppression as including either bodily oppression of her, or abuse that damages her reputation, or both.[56] So Bentham criminalized wife-beating by providing two separate offences against the practice in his penal code, 'detrection of husbandship', and 'matrimonial oppression'. By doing so, he gave physically or mentally abused wives the means of legal redress against their husbands.

WIFE-BEATING AND PATRIARCHY

Wife-beating was sometimes understood to be part of a husband's exercise of his patriarchal authority. We have noted that Bentham rejected any violence inflicted by a man on a woman, or by a husband on his wife. But did he nevertheless subscribe to the prevalent eighteenth-century notion that the exercise of patriarchal authority included the use of physical force? For example, Bentham explained that sometimes an assault of one person by another can be justified in law by the consent given by the victim. Thus, the consent given by a sick person to his doctor changed an action from an assault into an agreed medical treatment, a precaution taken against a greater mischief.[57] Following from this, did Bentham consider a man's patriarchal authority over his family justified his use of physical force against them?

First, some explanation is needed for what Bentham understood by 'family'. He did not consider 'family' to be restricted to the nuclear family of a man, a woman and their children, or to be confined to blood relationships alone. Instead, he would have understood family in the eighteenth-century sense in which it included all the dependent persons living within a household. These could include apprentices, labourers and household servants as well as a wife, children and other blood relations. Samuel Johnson, who had several unrelated people living with him in his house at 17 Gough Square in the City of London, defined a family simply as 'those who live in the same house'.[58] Bentham too understood that family included relationships of 'co-residence and authority'.[59] So no doubt he considered his housekeeper, his secretaries and his servants all to be members of his family to whom certain obligations were owed and from whom certain duties were expected.

This model of a family gave a man, as the head of the household, the right to exercise authority over all of his dependents in order to correct their behaviour and to maintain order. In this context, Bentham considered that the exercise of authority within a household justified blows restricted to 'simple personal injuries': in other words a slap given to an aggravating child or servant but not a violent blow.[60]

But Bentham made one significant exception to this rule about household authority: nothing ever justified a physical assault on a woman by a man,[61] and so a man who assaulted his wife could not claim his authority to do so as a defence. On the contrary, Bentham thought that a 'peculiar protection' should always be given to the female sex against the male because 'perhaps by nature' a man generally has the advantage of superior bodily strength over a woman, and undertakes greater physical exercise. A man also has the advantage of strength of mind over the women, and therefore 'a constant disposition in the person of the male sex to respect the female' should be maintained.[62]

Bentham employs here the language of sensibility, a language increasingly in use from the mid-eighteenth century. It is found, for instance, in court records of domestic violence, where a woman could claim not only that her life was at risk, but that her husband's behaviour was an irrational 'passion, fury rage'.[63] We might add that Bentham's exception of a wife from those whom a male householder was entitled to discipline physically supports the claim that he regarded a wife as an equal partner in the household with her husband, who should not therefore be subjected to 'correction' by him as his subordinate. On the other hand, his use of the language of sensibility should not wholly divert attention away from the fact that Bentham did subordinate a wife to her husband's authority in the marriage code.[64] In summary, we can conclude that Bentham gave authority within marriage to a husband in his penal code (as we saw in Chapter 4), but that authority did not extend to the right to beat her.

Bentham's writings on the Poor Laws indicate he was well aware of the prevalence of contemporary domestic violence. He mentioned the unhappy situation of poor women who lacked the means to seek the legal remedies that were available to wealthier women from the middling class and the aristocracy.[65] He drew up plans for an 'Industry House' which would provide an asylum for 'exposed girls' and others, and which would also act as a place of refuge for wives against bad husbands.[66] The purpose of this home for 'suffering wives against ill-usage from tyrant husbands', was to extend to the poor the church court remedy of divorce *a mensa et thoro* allowing a wife to live apart from her husband in safety, a remedy at the present time 'confined to and monopolised by the rich' because of the expense.[67]

By the nineteenth century, Harriet Taylor Mill and John Stuart Mill were together campaigning vigorously to focus public attention on wife-beating, which they identified as an outcome of the subjection of women. They compiled newspaper reports and published case studies of atrocities which make particularly harrowing reading.[68] But domestic violence, unless it resulted in murder, continued to be treated by the machinery of law enforcement as a 'domestic disturbance', and for various reasons was not accorded prominence as a social ill until the late twentieth century. Bentham recognized the social ill, and in the 1780s his solution was to make wife-beating a crime in the penal code – an offence against the domestic condition of husband and wife.

PETTY TREASON

Petty treason, the killing of a husband by his wife, was a felony. Although a married woman had a diminished legal personality – she could not sue or be sued in her own name – she was still liable for her own criminal acts unless she could show that she had been coerced into committing the crime by her husband. She was always held accountable if she committed treason or murder.[69] The Treason Act of 1351 made the killing of a husband by his wife, or a master by his servant, or prelate by his curate, a felony known as petty treason.[70] According to feudal theory, all men owed a duty of obedience to their lord, analogous to the duty owed to a king by his subjects. Killing a king was treason, so a wife who killed her husband was guilty of petty treason, because her husband was her *baron* or lord. The guilty wife was subjected to the most severe punishment – she was burnt at the stake. In *IPML* Bentham questioned whether 'so horrible' a punishment could ever be justified. In contrast, a husband who killed his wife was guilty of murder, to which the lesser capital punishment of hanging applied.[71]

Bentham evidently considered that the hierarchical feudal context of petty treason made it a complete anachronism, and indeed after 1790 trial juries stopped convicting women prosecuted for petty treason altogether. In 1828 Parliament legislated to reduce the offence to murder.[72] Kugler claims that later eighteenth-century judges were generally reluctant to send women to the gallows, and that with the growth of sensibility in the early nineteenth century the wronged woman had become instead an object of pity.[73] Bentham, writing in the 1780s, was angry that he should be forced to consider including petty treason at all. He wrote scathingly that as a crime it was 'ornamented with its embroidery of modifications and distinctions with which the mass of the people is just as much acquainted as with the Koran: spun out of a heap of statutes jumbled with the Fragments [remnants] of common law'.[74] He claimed that he could fill 20 or 30 pages 'with what is called learning' the only use of which was to 'encumber and perplex the law'. Only professors knew anything at all about this subject, which made as much sense as shaking out a 'bag of letters of the Alphabet'.[75] Given his strongly expressed opinion that as a crime petty treason was nonsense, Bentham chose to disregard it altogether and it does not appear in his penal code. He substituted no other offence to make good the lack.

THE CONFINEMENT AND HARBOURING OF WIVES

A husband's right to confine his wife, that is to imprison her in her house or elsewhere in order to correct her behaviour or restrain her extravagance, had long been considered to be part of the common law and another exercise of a husband's patriarchal authority.[76] But by the eighteenth century the extent, and indeed correctness, of the exercise of this authority was being questioned. Notorious cases heard in court typically concerned a wealthy woman whose husband had imprisoned her in order to force her to confer some financial benefit on him.[77] An imprisoned woman – or rather her family – was able to seek a writ of habeas corpus for her release, just as an abused woman was able to seek articles of the peace from the justices. For instance, in 1787 Andrew Robinson Bowes imprisoned his wife, the Countess of Strathmore, until she was released by writ of habeas corpus.[78] In 1818 Peregrine Bingham, referring to this notorious case, commented that if it appears that her husband has mistreated her and a wife exhibits articles of the peace against him, then a court will not 'order her to be delivered to him'.[79] Neither could a husband seize his wife and force her to live with him if they had previously entered into a separation agreement. The number of cases brought would lead to the conclusion that not all husbands agreed with Bingham, at least not in the 1780s.

Bentham dealt with the enforced confinement of wives in the 1780s in an offence he described as 'kidnapping' which he defined as where a man is concerned in 'conveying a person against his will to a place beyond the sea or out of the dominion of the state; knowing himself to have no right so to do'.[80] He allowed a possible defence, or 'justification', of consent: for example, the consent given by the victim to medical treatment.[81] He then continued by questioning whether the exercise of domestic power by a man over his family ever justified kidnapping: 'shall a Husband in any and what cases and upon what terms be allowed to exercise this authority over his wife? A parent over his Child who is a Minor? A Guardian over his Ward?' Bentham concluded that these questions were the business of the civil code and not the penal code;[82] he nevertheless proceeded to answer them by setting out an offence of 'matrimonial disturbance' which make it clear that he rejected any notion that a husband had a right to imprison or kidnap his wife.

MATRIMONIAL DISTURBANCE AND HARBOURING

Bentham listed matrimonial disturbance and harbouring as two offences against domestic condition in his penal code. Matrimonial disturbance was defined as the disturbance of conjugal rights, which he explained to be hindering a husband from enjoying the privileges of his position without lawful cause.[83] Therefore, this offence was committed by a third party who interfered in a marriage to the detriment of a husband. Bentham listed the justifications that could be made in response to an accusation of matrimonial disturbance as: '1 Medical practice. 2 Precaution against greater mischief. 3 Defence. 4 Military power and subservience thereunto. 5 Judicial power. 6 Sovereign power and subservience thereunto.'[84]

This offence was Bentham's replacement for the numerous common law actions of 'criminal conversation' which were brought to the Court of King's Bench in the 1780s and 1790s. Here an aggrieved husband sued his wife's lover for damages – that is monetary compensation – for loss of his wife's *consortium*, or companionship and society.

There were two significant differences between the common law action for criminal conversation and Bentham's action of matrimonial disturbance. First, Bentham's offence was a crime, whereas eighteenth-century criminal conversation was a trespass, or civil wrong. Secondly, although Bentham's punishment for matrimonial disturbance included payment of compensation it did not involve payment of damages or a fine, and so a wronged husband lost the right to take financial revenge on a wife's lover. Bentham also employed 'presence banishment' as a punishment: the offender was banished from presence of husband or wife, or both, and ordered not to correspond with the wife.[85] Because adultery was also an offence against domestic condition, and a ground for divorce in Bentham's penal code, presumably a successful verdict of matrimonial disturbance against a lover would provide grounds for divorce.

Bentham added some further explanation of what he meant by 'hindering' a husband's enjoyment. In this situation the offender had carried away a man's wife, or harboured her, or detained her with or without her consent but against the will of her husband, with or without any personal injury to her.[86] If the wife did suffer some physical injury in the course of the crime then this was a separate criminal offence and the wrongdoer could be punished for it separately. This last case should be distinguished from the offence of matrimonial disturbance, because the latter was concerned only with the injury suffered by a husband when his wife was 'taken away'.[87] Presumably as an alternative a husband could pursue a third party for kidnapping or harbouring his wife.

But Bentham stopped short of allowing a wife to pursue a third party (presumably usually another woman) for matrimonial disturbance if her husband had left her and she was hindered from enjoying the privileges of her condition as a wife. Here there could be no remedy for the wronged wife because 'of the subordination of her condition and the modesty of her sex' he concluded.[88]

What if a wife had left her husband of her own free will? Church court suits for restitution of conjugal rights – that is, cohabitation – ordering a deserting spouse to return home, had more or less ceased by the eighteenth century. In earlier times church wardens brought such cases before the court largely from financial motives, anxious to prevent a separated wife and children from becoming a financial burden to the parish. A deserting wife could defend herself by explaining why she would not return home, often citing cruel treatment or her husband's adultery. Actions for restitution of conjugal rights were also often brought in order to trigger a separation order,[89] and by the late eighteenth-century church court matrimonial suits for restitution of conjugal rights were commonly employed not to force a runaway wife to return home but as a tactical device by an embattled spouse to force an agreement on the finances of a separation agreement.[90]

If a wife had left of her own free will, then Bentham's offence of 'harbouring a wife' addressed this situation. He defined harbouring as keeping a woman with her consent, but against the will of her husband.[91] At the time a common law action was available to a husband in such circumstances, which was popularly known as the law of 'harbouring'. Here a husband pursued a third party for the loss of his wife's *consortium*, which meant loss of household rather than sexual services. A husband typically used the threat to bring such an action in order to force his wife to return home, especially if she had left taking the children with her. An aggrieved husband could advertise in the local press his intention to bring an action against anyone harbouring his wife, and this threat would deter anyone from offering a runaway wife a place to live or work. Therefore, just the threat alone could make a woman destitute. Allegations of cruelty in suits for church court separation orders often mentioned such threats. The third parties who helped a runaway wife would usually be her family or friends, but neighbours and servants too often intervened between husband and wife in cases of cruelty, and their intervention could take the form of providing a wife with somewhere to live.[92] A husband could also exert pressure on his wife to return home by informing the public that he was no longer liable to pay her debts. This would effectively cut off her access to credit for 'necessaries' including food. Husbands would place advertisements to this effect in newspapers, or would pay for announcements to be made by the bell-man in the churchyard on a Sunday or in the market-place on market-days, or else pay for the distribution of handbills.[93] Thus any third party who provided a runaway wife with a home and work did so at considerable financial risk to themselves.

To some extent Bentham's offence of harbouring, and the defences he made available, put into codified statutory form the existing practice of the courts, at least according to Bingham's explanation of it. In Bentham's code third parties could defend themselves against the husband's action by pleading 'lawful cause' – that is, that the wife had left because of her husband's cruelty: 'Where the wife having reasonable ground to apprehend *cruelty* on the part of her husband, absents herself from him in the intention of seeking her remedy at Law.'[94] Two other defences available to a third party were: first, 'where the Husband openly cohabits with another woman in the same house in which he would have his wife be'; and secondly, where a wife had 'no sufficient maintenance of her own, and her husband cannot or will not give her any', as a consequence of which the third party had intervened to help.[95] Bentham's punishments for a defendant found guilty of matrimonial disturbance included presence banishment and payment of compensation. But if there were extenuating circumstances then compensation could be reduced or denied, and costs might be evenly distributed between the parties at the discretion of the judge.[96]

In this manner Bentham's penal code brought an end to a husband's common law rights to confine his wife, and by providing defences of lawful cause to a third party who had intervened; he also nullified the canon law duty to cohabit imposed on all married people.

RAPE AND MATRIMONIAL OPPRESSION

Bentham wrote extensively on rape on two separate occasions in the 1780s. One set of manuscripts offers greater definition and severe punishments for the crime, but in general the two sets of manuscripts complement each other.[97] Bentham defined the crime as 'where a man has carnal knowledge of a person not consenting'.[98] He wrote extensively in Latin for much of this work, presumably for the sake of privacy. He deemed consent to have been given where a woman 'omits' to do everything in her power to prevent the rape by struggling and calling for assistance.[99] However non-resistance did not constitute consent if the victim was drugged or 'in a swoon', and neither can it be consent if the victim was illegally confined by force or fraud with the intention of extorting her consent.[100] Bentham would punish an 'immediate attempt' to commit violent rape, a serious felony at common law, by a sentence imprisoning the offender to not less than half a year of hard labour. He was to be utterly removed from the 'society of the other sex'.[101] The punishment for a 'remote attempt' to commit rape, defined as where a man 'unlawfully confines a woman with intent to force her by hardships or actual violence to let him have carnal knowledge of her', was a sentence of imprisonment half the length of that for an immediate attempt.[102] He explained that his purpose was to punish a man by repressing the gratification 'of that appetite which he had endeavoured to abuse'.[103] The punishment could be more severe too: 'He shall be punished in the offending parts', declared Bentham, and followed this with a description in Latin of whipping for a first offence followed by castration for subsequent offences.[104]

A victim was not to be compensated for rape unless she was unmarried, and of good fame of chastity. But this did not apply if the victim was injured,[105] or if the offence was committed 'against the order of nature'. In this last case the offender was to be punished by being exhibited with ignominy in the 'tub of uncleanliness', and might be banished from the victim's presence.[106]

Bentham included an offence of 'Lasciviousness' in the penal code. This seems to address sexual attacks less than rape. He defined lasciviousness as treating the person of another with indecent freedom without consent. 'What shall be reputed to be indecent will depend in good measure on the customs and manners of the country and upon the rank of the parties', he concluded.[107] The punishments included fines, imprisonment, presence banishment, or being required 'to ask pardon with circumstances more or less humiliating'.[108]

Was the rape of a wife by her husband also punishable as an offence against domestic condition? Bentham provides no clear answer to this question, which quite possibly would not readily have occurred to him. Eighteenth-century opinion was that a husband could not rape his wife because by virtue of the marriage contract she had consented to have sexual relations with him;[109]

after all, rape within marriage did not become unlawful until more than two hundred years later in 1991.[110]

Moreover, Bentham provided defences for the offence of rape that would suggest that a husband might well have considered himself justified in raping his wife, and again Bentham chose to write much of this manuscript in Latin. Justifications for rape include the fact that the victim was the 'wife of the Ravisher', or that he believed her to be.[111] Bentham concluded with the proviso 'But see the Law of Man and Wife' – unfortunately without any further comment.

Later, in the 1820s, when writing on contractual services as part of the civil code, Bentham argued that 'Every person is entitled to services the non rendition of which constitutes a negative offence.' Some services may be required 'by virtue of contract' he declared.[112] Among the examples he gave of such contractually required services was 'sexual intercourse [required] by marriage'.[113] But it is most unlikely that by this Bentham intended to condone a husband's rape of his wife. Such behaviour would not conform to the dictates of the principle of utility because of the harm it caused, and refusal of sexual relations did not number among Bentham's grounds for divorce. This would suggest that, while sexual relations were a required part of marriage, a husband was not justified in raping his wife. However, Bentham thought refusal of sexual relations sufficiently serious to make this an offence against the domestic condition of husband and wife.

Bentham listed another offence, that of matrimonial oppression, which he may have intended as a remedy for a raped wife. He defined matrimonial oppression as the sexual oppression of a wife by her husband by means of offences affecting her body, person or reputation,[114] which would certainly fit a modern understanding of rape within marriage. But this modern understanding may not have been the understanding of an eighteenth-century legal philosopher.

Bentham's remaining four examples of matrimonial oppression make criminal the denial of sexual contact rather than the violently forcing of it. 'Uxorial oppression' occurs when a wife withdraws herself from sexual intercourse with her husband;[115] while 'marital elopement' is where, in breach of the marriage contract, 'a husband withdraws himself out of the reach of conjugal intercourse with his wife'.[116] 'Wrongful subtraction of uxorial service' occurs when a wife 'omits to hold' sexual intercourse with her husband;[117] and 'wrongful subtraction of marital service' occurs when a husband 'omits to hold' sexual intercourse with his wife.[118]

WRONGFUL DETRECTION OF HUSBANDSHIP

Bentham explained this offence against domestic condition as being when a husband either does some unlawful act, such as the use of bodily or mental force against his wife, or fails to do some act in order to avoid becoming subject to an obligation he owes his wife.[119] In existing common law, as the corollary of coverture, a man was expected to provide his wife and children with the necessaries of life appropriate to his station in life – necessaries being legally defined as food, clothing and shelter. So, if a husband barred his wife from the family home, or forced her to leave home by cruel treatment, or if he deserted her, he still remained liable to maintain his wife and children.[120]

Bentham's offence of wrongful detrection was probably directed against defaulting husbands who left their families dependent on parish funds. Parish officers administering the poor law would frequently seek an order from the Justices to recoup from a husband's property monies given from parish funds to support his deserted family. Presumably Bentham hoped his codified offence would simplify and expedite this process of reimbursing public money.

A man had a common law duty to maintain his children as well as his wife, and Bentham included two further offences addressing the problems caused by defaulting men. The first, 'wrongful detrection of fathership', which he described as a breach of the domestic condition of fathership, reinforced a father's duty to maintain his children. Failure to do so was a punishable offence. Here Bentham's analysis of the duties owed by a father to his children owes much to the canon law rules followed by the church courts, rather than to the common law. In particular he wrote favourably of the 'Rome-bred' canon law which would confer legitimacy on a child born to a woman whom the father later married, whereas in common law the child would remain illegitimate. Bentham pointed out approvingly that in canon law if a man failed to marry the mother of his child he would still have an obligation to maintain the child, and could be ordered to do so.[121]

Lastly, Bentham's penal code listed several other offences against domestic condition that address failures to care for a dependant. These include 'wrongful evitation of mastership',[122] 'wrongful desertion of guardianship'[123] and 'wrongful evitation of fathership'.[124] The *Oxford English Dictionary* defines evitation as avoiding, shunning or shirking, so here Bentham was addressing a father's duty to maintain his children, which he extended to stepchildren. In the eighteenth century, agreements were frequently made before marriage by men and women who had children by a previous marriage. The husband-to-be typically promised to pay portions to the children of his wife's first marriage, because any property she had on marriage, or which she had inherited from her first husband, would become his.[125] Bentham's offence of evitation of fathership addressed this matter by inserting it into the penal code as an offence, rather than leaving it to private agreement. His offence covered not merely failure to maintain children, but also taking steps actively to avoid meeting the duties of a father.[126]

Addressing the same social ill in an alternative action, Bentham explained that the offence of desertion or elopement applied to the children of a family as well as a wife. In fact, a father who left his child, or his ward, without making provision for them, would be guilty of an offence. Even a temporary, limited absence and failure to maintain would suffice to incur punishment because it would not be necessary to prove that the father intended never resuming his role.[127]

6

Adultery

Bentham defined adultery as 'where a man and a woman have carnal knowledge of each other; one at least of them being married but not to each other'.[1] He went on to complete 52 densely written large manuscript pages on the subject of adultery, some of which are set out as a code of law under the heading of 'Offences against conditions. Adultery'.[2] For the most part these manuscripts are dated by archivists to the 1780s, while a few are dated 1773 by Bentham himself.[3] If the sheer number of words and pages are counted, then Bentham's treatment of adultery far exceeds that of divorce or any other single topic within his discussion of the law of marriage. Yet neither Etienne Dumont nor John Bowring published the adultery manuscripts, and we have to ask why? Also, why did Bentham consider adultery such an important subject?

No doubt his interest is explained in part by Bentham's plans for new divorce laws, for adultery was to be a ground for divorce. As part of this project he wanted to provide legislators with a clear definition of adultery as an offence, together with appropriate punishments (one of which would be the right to divorce).[4] But his interest in adultery was not limited to its role as a ground for divorce. In fact, except in the adultery code itself, Bentham's 52 pages make little or no mention of divorce. Instead, he used the example of adultery to make an exhaustive practical application of the principle of utility to what he (mostly) regarded as behaviour of private, not public concern. His proposition is that all private behaviour has an effect on wider society too, and may cause harm. So, in these pages he explains how to calculate these risks.

History reveals the reason for Bentham's choice of adultery as a subject for lengthy examination. The interval between 1770 and 1800 was remarkable for a great number of what were popularly known as 'trials for adultery'. These comprised matrimonial suits in the church courts (where adultery was a ground for a divorce *a mensa et thoro*), common law courts (where adultery was the ground of criminal conversation trials) and in Parliament (where adultery was the ground for parliamentary divorce).[5] As early as 1765 Blackstone had noted the increased number of 'adultery trials', without conjecturing the cause.[6] Their increase attracted much comment, so much so that the 1790s in particular have been described as a time of moral or sex panic in England.[7] In recent years historians have attributed the English preoccupation with adultery trials to a fear of the libertinism associated with the French Revolution, underlining a perceived correlation between sexual behaviour and political stability.[8] Certainly, one early nineteenth-century author blamed the evils of 'French morals', complaining that because the French could not defeat the English in battle they sent female dancers across the Channel to undermine and corrupt English youth.[9] But in France too the years between 1789 and 1804 (when family law was revised by the Napoleonic Code) witnessed a 'widespread obsession' with adultery, according to a scholar who also notes that the family as an institution was at that time the site of 'multiple and highly contested issues', including the role of women, inheritance of property and patriarchal authority.[10]

While canon law had long regarded adultery as a most serious offence,[11] by the mid-eighteenth century prosecutions for adultery in the provincial church courts had become very rare, and not many cases were heard in the London consistory court at Doctor's Commons.[12] Instead, by the 1780s adultery trials were most likely to be heard in the central common law courts of King's Bench or Common Pleas at Westminster Hall, where petitions for damages were brought for the trespass known as criminal conversation, popularly known as crim. con. Here an aggrieved husband sued his wife's lover for monetary compensation for loss of his wife's 'consortium', meaning her companionship and society. A successful suit was usually the first step towards obtaining a parliamentary divorce.[13] Lawrence Stone claims that the shift in the late eighteenth century from male violence and duelling to inflicting crippling financial damages following an action for criminal conversation action is evidence of the change to a more commercial age. Relationships, including those between husbands and wives, were increasingly being expressed in terms of property relations.[14] Bentham too connected duelling to criminal conversation cases, but not in order to draw a parallel with property relations. Instead, he remarked that adultery trials served 'to expose the observance of humanity', or lack of it, by a husband towards his adulterous wife, in much the same way as duelling had in the past on the part of one gentleman towards another.[15]

Bentham's reference to duelling was apt. Duels had been central to the aristocratic code of early modern England, and still had relevance because they embodied some of the fundamental characteristics of elite masculinity: honour, reputation and 'a certain amount of military expertise'.[16] Similarly, a successful criminal conversation case would restore a wronged husband's honour and reputation, and hurt his wife's lover. The large sums of money awarded by the court might fund the husband's divorce, and at the same time enable him to revenge himself on his wife's lover by inflicting financial damage on him. A defendant could face financial ruin, remaining incarcerated in debtor's prison until friends or family met his debts, or until death released him.

A large, and sometimes controversial, literature fed the public interest in adultery trials. This included the publication of the evidence from trials, newspaper reports, verse satires and collections of trial reports.[17] Caricatures and engravings of characters and scenes from the latest, or particularly notorious, trials were hung in print-shop windows for all to see and remark upon. It would have been difficult, if not impossible, for Bentham to ignore all this activity.

Much of this literature was regarded as disreputable,[18] but serious anxieties were also expressed about the numbers of widely reported scandalous 'intrigues' and 'gallantries'. One author claimed that the 'crime' of adultery prevailed to such an extent that it threatened the 'very existence of society'. Another blamed novel-reading which produced heated imaginations and weak minds in young women, leaving them prey to the 'Lovelaces and Lothários' of the day.[19] Disapproval of novel-reading, famously spoofed by Jane Austen in *Northanger Abbey*,[20] was not confined to young women; young men too should be protected from the perils posed by fiction. John Bowring reports that Bentham himself recollected that storybooks were forbidden reading in his childhood home.[21]

Adultery was popularly condemned as an aristocratic, fashionable vice. There is little doubt that Bentham agreed that, if not a vice, it was a pastime for the rich.[22] In some ways his writings on adultery provide a lively, though doubtless unintended, picture of late eighteenth-century fashionable metropolitan English life. Fashionable because, in his eighteenth-century language, 'intrigues' and 'gallantries' were more or less exclusively indulged in by the men (and some women) of the upper and middling sort. In fact, Bentham worried that the effects of adultery would be 'most pernicious' among the 'labouring class of people', but concluded that they were the least at risk because they 'have in comparison but little time to engage in intrigues'. Bentham must have had second thoughts about this because he added in a footnote: 'But Qu [query] on Sundays and Holidays.'[23]

Most people accepted without question the wrongfulness of adultery. But Bentham asked why adultery should be defined as a wrong at all, in a utilitarian scheme of law. His answers to that question provide an example of the application of the greatest happiness principle to private behaviour.

THE CRIME OF ADULTERY

Bentham defined adultery as a crime. In the 1780s it appeared in his penal code as one of a number of sexual offences, along with seduction and rape.[24] But earlier, in 1773, it had appeared in another guise in a detailed chart of crimes he had carefully constructed. This was a large sheet divided into several columns. The top of the columns were headed Avarice, Hatred, Lust, Self-preservation, Conscience, Sport or Curiosity, Ambition or Avarice, indicating motives for the various crimes listed beneath them.[25] Not all of Bentham's offences would be considered crimes today, and some of them bring to sudden life the eighteenth-century world he inhabited.[26] The crime of adultery appears under the heading of Lust. Crimes of Hatred include disfigurement, wounding, battery and assault. Crimes of Avarice and Lust include polygamy and clandestine marriage. Self-preservation crimes include abortion and child murder, while Sport or Curiosity crimes include animal cruelty. The column headed Lust lists first the crime of rape, but also includes fornication.[27]

In the 1780s Bentham turned again to definitions of adultery, changing his focus from lust as a motive in 1773, to 'domestic condition' as the target of the offence. Here adultery appears on a large sheet divided into four pages, one of which is crossed out in pencil. Adultery is one of a number of offences under the heading of 'Offences against Domestic Conditions'.[28] As we saw earlier, these 'domestic conditions' were a number of private relationships, one of which was the relationship between husband and wife. Adultery was therefore an offence –in fact a crime – against the 'domestic condition' of marriage.

Bentham's criminalization of adultery need not surprise us too much, even though adultery was not a criminal offence in English law at the time, any more than it is today. Ever since the twelfth century, punishing adultery had been understood as reserved to the church courts. The church courts' jurisdiction included the policing of religious, sexual and public order offences, as well as a general jurisdiction over marriage.[29] Jurisdictional boundaries overlapped, and the eighteenth-century Justices of the Peace sitting at Quarter Sessions also punished public and sexual disorder offences like prostitution and bastard-bearing.[30] There were also precedents in the past for defining adultery as a crime. During the Interregnum, the Commonwealth Adultery Act (1650) made adultery a capital offence, albeit for adulterous wives.[31] In Bentham's own time, in 1779 Lord Auckland's Adultery Prevention bill planned to criminalize adultery and prevent the remarriage of adulterous wives,[32] and an anonymous author called on Parliament to legislate and provide punishments for adulterous women.[33] In 1771 the ambiguity in law about the nature of adultery was argued at length in King's Bench by counsels for the plaintiff and defendant during Lord Grosvenor's much publicized action for damages for criminal conversation against the king's brother, the Duke of Cumberland. One of the questions that perplexed the court was whether Lord Grosvenor's suit was a private or a public matter, and whether the action was a matter of civil damages to be paid in reparation for a civil injury, or fiscal punishment for a crime.[34]

Bentham's classification of adultery as a crime also owes much to the distinctions he made between civil and penal law. In 1828 he concluded that there was in fact 'no demarcation between Penal and Civil codes'. The civil code was an appendix to the penal code, the subject-matter being common to both.[35] To explain this he likened a body of law to a human body. The penal branch is the skeleton, or 'outline of the whole', and contains the catalogue of offences. The civil code sets out the explanation of the subject-matter of the offence.[36] Thus penal law is imperative, and its subject-matter is the punishment of an offence in order to secure compliance,[37] while the civil law is expositive.[38]

Bentham's proposals for criminalizing adultery differed from those of others because he based his arguments on the principle of utility, rather than on moral or religious belief. Why Bentham thought adultery was a crime will be examined next.

ADULTERY AND THE PRINCIPLE OF UTILITY

Bentham recognized that sexual pleasure was not confined to marriage. He asked why adultery should be considered a wrong at all in a utilitarian scheme of law. For, as we have seen, in accordance with the principle of utility, Bentham saw that 'every particle of [sexual] pleasure . . . is *prima facie* when considered by itself a good and must be taken for so much good (until) some evil can be proved to arise from the same source'.[39] If sexual pleasure was a good, and if anything that has the effect of preventing sexual pleasure 'must *pro tanto* and *prima facie* be deemed an evil',[40] then it would follow that enforcing fidelity in marriage would be an evil because a married man and woman were prevented from enjoying the pleasures of love with other people.[41] This being the case, why did he not include adultery as a good according to the principle of utility? Adultery brought pleasure, but did any harm result?

Bentham explained that in a utilitarian scheme of law harm could be one of two kinds: 'primary harm' (i.e. adverse consequences resulting to an individual or 'multitude of assignable individuals' from a 'mischievous' act), or 'secondary harm' (i.e. harm that extends to the whole community, or to unassignable individuals).[42] Applying the principle of utility to adultery he concluded that an adulterous relationship may bring with it certain dangers, but 'it produces no certain harm'.[43] He pointed to the example of some other cultures where a husband's infidelity, and sometimes a wife's too, was either tactically ignored or else not treated as an offence of any sort.[44]

Looking at the customs of other nations, and surveying the differences between cultures, Bentham found that two systems of morality divided the world: the lax or loose system, and the rigid system. He believed that the distinction between the two was made particularly clear by the way in which adultery was treated.[45] According to the loose system adultery is condemned, or not, according to the particular circumstances of the case, but under the rigid system adultery is always strongly condemned and always punished, whatever the circumstances. This latter approach, Bentham added, very effectively policed fornication, but adultery was condemned on 'a footing of its own'. Presumably by this he meant adultery was punished for being an offence more serious than unmarried sexual incontinence.[46]

Looking at England, Bentham was well aware that, despite a huge fascination with criminal conversation trials, most people generally condemned adulterous behaviour as immoral. Noisy public demonstrations by neighbours still sometimes policed the extramarital affairs of the poorer and middling sort of people in the eighteenth century, giving expression to community disapproval of the sexual incontinence of husbands and wives. The scandalous behaviour of the aristocracy and the wealthy was exposed to shame and ridicule by the humiliating publicity that appeared in newspapers and print-shop windows. This has been likened to the earlier tradition of rough music because through it society deployed humiliation as a weapon against sexual transgression.[47]

Thus the community, or as Bentham was to call it in his constitutional code writings, 'the public opinion tribunal',[48] condemned adultery as a wrong. But Bentham thought sexual behaviour should be regarded as a matter of individual taste – 'you like oysters: I do not' – and therefore it should be legislated for according to the principle of utility, and not on the basis of popular prejudice.[49] So, if adultery was to become a crime in a utilitarian code of law, how should a legislator proceed? Bentham trod a careful path. As a general rule, as we have seen, he was wary of legislating to enforce moral behaviour. There was also the problem that all laws inevitably brought with them some pain: 'A law is good, according to the more or less clear happiness it produces. Every law, as such, necessarily produces a certain quantity of unhappiness.'[50] For example, the law preventing murder undoubtedly makes the prospective victim and his friends happy, but brings unhappiness to the would-be murderer.[51] If all laws bring pain to some people, then in order to justify criminalizing adultery great attention must be paid to the primary and secondary harm that adultery brings about.

PRIMARY HARM: MARRIAGE AS PROPERTY AND ADULTERY AS THEFT

Adultery can be considered in one of two ways, wrote Bentham: first as an injury done to an individual, and secondly, as an offence against morality. But in a utilitarian code, adultery is neither of these. Because Bentham saw marriage as a secular contract in which husband and wife agree to certain terms, he defined adultery as the 'breach of that contract whereby a man and woman engage to live together for the sake of each other's company . . . and [for] the pleasure of love or the pleasure of having children, or both'.[52] On this understanding, adultery 'is nothing but a violation of a species of property' which married people have in the person and personal services of each other.[53]

The idea of adultery as a violation of a kind of property right should really not be startling, he added, because anyone who agrees to render services of any kind to another becomes to a certain extent the property of that other.[54] He went on to explain that whatever existences are capable of becoming the objects of property can be put under the heading either of things or of persons. Things become a man's property by the uses he puts them to, while a person can be said to become another's property by the services he may be made to render to him. But really, Bentham concluded, this distinction between things and persons exists more in words than anything else, because when you contract with a person to render you 'such or such [a service] what is it but the putting him to such or such a use?'[55] Considered in this way, the wife is the property of the husband, the husband is the property of the wife, and adultery is a kind of theft.[56]

Bentham's understanding of marriage as a contract for services resembles that for other domestic relations. For example, in common law a master could sue for his own loss in tort if his servant were injured or 'enticed' away from his employment. The master's loss was the loss of his servant's services.[57] By the eighteenth century this action in tort had been extended to a husband who had lost the services of his wife because of some injury done to her, usually adultery; the husband sued for loss of her services.[58] These actions in tort protected relationships based on status rather than contract. By insisting that marriage was based on contract Bentham in effect rejected status, with its customary hierarchical relations, in favour of contract with its potential for more equality in bargaining an agreement for services between any two people.

Bentham distinguished between a property right in another person in marriage and actual slavery because in marriage the party to be benefited by another's service does not have absolute dominium over the provider of those services.[59] He also drew a contrast with Roman law, in which a man's family was considered his property and a husband could sell his children, repudiate his wife, or hand her over to another man.[60] Here he was referring to a form of marriage in Roman law known as manus-marriage. Before marriage a woman was subordinated to her father, and then after marriage to her husband instead.[61] Marriage in Bentham's code was none of these things, but instead a secular contract entered into by husband and wife. Nevertheless, he maintained that a more or less exclusive property right to the contractually agreed services (whether active or passive, corporeal or mental, or a mixture) did exist.[62]

PRIMARY HARM: THE ADULTEROUS WIFE

Having established the property right that husbands and wives have in each other, Bentham went on to describe the harm caused by adultery, in order to explain his reasons for criminalizing it. In a numbered sequence of 20 pages he describes what he calls the 'mischiefs' that would result from an adulterous relationship.[63] These mischiefs did not depend on popular prejudice, but instead on the psychological and other harm that adultery brings to an individual. For both husband and wife, loss of a spouse's affection and miscellaneous services are undoubtedly the main mischief of adultery, but there are others too. The harm is not limited to a husband and wife: children and the lover were damaged too.[64]

Bentham concentrated his attention on the wrong done to a man by his adulterous wife. He noted that in France while canon law did not distinguish between adultery committed by a man or a woman, civil law did.[65] Customary French practices of arranged marriages were 'slowly giving way' to modern concepts of companionate marriage. A husband's infidelity (unlike his wife's) had traditionally been regarded as unimportant, but it has been claimed that in the eighteenth century female infidelity 'functioned as a lightening rod' for the confrontation between revolutionary ideas and traditional values.[66] In 1852 Alexandre Dumas advanced a reason for this. Once primogeniture was outlawed in 1789, he wrote, and all children of a family inherited equally, then illegitimate children suddenly represented a real threat to the stability and finances of a family. Mainardi claims that as a result private morality became a public issue, and relations between men and women assumed societal and political significance.[67]

Public outcry against a wife's infidelity suggests that similar sentiments prevailed in England, even though primogeniture was retained as customary law. So, Bentham asked, was adultery more acceptable and permissible in a man than in a woman? Confronting a question fraught with difficulties for an eighteenth-century man of means, Bentham went on to question whether a man's sexual fidelity was really quite as serious a matter as that of his wife. Popularly, an adulterous woman was regarded as immodest, devoid of shame, and among civilized people as 'a kind of monster', but male adultery was often condoned.[68] Bentham set out several reasons frequently advanced to explain this more lenient attitude towards male infidelity, but to what extent he himself subscribed to them is not clear. For example, he asserted that without 'connections of the amorous kind' a man's health would suffer, and that infidelity in a husband was more excusable because wives were likely to be incapacitated by pregnancy or parturition. Anyway, women were more often ill than men. Also, men were much more likely to make long journeys away from home than their wives, and so, presumably, meet with greater temptation.[69] In general women were less interested in sex than men, and because a married woman did not usually have 'physical want to activate her', she had no excuse.[70]

Bentham also considered women were usually more 'modest' (understood in the sense of 'chaste') in their behaviour than men. Modest behaviour, in both men and women, was valued by anyone with any degree of refinement, and here, Bentham reported, the popular understanding of modesty coincided with Christian teaching. Both required the same standards of behaviour, and in both the act of adultery was in general looked upon as shameful and wrong.[71] So if a wife committed adultery it probably proved that, unusually, this woman was not modest and also that she already hated her husband. But this was not equally true if the husband was unfaithful.[72]

So, should an unfaithful wife be more severely punished than her unfaithful husband? Bentham pointed out that popular opinion judged that she should.[73]

She was not punished in any other way but by 'the censure of the world', but this censure was undoubtedly harsh.[74] But at the time in which he wrote, attitudes towards adulterous women had changed in certain ways, changes exemplified in the many reports of trials for criminal conversation. Whereas in the seventeenth century men whose wives had been unfaithful were derided as cuckolds, by the late eighteenth century there was public sympathy for the unfortunate husband, but at the same time an increased condemnation of him if he had been the architect of his own misfortune. For example, if a husband 'neglected' his wife, he had only himself to blame if she subsequently fell prey to a seducer. This attitude is seen clearly in the calculation of damages awarded to a wronged husband in the criminal conversation cases discussed below.[75] Whether 'neglected' or not, an unfaithful wife was always condemned.

The 'mischiefs' resulting from adultery listed by Bentham inevitably reflected the hierarchical structure of eighteenth-century life, which included the inferior status of women. A wife, Bentham wrote, was everywhere in 'that state of subordination in which nature and the Laws of almost all countries place her with respect to her husband'.[76] The result was that the infidelity of a wife would be regarded by most people as much more mortifying to a husband than a husband's infidelity would be to his wife.

He then explained the greater significance accorded to a wife's infidelity in hierarchical, rather than political, terms. He asserted that a slight from an inferior to a superior (especially from people who are constantly in each others' company) is much more mortifying to receive than a slight from a superior to an inferior. From this he concluded that a husband's infidelity with a woman of inferior rank – for example, a servant – would be less mortifying to his wife than his infidelity with a woman of equal rank. In the first case the infidelity was likely to be a transient passion for mere beauty, but in the second it was likely to indicate a real preference for another person. For this reason too, if a liaison between a married man and a woman is open knowledge to all the world, then it is much better that the liaison should be with a person of inferior rank so that the wife is not slighted.[77]

Bentham's views also reflected contemporary male honour codes. By the eighteenth century a man's honour was less susceptible than it had been in the seventeenth century to damage from sexual insults levelled at him, but he remained vulnerable to an attack on the reputation of his wife. An important attribute of 'manliness' was considered to be a man's ability to form a household, protect it and control it.[78] An accusation of cuckoldry therefore damaged a man's honour and public reputation, because he was seen to be deficient in managing his own household, and particularly his wife.[79] Bentham thought that an adulterous wife might be tempted to betray her husband's interests to a blackmailing servant, or to the adulterer himself, or to anyone else who discovered the relationship. The result would be a 'shamed' husband whose interests could be jeopardized.[80]

Bentham's views are not, however, representative of those, who fearful of female sexuality, found more to condemn in adulterous women than men because errant women, (a weaker sex, or 'lower creation') 'generally exceed men' in wickedness.[81]

Although Bentham concentrated on the wrongs suffered by the husband of an adulterous wife, this does not reflect his lack of sympathy for the wife of an adulterous man. On the contrary, as we shall see, his adultery code gave a (not quite equal) right to a wife to punish and to divorce her adulterous husband. This proposed innovation contrasted with the legal position in the 1780s and 1790s: a man was able to petition Parliament for a divorce from his adulterous wife, but women were not to succeed in divorcing adulterous husbands until the nineteenth century. His comments also reflect the concerns of contemporary case law. In the 1780s and 1790s criminal conversation trials were brought by husbands, and as a result much jurisprudence was already in place for the wronged husband, but little for the wronged wife.[82] Bentham remedied this in his adultery code.

Summing up, Bentham pointed out that while adulterous men were judged according to circumstances, adulterous women were always judged severely whatever the circumstances. This resulted in curiously contradictory attitudes towards one and the same offence. Adultery was generally condemned, but 'gallantry' (the male pursuit of intrigues or affairs) was not. Disapproving of what would later be described as the 'double standard', Bentham wrote 'mention [the same act] under the name of adultery there is never anyone who will not venture to condemn it: the very same practice under the name of gallantry will be received by the very same person with a smile of approbation'.[83]

Bentham concluded that public opinion judged adulterous women much more harshly than it did either their husbands or their lovers. In 1830, when the unmarried John Stuart Mill and the married Harriet Taylor began their supposedly platonic 'open friendship', their liaison was considered scandalous. Harriet was ironically dubbed Mrs 'Platonica' Taylor and not accepted into polite society, even after her marriage to Mill in 1849.[84]

PRIMARY HARM: QUANTIFICATION OF LOSS

Bentham wrote at some length on how the loss suffered by a wronged husband should be quantified, a question frequently raised in criminal conversation cases. For him, the payment of damages had two ends: first, the prevention of wrongdoing, and secondly, to compensate the injured person. The first was more important, declared Bentham, because (by addressing secondary harm) it prevented many crimes, while the second (by addressing primary harm) compensated only one.[85]

In general, Bentham placed great emphasis on monetary punishments ordered by a court, although in 1775 he had opted for corporal punishment as an alternative if the offender could not pay.[86] By the 1780s Bentham wanted punishment to act as a deterrent to others too, so wealthy adulterers might be ordered to pay a fine to the court as well as paying compensation to the husband.[87]

The rules applied by courts in the late eighteenth century to determine the amount of damages to be awarded to a wronged husband addressed what Bentham might have identified as primary harm. First, a husband seeking damages from his wife's lover in King's Bench had to satisfy the court that he had indeed suffered loss by his wife's adultery. Next, he had to show that he was not already separated from his wife, whether formally, by an order of divorce *a mensa et thoro* from the church courts, or informally by mutual agreement.[88] Then the amount of damages awarded was assessed depending on the value that a husband was perceived to have placed on his marriage. His damages would be reduced by any suggestion of neglect or indifference towards his wife or, worse still, if he had actually condoned her adultery.

On such principles, in several much-reported King's Bench adultery trials, the court calculated the degree of a betrayed husband's loss, and thence the appropriate amount of damages to be awarded to him as compensation.[89] Bentham paid close attention to these trials, and frequently made use of the arguments deployed in them. For example, in the 1780s he echoed the language used in a 1771 trial to claim that a betrayed husband might well consider the loss of his wife as the loss of 'much the most valuable part of the property a man possesses'.[90] He accepted that such a loss was, of course, 'liable to infinite variation', and could even be no loss at all, but frequently a husband placed great value on his marriage and therefore his wife's adultery was 'a very cruel injury' to him.[91]

Bentham evidently knew of *Biscoe v. Gordon*. In this criminal conversation case Lord Erskine, famous for his emotional rhetoric in court, represented Mr Gordon, a gentleman of means. Erskine declared that 'an injury of this nature is more severely felt by a man of sensibility and honourable birth, than it can be by a person of a different description'.[92] Bentham, and probably Erskine too, may well have read the anonymous *Free Thoughts on Seduction, Adultery and Divorce* (1771), where this point was made at length.[93] Bentham agreed that a husband's loss depended to a great extent on his sensibility, taste, moral sentiments, rank and education.[94] He listed the husband's loss as the loss of his wife's affection for him and for his children, the burden of the upbringing of children who were not his own,[95] and the possibility of disease because of his wife's infidelity. The family would suffer because the children of the family would not have the same affection for each other if they doubted they had the same father.[96]

When he turned to the problem of calculating the amount of monetary damages the court should impose on a defendant in a criminal conversation case, Bentham argued that the sum should not be fixed but be assessed according to the adulterer's means, because 'otherwise a Duke . . . [could amuse] himself by virtue of a law made in times of poverty'.[97] There really was 'no more reason why a peer should be entitled to purchase the chastity of his neighbour's wife, than a peasant of his'.[98] In other words an award of damages should act as a positive deterrent to the defendant and to others.

Bentham's language made reference to a particularly notorious case criminal conversation trial brought in 1770 by Lord Grosvenor against the king's brother, the Duke of Cumberland. In court, the question of what damages should be awarded led to a discussion between counsels for the plaintiff and defendant on the nature of the criminal conversation action itself.[99] Lord Mansfield, who defended the duke, claimed that 'An injury done to the bed of any commoner of England is as much an injury to him . . . as to a peer of the realm.'[100] His support for a fixed level of damages attracted much public criticism because it was seen as trying to mitigate the severity of the law in favour of a royal offender. In the press 'Junius' wrote that damages should be proportionate to the rank and fortune of the parties involved, because what is a penalty to one man is nothing to another. Otherwise, the seduction of a duchess and a milliner will stand on the same footing in respect to the compensation payments awarded. He added that while it was true that the crime was the same from the moral point of view, the punishments should not be regulated by the rules of morality but should depend on the circumstances of the case.[101]

Despite Bentham's admiration for Lord Mansfield, it appears that he agreed with Junius.[102] He was concerned that an order for damages should not act as an incentive to litigation. Otherwise, he wrote, it might be 'thought odd to allow Husbands to sell their wives in this way'.[103] He then added a further note 'But the law itself sells them from their husbands.'[104] His last words alluded to another notorious and well-reported criminal conversation trial which had taken place in 1740. Theophilus Cibber, the son of the famous actor Colly Cibber, brought an action against a wealthy young gentleman, William Sloper, for adultery with Cibber's wife Susannah, a singer who played the part of Polly Peachum in John Gay's *The Beggars Opera*. It appears that Cibber had gained financial backing from Sloper for his theatrical ventures, while turning a blind eye to Sloper's affair with Susannah. The court decided that Cibber had actually connived at his wife's behaviour, and remarked on the ill consequences of letting it pass for law that men may sell their wives, which would have been the consequence of a verdict for Cibber. Cibber was awarded a nominal and derisory £10 in damages.[105]

However, Bentham evidently thought the danger of encouraging litigation was not great, because in practical terms a cuckolded husband was in a difficult position. While he might very well be the best witness, he would also be unlikely to want his own shameful status made public.[106]

What if a husband had not suffered any loss at all by his wife's infidelity? Should adultery be punished where no one was harmed, as where, for example, a husband was indifferent to his wife or even actively promoted her infidelity? Bentham considered this question at some length in the context of two hypothetical situations. The first was the example of a husband who is perfectly indifferent to his wife's infidelities because he cares little or nothing for her. He argued that if a wife committed adultery only when her husband is cruel or neglects her, then, just possibly there might be no harm in it.[107] He went further and suggested that in these circumstances public opinion might think it acceptable for her to live with some single man if she did so 'with an abundance of reserve'.[108] By this, Bentham most likely meant that the woman should live a retired life and exclude herself from polite society.

In most cases, the more public an affair becomes, whether because of the woman's wrongdoing or because of her misfortune, the greater the public censure. But even where the adulterous woman meets with some public sympathy, Bentham advised that this should be understood 'as an indulgence of our infirmities', and because of the particular exceptional circumstances, rather than because the public judged it right. At the least allowing a married woman to live with a single man when her husband has been cruel, or has deserted her, is necessary for the continuation of the species, he added wryly.[109]

Bentham's second hypothetical context for assessing the primary and secondary harm caused by adultery was one in which a husband is not indifferent to his marriage, but is still deceived by his wife and her lover. He thought this situation particularly wrong if the 'gallant' had used 'the mask of friendship' with the husband in order to seduce the wife. Indeed, by the late eighteenth century, men were often portrayed as manipulative seducers exploiting friendship with a husband in order to seduce his wife.[110] Bentham criticized behaviour that, for the sake of what was almost always no more than a transient pleasure, brought 'a fund of unhappiness' to a wife, her husband and their children, and which had no end but with the end of their lives.[111]

Bentham reported that in such circumstances adultery was censured more or less severely according to the loose system, and was always harshly censured in the rigid system. The gallant would be more severely censured by public opinion if, for example, there had been great love between husband and wife, or if the gallant used particular acts to weaken that fondness, or if he had been treated by the husband with hospitality as a guest, or if he had insinuated himself into the family by pretending an extraordinary friendship with the husband. The gallant would also be especially condemned if he had been under a particular obligation to the husband, or if he had taken advantage of the confidence reposed in him when the woman had been entrusted to his care, or if through the gallant's imprudence some secret was betrayed which brought 'prejudice' to the whole family.[112]

He went on to describe the difficulties encountered by a gallant embarking on an affair with a married woman from the gallant's perspective. Affairs of that sort need time and privacy, he advised. Privacy was difficult to come by in the eighteenth century; historians have indeed remarked on the 'the near-total absence of privacy in domestic life', because 'servants and neighbours were everywhere, and prying eyes and listening ears were constantly on the watch'. Therefore, among the wealthy, it was 'virtually impossible' to conduct a love affair 'without it becoming known below stairs'.[113] Bentham mentioned that in those countries where a woman's chastity is considered a matter of great importance, a husband would place people around her to prevent the gallant's approach. In some countries a man would ward off gallants by the deliberate placing of relatives or companions for his wife's company. If such a companion were corrupted by the gallant, the husband's cuckolding may well 'furnish incidents for plays', commented Bentham, but even in fiction he thought such events uncommon enough to appear extraordinary. In his opinion the difficulties that civilized society placed in the way of any project for the seduction of a married woman must surely make a husband feel secure.[114]

Eighteenth-century adultery trials confined their consideration of the damage caused by an adulterous relationship to the wronged husband, but Bentham considered also the damage done to the gallant himself.[115] He did not condemn sexual pleasure, but believed that the deceit employed to obtain it will 'corrupt the heart'.[116] A man who is about to seduce, or to meet the advances of, his friend's wife must learn to behave in a manner very unfavourable to his own happiness. He must shut his heart against the prospect that discovery of the affair will bring grief to his friend and his friend's family. To avoid discovery, he must learn to lie well and to be determined to persevere in a bad cause.[117] Therefore, his behaviour will inevitably bring the gallant himself great and long-lasting misery.[118] Bentham compared success in carrying out intrigues with success in the political world: if a man's ambition to make conquests is flattered by success that success will lead on to evils of which he could have had no conception when he started.[119]

Things were different in France, said Bentham approvingly, particularly in Paris. There among 'people of quality' allowing a partner to commit adultery was not regarded so much as a form of generosity on the part of a husband, as of good breeding. When a French wife has an affair it should not be understood that this is because her husband has given her permission. His behaviour is not that of one man extending a favour out of friendship to another man. On the contrary, the husband allows his wife to act as she wishes 'as a (species) of justice to the wife'.[120] The Parisian husband realizes how little he can bear to confine his own 'amours' to a single object, and he is ashamed to exact a fidelity from his wife that would form 'so unreasonable' a contrast with his own laxity.[121]

Bentham's views here reflected the permissive behaviour of the European propertied classes before 1815.[122] He would doubtless have known, for instance, about Voltaire's long love affair and intellectual partnership with Emilié du Châtelet, a friend of Fontenelle and admirer of Newton. In 1725, at the age of 17, Emilié married the Marquis of Châtelet-Lomont, who, once married, rapidly resumed both his military career and his amorous adventures. The marquis made no objection when Emilié and Voltaire began their decade-long partnership, and when Emilié became pregnant in 1749 the marquis averted scandal by taking up residence with Emilié (and Voltaire) and allowed the world to assume him to be the father.[123]

ADULTERY CONDONED

Bentham turned to the situation where a husband was not merely neglectful but actually condoned his wife's adultery. The scandalous adultery trial of *Worsley v. Bisset* was heard by Lord Mansfield in King's Bench in Westminster Hall in 1781. The publicity was great and Bentham could not have failed to hear of it, particularly as he was soon to meet the plaintiff himself, Sir Richard Worsley, in Constantinople and then in Kritchev, Russia, when Worsley made an unwelcome visit to both the Bentham brothers in 1786.[124] Worsley claimed damages of £20,000 (the equivalent of £12.7 million today) from Captain Bisset for adultery with his wife, Lady Seymour Worsley. This sum would have ensured that Captain Bisset remained in a debtor's prison for the rest of his days. Lord Mansfield told the jury that if they decided Worsley 'had been privy to the prostitution of his wife' he should not recover any damages. As in Theophilus Cibber's case against William Sloper discussed above, Worsley was held to have connived at his wife's seduction and he was awarded a shaming one shilling in damages.[125] Although he went on to divorce Seymour, Worsley's reputation never recovered.

At the time, a defence of 'connivance' was available to a defendant in a church court adultery trial, and Bentham's attempts to define harm, and to set limits to such a defence, reflect case law.[126] But the church courts were more likely to hold that a husband had merely behaved foolishly rather than actually connived at his wife's adultery.[127]

Even if there were plainly no direct mischief and no immediate primary harm to a husband who condoned his wife's adultery, Bentham thought that nevertheless there was something in the nature of the property that men and women had in each other in a marriage that made it 'inexpedient' to allow the transfer of it.[128] But there was a risk of secondary harm because a law that treats adultery as an offence presupposes it to be committed without the consent, and against the wishes, of the other spouse.[129]

Bentham elaborated at length on the primary and secondary harm caused by a condoning husband. For example, if a husband has been content to accept his wife's adultery, then public opinion will conclude that this must be either because he has some interest in it, or because he has been deceived by his wife.

If the husband failed to see the danger, and was deceived, this shows a regrettable 'want of sagacity' on his part and he will be in general be condemned. If he knew of the adultery and did nothing to prevent it (when he had the legal power to do so), then public opinion will think he must condone the situation and he will be condemned for that too.[130] In fact, because as far as the outside world is concerned it is more common that a husband should want to prevent adultery than condone it, the husband will find himself in the damaging position of being regarded by the public as a dupe, whether or not he condoned his wife's behaviour.[131]

Alternatively, if a husband knowingly permitted his wife's adultery in return for some advantage, the result would be no less damaging. Again, he will be regarded by others as a dupe: for the sake of some advantage he has put himself in a position that makes him an object of contempt. Whatever the true situation, people will perceive that a woman has preferred another man to her husband, and his reputation will suffer. Public opinion will censure the situation either as a mischief or a sin. 'They will differ on the grounds of their sentiment but agree on the sentiment itself: so between one and the other it will be pretty generally condemned.'[132]

Bentham wrote about 'the virtuous Cato', who lent his wife to a friend.[133] Cato was persuaded by his friend Hortensius to divorce his wife Marcia so that Hortensius could marry her instead. Then, after Hortensius died, Marcia and Cato remarried. Bentham pointed out that in his day Cato's motives would no longer be seen as 'generous friendship', but instead a meaner motive would be attributed to him.[134]

Even if there were no primary harm in condoned adultery, there was nevertheless a danger of secondary harm because while a husband's indifference would not necessarily be known, his wife's adultery might very well be. The more public adulterous offences become, the less they are seen as wrong, and the more excuses people find for committing them. Thus, even in cases where no one appears to be harmed, adultery can nevertheless contribute to producing future harmful cases. Bentham considered this to be one reason, even if there were no other, why adultery should be forbidden: prohibition would force people to keep it secret.[135]

In a curious way, Bentham's discussion of gallantry and gallants provides a conduct book for an eighteenth-century gentleman's management of sexual intrigues with married women. For example, if the woman's husband was considered socially inferior to the gallant, then the correct conduct for the latter was to assume a sort of duty to patronize the husband in return for the pleasure enjoyed at his expense.[136] Also, if at first a married woman indulgently accepted the advances of a man, but then later refused him, it was to be understood that it was not that she disliked gallantry as such, but the gallant himself.[137] In general, Bentham maintained that men do not persist in their attempts at seduction without encouragement.[138] He illustrated this by making reference to the famous fifteenth-century Florentine love affair between Petrarch and Laura. If Petrarch persisted in his passion for his Laura, Bentham explained, either she must have given him some encouragement at first, or else her subsequent behaviour gave him hope. Downplaying sexual attraction as a motivating force for women, Bentham added that possibly Petrarch hoped that in time the éclat of his reputation would add to his personal accomplishments and help him to conquer her.[139]

Bentham observed that in many ways a man who is thought to be committing adultery becomes an object of affection to women and of envy to men. Declining to become involved in adultery could be considered reprehensible where a man receives an invitation from a woman and refuses it, especially if he refuses on the pretence of virtue and not from want of inclination. Bentham reported that such a man would be treated with scorn and derision by a majority of both sexes.[140]

He concluded that there would always be a schism among mankind on the subject of adultery. In general, a man will judge adultery with a greater or lesser degree of severity according to the pleasure he personally derives from it, or according to the harm produced by it within his own circle of acquaintance. As a result a legislator may treat this practice with a considerable degree of severity, or with no severity at all without being in any way to blame. But a legislator will be very much to blame in one circumstance: if he fails to provide punishments for adultery adequate to protect 'the most valuable part of a marriage' for a husband who does not choose to part with it.[141]

SECONDARY HARM: BENTHAM'S VOLTAIREAN TALE

In order to illustrate his belief in the necessity of fidelity in marriage, Bentham invented a tale or fable about a group of six people living together in a state of nature.[142] In this primitive society, infidelity produces serious secondary harm by endangering the survival of the whole community.

His fable begins when Deaclion meets Phyrrha and begins to live with her. Two children are born to them. However, just before the birth of their second child Deaclion meets Calliame and thinks her more beautiful than Phyrrha. Abandoning Phyrrha and their children, Deaclion goes to live with Calliame with whom he has a third child. Sophrena, witnessing Phyrrha's distress resolves to live a single, celibate life. As a result Sophrena rejects Caleb's advances. Caleb meet no other single woman so both Sophrena and Caleb remain alone and childless.

Bentham's narrative moves swiftly towards tragedy when another man, Callion, happens to meet Calliame while Deaclion is away hunting. On his return home, Deaclion is enraged to find Calliame in the arms of Callion and the two men fight violently. Deaclion is injured. Callion and Calliame, snatching up Deaclion and Calliame's child, flee from Deaclion, but he slowly gains on them. Callion urges Calliame to drop their child in order to travel more swiftly, and she unwillingly agrees. Wild beasts then make an appearance in Bentham's brutal landscape. A wolf spies the abandoned child and quickly devours it. Underlining the moral of his gruesome tale, Bentham concluded: 'Such then are the inconveniences resulting from unlimited licence [for people] of seeking their pleasures wherever they are to be found.'[143]

He then summed up these 'inconveniences', by which he meant losses, for each member of the group. Phyrrha's loss was 'the pleasure of love' and the possibility of bearing more children. Bentham admitted that Deaclion did enjoy much more of the pleasures of love, but probably no more than if he had stayed with Phyrrha. Anyway, Deaclion had been 'soundly beaten' and left in a far worse condition than he would have been if he had never left Phyrrha. Sophrena and Caleb meanwhile, have never so much as tasted the pleasures of love, and worst of all, 'an infant perishes miserably being deserted by its mother'.[144] Bentham did not describe the infant's death as a parent's loss, but instead as the tragic infant's own suffering. He apportioned blame too: the child died because it was abandoned by its mother.

Bentham's story concludes when Hymenaus (the god of marriage in Greek mythology) intervenes by calling everyone together to resolve their difficulties. Hymenaus, who had lived happily for many years 'in the company of his Delia' (an anagram of ideal), has heard about the disasters that have befallen the group. He brings everyone together and suggests that Deaclion return to Phyrrha, that Callion live with Calliame, and that Sophrena live with Caleb. Then each pair should remain constant to each other, just as he and his Delia have done. If any one of them fails to do so, then all the others have the right to expel them from their society. The group of men and women hear Hymenaus out and decide to accept his suggestions, exchanging solemn public promises to remain faithful to each other.

One year later, the meeting reconvenes and all report that they have enjoyed pleasure 'derived from the possession of their respective children', and additionally have enjoyed threefold 'that pleasure which by inconstancy they had attempted to increase'.[145] It may be true, Bentham concluded, that 'the adventures that might happen from the promiscuous embraces of the sexes may admit of infinite variety', but nevertheless the harm resulting from promiscuity must have contributed to the institution of the marriage contract, and the very same circumstances which brought about the institution of marriage show the reasons why it should be enforced by a legislator.[146]

Bentham is not known as a writer of fiction, so his choice of such a literary device to explain his philosophical and legal ideas is unexpected.[147] His fable is reminiscent of the foundational narratives of Thomas Hobbes, John Locke and Jean-Jacques Rousseau describing the origins of civil society.[148] In 1651 Hobbes considered that life for man living in a state of nature was unpleasant: 'no society; and which is the worst of all, continual feare, and danger of violent death; And the life of man, solitary, poore, nasty, brutish, and short'.[149] Like Hobbes's stories of the law of nature, Bentham's story indicates a similar belief that, without government, human nature must inevitably lead to conflict.[150] Therefore, Bentham's men and women also agree to give up some of their rights in order to live in peace.

Locke's influence on Bentham is evident too. In 1690, Locke wrote that men in a state of nature lived in a '*State of perfect Freedom*' to do as they thought fit.[151] They also lived in a state of equality with each other. This Lockean state of nature is not a state of licence but is governed by a Law of Nature, discoverable by reason, which is that, all being equal under God's authority, no one should harm another. Everyone is bound to preserve himself and also 'to preserve the rest of mankind' too.[152] Every man also has a right to punish someone who does him an injury, a right held in common with everyone else.[153] In accordance with this principle, Bentham's group of people have the collective right to expel a wrongdoer from their society.

Bentham's contemporary William Paley also reflected Locke's theories of government as they apply to marriage. Writing in 1785, Paley held that the institution of marriage increased the peace of human society, because restricting one or more women to a man, and protecting his exclusive right by sanctions and moral codes, removed a principal source of conflict.[154] Distributing the community into families also made for the better government of society. Certainly, it was sexual jealousy that led to conflict among the characters in Bentham's story.

But Bentham also knew and admired the philosophical tales of Francois-Marie Arouet de Voltaire. In October 1760, the twelve-year-old schoolboy Bentham had drawn up a list of books to take with him from Westminster School to Oxford. His lengthy list of mainly Latin authors also included Voltaire's *Essays upon General History* in seven volumes.[155] Later, six years before he wrote his Voltairean tale, Bentham worked for publishers as a translator. He was paid to translate Voltaire's philosophical tale, or *conte*, *Le Taureau Blanc* into English.[156]

Voltaire's *White Bull* satirized biblical exegesis. The heroine, the 'fair Princess Amasida', rejected Old Testament stories as 'boring' for educated people who, like her, had 'read the *Essay Concerning Human Understanding* of our wise Egyptian philosopher Locke'. Amasida likes stories to be 'essentially plausible . . . I particularly like the ones which, from beneath the veil of the plot, reveal to the experienced eye some subtle truth that will escape the common herd.'[157] Thus, Voltaire described his own method.

Taking Amasida's instructions to heart, Bentham's own philosophical tale set out the familiar and recognizable Hobbesian and Lockean picture of primitive man living in a state of nature. He then added an underlying 'subtle truth', which was to make very clear the central importance of monogamous (and here secular) marriage in bringing about civilized society.

In his story his imaginary world faced a serious threat of depopulation, so that if men and women lost the chance of procreating, or a child died, this had to be regarded as loss to the whole group. Bentham was, of course, writing before the 1798 publication of Malthus' *Essay on Population*, and in 1780 underpopulation and not overpopulation remained the greater fear.[158] So he thought that the institution of marriage would benefit the whole community by encouraging population growth, as well as bringing happiness to each individual. He wrote, as well, that without marriage there would be constant sexual competition between men, and that the 'prettiest' women would have such a variety of lovers that they would be rendered unprolific while the 'ugliest' would be neglected.[159] In fact, far too much of everyone's time would be taken up hunting for new *amours*. At this point in his narrative Bentham evidently had second thoughts because, recalling travellers' tales of faraway sexual utopias, the manuscript indicates he later added a short note, 'was this really so in Tahiti?'[160]

BENTHAM'S ADULTERY CODE

At some time during the 1780s Bentham set out his legal definition of adultery in the form of a code of law under the heading 'Penal Code of Offences against domestic conditions. Adultery'.[161] An 'Analytical View' immediately followed his brief definition of adultery. In this he explained that adultery could be single (where only one of the parties is married), or double (where both parties are married).[162]

Bentham's own law of marriage was secular, and in it adultery was a criminal offence and not a sin, yet he concurred with the canon law's position that adultery was a most serious offence. He provided many punishments, together with lists of extenuating circumstances which the judge was to take into account when passing sentence. Divorce was a last resort.

In Bentham's adultery code, the first situation was that of a married man who, without any extenuating circumstances, commits adultery with an unmarried woman. For a first offence, the offender was to be reprimanded and his name was to be registered in a Book of Adultery.[163] Bentham provided no further details, but presumably registration in this book would act both as a record of the offence and as publication of it. That would be in accordance with Bentham's plans for the reform of the law of evidence by making use of what he termed 'pre-appointed evidence'. The Book of Adultery provided just such evidence.[164]

For a second offence, the offender 'may be made to wear the Adulterers coat, for a certain time in a manner more or less public'.[165] This punishment again relied on the deterrent effects of public humiliation, and called to mind the public appearances draped in a white sheet formerly required by the church courts. Lastly, a third or subsequent offence gave the offender's wife rights that were not available in canon law; she could 'put him away', that is, divorce her husband and marry again.[166]

In circumstances where a thrice-betrayed wife did not want to exercise her right to 'put her husband away', Bentham provided two alternatives: restraining orders, and financial penalties. That is, a wife could be given the power to subject her adulterous husband to some sort of confinement or restraint for a certain time,[167] a provision that would certainly have startled Bentham's eighteenth-century contemporaries because while a husband's legal right to restrain and confine his wife was well recognized, wives had no rights to restrain husbands.[168] Bentham may have had in mind the *lettre de cachet de famille* which in pre-revolutionary France allowed fathers to imprison sons, daughters and wives too.[169]

If a convicted adulterous husband were sufficiently wealthy, then he could be ordered to compensate his wife by means of some form of pecuniary payment. At the time in matrimonial suits for divorce *a mensa et thoro* the church courts would award an allowance to a wife who succeeded in separating from her husband. Here, though, Bentham was not suggesting augmenting a wife's alimony, but rather compensating an injured wife who wished to remain living with her husband. He suggested that a husband might be ordered to augment his wife's separate allowance, if she had one, or agree to leave her a certain sum in his will.[170] Again, this order would not have been popular with husbands. Aware of this, Bentham remarked that enforcing it might do far more to disrupt family life than to maintain it.[171] He explained that his main purpose was to subject the adulterous husband to a kind of judicial disgrace in order to give force and direction to the 'censure of the World'.[172]

In order to achieve this end, and at the same time to limit possible damage to the marriage, Bentham restricted prosecution to the wife alone: neither her family nor anyone else could bring an action for adultery, and an information on oath by an actual eyewitness was necessary in order to begin the prosecution. The church courts, applying canon law, required two witnesses to an act, so here Bentham's proposal conformed more closely with the common law courts' rules of evidence. Canon law also excluded the evidence of the husband, wife or lover on the basis that their evidence would be unreliable, whereas Bentham did not. Finally canon law accepted circumstantial evidence, but Bentham did not.[173] He also made provision for the difficulties caused by unreliable witnesses who were sometimes paid to give evidence in trials for adultery. For example, he proposed that witnesses faced by threats of a defamation suit by a defendant were unable to raise a defence of fair comment unless they were actual eyewitnesses. Lastly, his code ensured that neither the husband and wife, nor close relatives and servants could be compelled to give evidence.[174]

Bentham's code punished not only the adulterous husband but also the unmarried woman who had committed adultery with him. Her name too was registered in the Book of Adultery, she could be banished from the presence of the married couple for a certain period of time, and she also could be ordered to pay compensation to the wife of the adulterer.[175]

Next, Bentham considered the case of an unmarried man who commits adultery with a married woman without any extenuating circumstances. This man could be banished from the presence of the husband and the wife, either for a period of time or forever. He was also to pay compensation to the wronged husband. If the single man was wealthy, a compensation order might mean little to him, so he could be ordered to pay a considerable additional fine.[176]

Orders for damages had also to take into account a husband's affection for his wife, and not just his wealth, because while a wronged man's rank and circumstances were visible to everyone 'the degree of his affection for his wife – his sensibility to such an usurpation of his rights' could not be seen.[177]

A further punishment available to the court was to issue an order compelling the unmarried man to marry the married woman. There were several preconditions to be met first. The woman's husband must have divorced her, the woman must be 'otherwise of good fame for chastity', and lastly, there must be no disproportion in rank between the new husband and wife.

By 'a disproportion of rank', Bentham meant distinctions not only of wealth but also of status. In England, rank and status had long determined legal and social relations, but, while still significant socially, they were probably of little legal relevance by the eighteenth century, except for the legal disabilities imposed on married women, children, criminals and the insane.[178]

When Bentham wrote that the woman must be of 'good fame of chastity', he used the language of the church courts which like other local courts, took account of public knowledge of a person's character and reputation when making an order. If the married woman was in fact a prostitute, or, in Bentham's words, if she prostituted herself 'for lucre', then the unmarried man would only be 'privately admonished'. In this situation, costs were to be divided between the unmarried man and the husband. If the unmarried man had probable reason for believing her to be a prostitute, or probable reason for believing her to be unmarried, then his compensation order should be adjusted accordingly.[179] If before he solicited the woman she solicited him, then he need pay neither fine nor compensation.[180] Envisaging a situation where a prostitute's husband acted as her 'protector', Bentham argued that if the husband consented to his wife's behaviour, then the adulterer should pay nothing.[181]

Other extenuating circumstances for an unmarried man were the same as those for the married man, but included, without explanation, his 'deference to authority'.[182] Bentham added a brief marginal note with no further comment: 'Forced Marriage'. It may be that his words merely sum up the nature of the punishment he proposed, but it is also possible that he questioned the efficacy of his plan because in canon law the use of duress to compel a marriage meant it subsequently be annulled.[183] He may also have been referring to the practices of parish officers who pressured men into marrying women whom they had made pregnant in order to avoid paying relief to the woman out of parish rates.[184] Alternatively, Bentham may have referred to another by then long-past church court practice which at one time had policed fornication by ordering couples to 'abjure' continuing relations 'under the penalty of marrying'. The next time they had intercourse they would be ipso facto married.[185] But it is most likely that rather than ancient laws on marriages that disparaged rank, or defunct church court practices, Bentham had in mind eighteenth-century social distinctions and notions of honour and reputation.

Lastly, Bentham considered the case of a married woman who committed adultery with an unmarried man. If on a first offence this was proved, her husband could 'put her away', that is, divorce her, and marry again in the same way that an innocent wife could put away her adulterous husband. But here, in her defence, a wife could rely on the extenuating circumstance that her husband had deserted her.[186]

7

Divorce and Separation

AN ANECDOTE

The curious structure of a village church in Hertfordshire bears unexpected tangible witness to the indissolubility of marriage in the eighteenth century. An anecdote on this church reveals much about why Bentham thought his plans for reform of the laws of divorce were needed. Tradition has it that in 1778–9 the recently knighted Sir Lionel Lyde, an eminent tobacco merchant and a governor of the Bank of England, began to pull down the gothic village church of Ayot St Lawrence in Hertfordshire. He planned to build a radically designed new church within view of his house, and to incorporate the ruins of the old one into his garden. Demolition had proceeded to the point of ruination when urgent appeals by parishioners to the Bishop of Lincoln put a halt to further destruction; but to this day the old church lies in ruins. Referring to the sensibilities of the age, Pevsner found it probable that those picturesque ruins provided 'a sight which would no doubt have pleased Sir Lionel and his friends'.[1] With certainty, the new church, designed by Nicolas Revett, was in accord with, even pioneered, the most advanced sensibilities.

Pevsner mentions that some of its most striking features made it 'an eye-catcher from [Lyde's] house'. These include 'its "gloriette"-like far-spreading front', although 'the church itself [was] no larger than, and rather similar to, an early C19 cemetery chapel' with a Grecian front. And then Pevsner mentions the feature of this ground-breaking church that has distinct relevance here: 'In the outer aedicules stand the urns to Sir Lionel Lyde and his wife'. That is to say, at the far end of long colonnades on either side of the church lie the tombs of the squire and his wife, one on each side, placed as far apart as is possible with the body of the church dividing them.[2] According to the parish guide, the wicked (or headstrong) Sir Lionel, who had so impetuously pulled down an older church without permission, vowed that since the Church had united him to his wife in life 'it should make amends by separating them in death'.[3]

EIGHTEENTH-CENTURY DIVORCE

Bentham's support for divorce is well known, but until now what he actually proposed has remained hidden among his manuscripts. Arguably, many of Bentham's contemporaries knew about his work, but because it remained largely unpublished its detail was lost. Therefore, nothing is known about what kind of divorce laws Bentham proposed: were they radical plans for a liberal law of divorce, or did he plan a more restricted extension of the existing laws? The answer lies in Bentham's manuscript proposals for a reformed, codified law of divorce based on the principle of utility, to be examined here for the first time.

Bentham would have sympathized with Sir Lionel's sentiments on the indissolubility of marriage, if not with Sir Lionel himself. He would also likely have sympathized with the plight of Sir Lionel's wife. Whatever the circumstances of Sir Lionel's own marriage, England in his day was 'neither a separating nor a divorcing society', and for most people marriage ended only with death.[4] If a marriage did break down then divorce was not (usually) an option, for despite the religious upheavals of the sixteenth century, eighteenth-century England remained unique among the Protestant countries of Europe in continuing to uphold the Catholic doctrine of the indissolubility of marriage. Divorce, together with remarriage, was soon accepted in most Protestant countries, although there was no common agreement about what actually constituted the correct grounds for divorce. Catholic humanists, for instance, Erasmus, Thomas More and Michel de Montaigne, also argued in favour of divorce.[5] But in England, implementing any major reform of the divorce laws was to prove impossible until the nineteenth century,[6] and divorce in the modern sense did not become available until the Matrimonial Causes Act of 1857, 26 years after Bentham had died.[7] In his time terminating a marriage so that the spouses could remarry was only rarely achieved.

Petitioners in the eighteenth century could seek a divorce by Act of Parliament or in the church courts. The church court decree of divorce *a mensa et thoro*, or from bed and board, ended the canon law duty to cohabit but because the marriage was not ended remarriage was not possible.[8] Alternatively, a church court divorce *a vincula matrimonii* annulled a 'marriage', but only if certain pre-existing legal impediments to the marriage were satisfactorily proved. As the marriage was void, remarriage was possible.[9] Protestant propagandists and some scholars have suggested that it was always possible for unhappily married couples to unearth some convenient canon law impediment to nullify their marriage, but investigation of the numbers of nullity suits leads other authorities to doubt this 'hoary' tradition in English historiography.[10] After 1753, such suits increased in number because Lord Hardwicke's Marriage Act made parental consent necessary for a valid marriage for those under 21 years of age. In 1770, three-quarters of the nullity cases heard in the church courts were based on underage marriage.[11]

Bentham rejected a divorce law that did not allow remarriage, and he made little reference to church court suits. He did, however, pay considerable attention to divorce by private Act of Parliament, which had been possible since Lord Roos's divorce in 1670. In practice this was limited to divorce on the grounds of a wife's adultery.[12]

Obtaining a parliamentary divorce was a lengthy process, which could take several years. First, the husband invariably brought an action for criminal conversation seeking an order for damages from his wife's lover, usually in King's Bench at Westminster Hall.[13] A wife was not a party to the criminal conversation action against her alleged lover, and therefore could not defend herself; this fact was criticized by some commentators.[14] In defence, it was said that this procedure was necessary to prevent collusion between husband and wife.[15]

Next, the husband was required to petition for divorce *a mensa et thoro* in the consistory courts, in practice often Doctor's Commons, for adultery. Only after he had succeeded in King's Bench and Doctor's Commons could the husband petition for a bill for divorce to be presented to the House of Lords. Here the written transcripts of the church court trial would be carefully read and oral evidence heard. The bill was then referred to the House of Commons select committee on divorce bills. After acceptance, the bill was returned to the House of Lords and eventually became law. If he was successful the petitioner was awarded costs and damages.[16] Aside from the expense, a further deterrent to matrimonial suits in any of these courts was the humiliating publicity given to trials for divorce in case reports, newspapers and pamphlets.[17]

Between 1670 and 1857 there were only 325 such divorces in England,[18] and it was not until 1801 that the first petition for divorce brought to Parliament by a woman succeeded. This was brought on the grounds of adultery aggravated by incest.[19] Between 1670 and 1857 only 4 women obtained parliamentary divorces.[20] Just why women were not successful is unclear. Scholars have suggested that either the wife had no right of action at common law, or else a right she could not enforce, because the operation of the doctrine of coverture subsumed a wife's legal personality into that of her husband. This meant that she would be required to join her husband as a party in any legal action she brought. Therefore, if he was the wrongdoer, she was effectively prevented from bringing an action against him.[21] But I can find no such arguments in the literature of the time. Instead, most writers on divorce restrict their comments to a husband's existing right to divorce his adulterous wife. Frequent claims can be found in eighteenth-century contemporary literature that a man's rights to a parliamentary divorce was necessary in order to protect great estates from damage inflicted by adulterous wives and their illegitimate children: in other words to safeguard elite male patrilineal descent.[22]

Earlier historians of divorce believed that parliamentary divorce had been the preserve of the aristocracy, and that 'middle-class' divorce was only available after the 1857 Divorce Act.[23] But Bentham's manuscripts reveal a different picture. He observes that petitions for divorce were increasingly being brought to Parliament by the 'rich', which would have included men of the gentry and middle ranks, as well as the aristocracy.[24] His accuracy has been confirmed by more recent studies,[25] but he wanted to extend rights of divorce even further; he called for new laws to deal with the needs of poorer people and of women.[26]

It was quite probably the increase in numbers of petitions brought between 1780 to 1800, despite the great hostility of individual Lord Chancellors, that fired Bentham's immediate interest in parliamentary divorce in the first place. The rights and wrongs of divorce gave rise to 'bitter divisions of opinion' among people of all sorts whether moralists, churchmen or parliamentarians.[27] Bentham criticized what he saw as the inadequate legal procedures and rules of evidence. He criticized too the popular prejudices that prevented women from petitioning Parliament.[28] But despite its limitations, Bentham recognized that divorce by private Act of Parliament remained the only alternative to divorce in the church courts until 1857. Although the procedure was lengthy and relatively expensive, it did allow for remarriage.

THE GREATEST HAPPINESS PRINCIPLE AND DIVORCE

Bentham based his law of marriage on the principle of utility which recognizes that all human actions are motivated by a wish to avoid pain and to gain pleasure,[29] and, as we have seen, he regarded sexual love as an important source of pleasure, possibly the greatest. Therefore, he instructed his ideal legislator to do all in his power to ensure that the quantity of this pleasure in society was as high as possible by regulating marriage contracts.[30]

Even though Bentham regarded the marriage contract as 'beyond comparison' the most important contract of any in law,[31] he did not think that all marriages should be enforced. Given a choice, most people would probably want their marriage to last for life,[32] but for some this might not be possible, or even desirable. The present laws left these unfortunate victims of circumstance facing a life either of deprivation of sexual relations, or of seeking 'improper satisfactions', by which he meant sexual relations outside marriage. He wrote that 'the former [i.e. the deprivation of sexual relations] is a wrong for which everyone repents, and of which no one speaks: the latter [i.e. sexual relations outside marriage] is a wrong for which, in most cases, no one repents, and which outrages everyone'.[33] Therefore, terminating an unhappy marriage by divorce sometimes accords with the dictates of the principle of utility. Divorce, especially if accompanied by remarriage to someone else, would increase happiness.

Likening a marriage contract to any other contract, Bentham asked why marriage should be treated any differently. After all, most people take great pains to avoid entering into a contract, or commitment, from which they cannot escape because 'no-one likes a prison, especially when the sentence is for life'.[34] Laws that prevented the termination of any other kind of contract would be regarded as either tyranny or folly.[35] 'See how logical English law is', Bentham remarked ironically, for in contracts made for the provision of services 'there is no tie that cannot be undone' but in the case of marriage 'there is no tie that can be undone'.[36] We would condemn the idea of enforceable lifelong contracts entered into with 'an associate, a steward, a nursemaid, a tutor, a companion' and yet in most civilized countries the only marriages we can have are lifelong.[37]

Bentham paid particular attention to the plight of an unhappily married woman bound by an indissoluble marriage contract. Such a life was wretched, even more degraded than that of a slave. 'To live under the perpetual authority of a man that one detests is in itself a form of slavery: being compelled to accept his embraces is a misfortune too great to have been tolerated even under slavery itself.'[38] Bentham rejected as illogical the argument that because men too were bound by indissoluble marriage contracts, and so 'shared the yoke', no change in the divorce laws was needed. This supposed reciprocity did not lessen the burden of lifelong unhappy marriages at all. On the contrary, 'reciprocity only doubles it'.[39]

Like Enlightenment thinkers before him, Bentham surveyed the laws of divorce of other countries. In Scotland, he reported approvingly, to obtain a divorce all that was required is the adultery of the husband. 'Here is a condition it cannot be particularly onerous to fulfil', he remarked.[40] But he complained that the dissolution of the marriage allowed only the innocent party the right to remarry. He mentioned too the laws of Prussia and Geneva. Under the Code Frederic in Prussia, voluntary separation could be followed by an order allowing remarriage, but only 'if one whiles a way a year in solitude', a period of time that could be put to better use. In Protestant Geneva he found even greater freedom to petition for divorce. There 'incompatibility of character is a sufficient reason for divorce', but despite this, divorce is said to be very rare.[41] Bentham, who probably obtained this information from Etienne Dumont, hailed this, if true, as yet another striking proof that laws requiring lifelong marriage were unnecessary, and anyway would be most inconvenient to enforce.[42]

He considered that there was a danger of depopulation in maintaining indissoluble unhappy marriages. Most politicians would agree with him, he wrote, that unhappy marriages were unprolific, and that inhibited population growth.[43] Here Bentham was in accord with those Enlightenment thinkers who linked fears about depopulation to the lack of laws allowing divorce. Montesquieu, for example, declared that non-Christian countries where divorce was allowed achieved the desired higher birth rates.[44]

During the revolutionary period in France, the law of marriage had been secularized, and the canon law doctrine of the indissolubility was rejected. Earlier in the century the *philosophes* had advocated divorce and many pamphlets and plans for legislation on divorce were published in the years before and after 1789. In 1791 marriage was declared to be a civil contract, and in September 1792 the Legislative Committee passed the first divorce law allowing divorce either by mutual agreement, or unilaterally for incompatibility. Fault-based grounds for divorce included cruelty, adultery and desertion.[45] Dumont reported Bentham's remark that in Paris alone, in two years between five and six hundred divorces had taken place, a very large number.[46]

It becomes apparent that Bentham's codified divorce laws presupposed a secular, contractual theory of marriage, and one that to some extent accorded with reformed Protestant traditions. As we have seen, the leading reformers of the sixteenth-century Protestant Reformation – Martin Luther, John Calvin, Huldreich Zwingli, Martin Bucer, Thomas Cranmer and John Knox – all agreed that marriage was a secular contract, and that divorce should be made available.[47]

Reformed Protestant ideas on marriage and divorce can be found in the writings of jurists and moralists throughout the eighteenth century, including the moralist William Paley.[48] Paley confessed that he was quite unable to find anything in a marriage contract that distinguished it from other contracts, or that prevented it from being dissolved by the consent of the parties, although he went on to retreat from his initial liberal position on divorce.

There is little doubt, however, that Bentham's divorce proposals would have caused much offence to some. Whatever had happened elsewhere in Protestant Europe, England still upheld Catholic traditions on marriage, especially on the indissolubility of marriage. Until the introduction of civil marriages by the Marriages Act of 1836 all English marriages, except those of Quakers and Jews, were solemnized in an Anglican church, in front of witnesses, according to the Prayer Book marriage service.[49] Marrying couples made promises to each other that were intended to last 'til death us do part'. Attacks on the established church's doctrines were widely feared, and many predicted that a breakdown in marriage would lead to a breakdown of political and social life.[50] Proponents and opponents of divorce respectively cited the Old Testament Books of Genesis and Deuteronomy, the New Testament, and natural law and reason, as authority for their opinions. Thus contending voices of the eighteenth century argued for and against the doctrine of the indissolubility of marriage.[51]

DIVORCE ON THE GROUNDS OF INCOMPATIBILITY

The most famous proponent of liberal divorce laws was the poet John Milton (1608–74), whose first wife had deserted him soon after their marriage. In four divorce tracts Milton claimed that a misinterpretation of certain New Testament readings had changed the blessing of matrimony into 'disconsolate household captivity'.[52] An unhappily married man and woman cannot be one flesh, he argued. Quoting Virgil on the tyrant Mezentius' cruel punishments, he compared the unhappy spouses to 'two carcasses unnaturally chained together', or even more horribly, 'a living soul bound to a dead corpse'.[53]

Milton also cited some sixteenth-century Protestants who campaigned for divorce, reasoning that an incapacity for 'the ends of marriage' would make that marriage void. Their arguments refer to the Book of Genesis (Eve was designed by God to be Adam's helpmeet),[54] and also to the purposes (or ends) of marriage set out in the marriage service in Thomas Cranmer's 1549 *Book of Common Prayer*. Here the three purposes were listed as procreation, the avoidance of fornication and sin, and lastly (innovatively) 'for mutuall society, helpe and coumforte'.[55] It is this last purpose that led to the Prayer Book's version of marriage being known as a 'companionate marriage'.[56] The reformers argued that if this purpose failed then divorce was permissible. Therefore, for Milton, marriage between two incompatible people was no marriage, especially if there were no children and both consented to the divorce.[57]

How well known were Milton's divorce tracts in the eighteenth century? Lawrence Stone claims that Milton's radical ideas on divorce were in fact more or less unknown for two centuries,[58] but similarities of language and ideas make it likely that Bentham was aware of Milton's ideas on divorce.[59] For Bentham is likely to have read Thomas Salmon's 1724 *Critical Essay Concerning Marriage*, which referred to Milton's arguments and set out the Protestant companionate marriage thesis.[60]

At first sight it seems that Bentham did not agree with Milton's radical ideas. Although he rather bleakly likened an unhappy marriage to imprisonment for life, and wrote approvingly of the great freedom to divorce in Geneva, where 'incompatibility of character is a sufficient reason for divorce', these were only discursive remarks and not substantive proposals.[61] But a closer look at Bentham's proposed marriage contract reveals that it did, in effect, support a liberal, non-fault-based regime for divorce. For, as we saw in Chapter 3, Bentham's marriage contract allowed the contracting parties themselves to decide on the duration of their marriage. Therefore, marriage contracts could stipulate that a marriage was to last for an indefinite term rather than for life, or, in Bentham's words, to last 'for the time that the two parties find appropriate'.[62] A legislator need only let people decide for themselves, or, as Bentham put it, 'instead of giving them the law, the legislator takes/derives it from them'.[63] Divorce would then be consensual: the woman would say to the man, 'without my consent you will no longer be free to leave me', and the man would reply, 'since it is like that, you will no longer be free to leave me either'.[64] In contrast, the marriage service in the *Book of Common Prayer* implies that marriage lasts for the lifetime of husband and wife. Only death ends a marriage.

Dismissing notions of romantic love as a foolish delusion, Bentham argued that even if it were true that love between a husband and wife could last a lifetime, this was an insufficient reason to make marriage indissoluble. Quite to the contrary, if love lasted a lifetime, then there would be absolutely no need to compel lifelong marriages.[65]

But if Bentham's marriage contract provided for divorce for incompatibility by mutual consent, it did not provide for unilateral divorce. Other more radical opinions, like those of Milton, did propose unilateral divorce. In Bentham's time, William Godwin achieved notoriety by asserting that men and women should remain together only for as long as they both loved each other. Relationships should be unilaterally terminated once love was gone. This idea greatly impressed his future son-in-law Percy Byshe Shelley, who left his wife Harriet for Godwin's daughter Mary. Moreover, despite the suggestions of recent scholarship, both Godwin and Shelley knew Milton's divorce tracts.[66] Unlike Bentham, and much more harshly, Godwin did not mention the care of the children of the family following a divorce.

Bentham accepted that divorce brought disadvantages, particularly to women and children. The problem was that men and women had different needs to be met during their marriage. A man's motive for marriage was 'to satisfy a passing desire: there are only advantages for him with no disadvantages whatsoever'.[67] A woman may have a similar motivation but, unlike a man, she suffered disadvantages in marriage and must 'pay dearly' for her happiness.

These 'disadvantages' were the discomforts of pregnancy and birth that a women must undergo. A woman knows that she assumes particular burdens in marriage and naturally demands compensation. She may want help during pregnancy, help with 'everyday chores' and help with child-rearing.[68] Because of these 'disadvantages', it is natural for a woman to stipulate lifelong marriage in her marriage contract, and even more natural for her father, or whatever authority she is subject to, to stipulate it on her behalf, in order to protect her interests and compensate her for her disadvantages.[69]

A wife had yet another vested interest of her own in wanting her marriage to be of indefinite duration. 'Time, pregnancy, nursing, cohabitation itself' all conspire to diminish what Bentham described as 'the value' of her looks, and so make it more difficult for her to contract a new relationship. In contrast, Bentham declared confidently, a man is little affected, or hardly at all, by the passage of time.[70]

He concluded that in order to complete the task of bringing up their children successfully, a husband and wife inevitably find themselves committed to each other for a number of years.[71] Does it therefore follow that by agreeing to a certain term for the duration of a marriage the husband and wife are bound together and cannot separate earlier if they want to? Bentham concluded that it is impossible to plan in advance for a woman to be indifferent to the early termination of her marriage. Nor is it possible for a man to postpone the rage and impatience he may feel from a tyrannical desire to do just that.[72] But, perhaps optimistically, Bentham suggested that if all the circumstances were made right for her, then the wife may be led to give her consent freely to the divorce her husband so much wants.[73] The manuscript is hard to read, but Bentham appears to suggest some form of communal living as a happy solution to some of the difficulties standing in the way of achieving a divorce by mutual consent.[74]

DIVORCE FOR ADULTERY

Bentham's proposals on divorce for adultery are novel for three reasons: his law on adultery took the form of a code; the right to petition for a divorce for adultery was available to both men and women equally; and after a divorce men and women could remarry.

Extending the right to divorce to women was a radical departure from established practice, where petitioners for divorce on the grounds of adultery were more or less exclusively male, in both church courts and Parliament.[75] So Bentham's proposals would have been controversial. As noted above, public opinion tolerated only a limited *male* right to parliamentary divorce.[76] Justifications for allowing exclusively male rights to divorce had a long history. Writers often cited Old Testament authority to the effect that a wife's adultery was such a serious and unforgivable event that it dissolved the marriage.[77] In Bentham's time, most of his contemporaries upheld a double standard: infidelity in a wife was serious, but quite forgivable in a man.[78] In pre-revolutionary France, an adulterous wife suffered severe condemnation and punishment. Her husband, whose own adultery was not punishable, could place her in a convent and retain her property and dowry. If the woman's husband did not take her back within two years, her head was shaved, and she must put on religious dress and live out the remainder of her days in the convent.[79] Voltaire, who thought this treatment barbarous, ridiculed it by imagining the reverse; a wife forcibly imprisoning her adulterous, shaven-headed husband.[80]

In late eighteenth-century England, criticism of adulterous wives led to the introduction, in Parliament, of number of bills to prevent the remarriage of a wife divorced for her adultery.[81] In support, Paley argued that allowing divorced women to marry their lovers rewarded them for their bad behaviour.[82] The author of one popular pamphlet condemned the lack of chastity and modesty in women, and went on to complain that adulterous wives would '*emasculate* the Age, consume the *Strength*, and melt down the *Courage* of the Nation'. The consequences of a wife's immorality included the risk of infection passed to her children, and sterility too, which thus destroyed one of the ends of marriage (i.e. procreation).[83] James Boswell recollected Dr Johnson's opinion that there was a great difference between adultery by a husband and adultery by a wife, and that 'confusion of progeny constituted the essence of the crime'.[84] Lord Brougham, Bentham's sometime friend, similarly declared in 1832 that a wife's adultery gave her husband 'a kind of right' to dissolve the marriage, but that a wife acquired no such right if her husband was unfaithful to her.[85]

Bentham probably subscribed to Dr Johnson's 'confusion of progeny' argument and, as we have seen, wrote at length on why adultery should be regarded as a wrong at all in a utilitarian code of law. But he made no mention of any undefined legal right that allowed men to divorce their adulterous wives. Instead, his adultery code gave either the husband or the wife of an adulterous spouse the right to divorce and marry again.[86] Yet he did make a distinction between wronged husbands and wronged wives: a wronged husband could divorce his adulterous wife after a first offence of adultery, but a wronged wife had to wait for a third or subsequent offence before divorcing her adulterous husband. Evidently he too saw a wife's adultery as a greater offence than that of her husband, even though his code extended the right to divorce to wives.

Bentham's code listed several circumstances that would provide an adulterous husband with an extenuation. If any of these were proven then his wife's petition for divorce would be refused and the husband would only be 'privately admonished'. They included his wife's refusal or unwillingness 'to receive his embraces' because she was absent or infirm of body. Others were, puzzlingly, a lack of intention, ignorance of the law, innocence of intention, intoxication, provocation and compulsion.[87] Bentham did not explain further but in a note squashed in at the bottom of the page speculated that most of these excuses were 'in a high degree improbable but all are possible'. In a finished body of law, he added, some explanation would be needed for each, but they did not appear to be sufficiently important to warrant it here.[88]

An extenuating circumstance for an adulterous wife was that her husband had deserted her, with or without notice. If she was able to prove desertion without notice, and subsequently did not hear from him for six months, then her husband's petition for divorce on the grounds of her adultery would fail. Or, if he deserted her with notice, and subsequently she did not hear from him for three years, then again her husband's petition would fail. Bentham made careful note that special provisions should be made for seafaring people on long voyages, in particular to the East Indies.[89]

An eighteenth-century divorced woman faced particular hardships, and so Bentham accepted that an adulterous wife may choose to defend her husband's petition for divorce on the grounds of her adultery, even if he had treated her with neglect or cruelty. Taking account of this reality, his third and fourth extenuating circumstances reflect the social hierarchies and problems of his day. A wife could defend her husband's divorce petition if, within the year before he presented it, he had lived in open adultery with a woman in the same house as him. Other defences were that he had been detected in adultery, or 'in solicitation', or in the practice of 'amorous familiarities' with a servant or other woman. If her husband had the authority to send such a woman away, but refused to do so within a week when so requested by his wife, then the husband's divorce petition would fail.[90]

Such improper intimacies were not unknown and could lead to serious abuse. For instance, in 1780 Mr John Foster seduced his wife's maid and then demanded that his wife depart their home, leaving their children with him. His wife was the daughter of the Earl of Bristol and so the affair was much discussed.[91] Similar circumstances lay behind the Countess of Strathmore's case in 1785.[92]

The fifth and last extenuating circumstance for an adulterous wife was that she was already separated from her husband in bed and board by judicial order. If any of these extenuating circumstances were accepted by the court, then the adulterous wife was only to be privately admonished. Other excuses for women were, again, want of intention, ignorance of the law, innocence of intention, intoxication, compulsion and deference to authority.[93]

Bentham intended his adultery code to apply to all men and women, and so he set out careful, detailed 'Instructions to the Legislator' on the post-divorce division of the family assets. Any decision on property was to be based partly on the circumstances of the parties and partly on the nature of their property. Realistically, Bentham knew that the 'great bulk of the people' had no property at all that could be subject to a settlement, and if this was the case then each should retain their own clothing and 'instruments of trade', but the household furniture should remain with the woman unless the 'Judge thought proper to make an express allowance of it to the man'.[94]

Where the husband had brought capital into the 'Commonstock' and the wife little or nothing, then Bentham expected that some allowance should be made for her.[95] Similarly, if the wife brought capital into the marriage and the husband did not, then some allowance should be made for him. But 'upon the whole', he insisted, the wife should be able to exercise her rights to an allowance on more favourable terms than the husband. For this purpose, the age of the parties and the length of their cohabitation was to be taken into account, because 'the power of pleasing the opposite sex, and therefore the chance of obtaining a new alliance is more diminished in the female than in the male'.[96]

Bentham stipulated that when family assets were divided after a divorce, an important factor to be taken into account was the sex, number and ages of any children so that provision could be made for their support. In the margin Bentham stressed, 'wife to be favoured'.[97]

Eighteenth-century condemnation of adulterous wives led to plans to impose financial penalties on them if they were independently wealthy. For example, Paley suggested that 'a penal check' be imposed on an adulterous wife, which could be achieved by directing that after her divorce her estate be distributed as it would have been on her death. She would be awarded an amount for her subsistence alone.[98] Similarly, Bentham's adultery code provided that if a wealthy wife had children by her husband, or any former husband, then she could be made to forfeit half her fortune: one-quarter to go to her husband, and the other to be divided among her children in equal shares. If she had no children then her husband was to have the other quarter as well, unless the judge orders otherwise.[99] Bentham's suggestion was less draconian than Paley's, but the result would have been that half the fortune of a divorced adulterous wife would remain with her family and out of the reach of her lover.

DIVORCE FOR DESERTION

Bentham asked whether a wife should have the right to divorce her husband for desertion. In particular, could a wife divorce a husband who treated her with aversion and/or contempt, and had left her to live with another woman? At first, Bentham merely identified this as a right in Roman law, but then as part of his penal code he drafted laws for divorce on the grounds of desertion.[100]

Bentham saw desertion as a breach of the marriage contract made all the more distressing because the deserted spouse, usually the wife, must remain 'deprived of the comforts of matrimony' not only during the lifetime of the deserter but possibly even after his death (because he might simply disappear).[101] So he gave the deserted spouse the power to take over the deserter's property for the duration of the marriage.[102] Then after a certain period of time, and after proper notice, the deserted spouse had the right to divorce and was free to choose to marry again. Failure to correspond with the deserted spouse for a certain length of time would be presumptive evidence of either death or desertion. Bentham took account of the problems of communication faced by people who lived overseas in the dominions – who after 1770, provided a considerable proportion of criminal conversation and divorce cases – and required such cases to be managed 'according to the Book of Procedure', but he did not explain what this was.[103]

Bentham knew that among the poor, desertion remained the most common way of separating from an unwanted spouse. He reported that 'among the lower classes of people this mischief happens more frequently than people of the higher classes are aware of',[104] an assertion that has been proved correct by recent statistical studies of applications for poor relief made in town and country parishes by abandoned wives and children. These indicate that between 1700 and 1830 in the countryside, between 4 and 6 per cent of all applications for poor relief were made by deserted wives, while in a London parish an estimated 12 per cent of applications were made by deserted wives in the first half of the eighteenth century.[105]

Because of such problems local parish officials administering settlement, vagrancy and poor laws provided support for wives whose husbands had deserted them, or who refused to supply them with maintenance. Where possible, the poor law officers would seize a deserting husband's property in order to reimburse the parish funds. If a deserting husband could be found, and refused to return to his wife, he could be punished by being publicly whipped and placed in a house of correction.[106] Bentham provided another solution: immediate financial disaster for a deserted wife and children was to be averted by allowing the wife to take control of her husband's property in order to fund provision for the necessaries of life. Thus, by dispensing with the disabilities of coverture, a deserted wife and children were saved worse suffering and the parish was spared more expense.[107] Bentham's suggestion indicates the extent of his concern with the social and administrative reform of the law of marriage, as well as with legal reform.

DIVORCE AND THE WELFARE OF CHILDREN

In the seventeenth century, John Locke had drawn an analogy between the human and natural worlds in order to argue that couples should stay together as long as their children needed their care. Locke admitted that this period of time lasted longer in humans than in other animal species, but argued that it should still be possible to terminate the marriage by consent, or on certain conditions, once the children no longer needed their parents.[108]

Bentham too admitted that there were difficulties about ensuring the continuing welfare of children once their parents had divorced. Like Locke, he thought there was a solution. For instance, a marriage contract could be drafted to allow a marriage to end when the last child that the mother might hope to bear had reached an age when it could look after itself.[109]

Thus Bentham was more optimistic than David Hume in 1741, and William Paley in 1785, both of whom argued that the welfare of the children must take precedence over their parents' interests. Indeed, Hume used this argument as the primary reason for rejecting divorce entirely, writing that divorce would give parents the power 'Upon every Caprice to render their Posterity miserable'.[110]

Paley, addressing contract theorists directly, agreed that 'if we argue, with some moralists, that the obligation of a contract naturally continues, so long as the purpose, which the contacting parties had in view, requires its continuance', then it is difficult to say that any man and woman should be compelled to stay together. However, the welfare of children provided the exception to this rule, and couples should stay married for the sake of their children.[111] It would be tempting to identify the moralist whom Paley addressed here as Bentham himself, and indeed it could have been, but most probably Paley, like Bentham, was referring to Locke.

By the mid-nineteenth century John Stuart Mill and Harriet Taylor Mill were also concerned to ensure that the liberal divorce laws they were proposing were compatible with the welfare of children. Mill thought the problem of providing for the welfare of children on divorce so difficult to resolve satisfactorily that he urged delay in having children at all, and proposed communal living as a solution. Harriet Taylor Mill, in contrast, thought women should assume the responsibility for their children on divorce.[112]

Bentham thought that the children should live with the parent whose care was most necessary to them, which was likely to be the father for sons and the mother for daughters.[113] This contrasted with the existing law, which gave a father a right in common law to custody of all the children of a family, and the right to prevent the mother from having access to her children.[114]

In the 1780s, marriages were far more likely to be ended by death than divorce, and Bentham suggested that children could be just as damaged by the death of a parent as by divorce. Within a family, he wrote, the parents' affection for each other is the 'strong cement to the ties which bind each of them to their children'. That 'cement' might cease to bind if one of the parents died. But on the other hand, Bentham realized, in the case of a divorce the parents might have already become estranged beforehand, and this situation was bound to bring unhappiness to their children.[115]

In his opinion if a widow and widower with children were to remarry and then go on to have more children themselves, the children of the second family would commonly receive far more attention than those of either 'former broods'.[116] In fact, such a likely outcome was well understood by those 'fond parents' who decided to forgo a second marriage in order to protect their children's interests. Perhaps events in Bentham's own life led to his reflections on the dangers for children of second marriages. His mother, Alice Bentham, died in 1759, and in 1766 his father married a widow, Mrs Sarah Abbot. Bentham's younger brother Samuel was 9 years old at the time of his father's second marriage, while Bentham was 18 and an undergraduate at Oxford. Bentham's experience of his father's remarriage was not happy and his relations with his stepmother were never completely amicable. Although he himself made no complaint about his father, the letters passing between them invite our judgement on his father's careless behaviour. Thus, we learn that on returning home from Oxford, Bentham was unexpectedly turned away from the empty family house at Queen's Square Place by the servants, at which time he was probably first given the news of his father's marriage to Mrs Abbot. Bentham was then informed by letter that his books and possessions had been taken to chambers rented for him at the Inner Temple, where he was now to live. Samuel, however, with whom Bentham had a lifelong close emotional attachment, was to continue to live at Queen's Square Place.[117] In this manner Bentham's family life was suddenly and conclusively brought to a close.

BENTHAM AND PALEY ON THE OBJECTIONS TO DIVORCE

In about 1789, Bentham wrote in manuscripts at some length on the several 'specious' objections to divorce that were often heard.[118] These objections correspond so closely to those published by William Paley in 1785 that we might conjecture that Bentham planned to publish a public response to Paley's comments on divorce.[119] Paley claimed that the divergence between the interests of men and women made it difficult to legislate for new divorce laws, because 'the power of divorce is evidently and greatly to the disadvantage of the woman', and as a result it would be far better for a wife not to have to rely on the continuing affection of her husband for the security she needed in her marriage.[120]

Evidently disapproving of Milton's ideas, Paley thought the difficulties for women would not be improved by allowing mutually agreed divorce. He saw little prospect of happiness for one spouse who opposed the other's desire for liberty if consensual divorce was the rule.[121] Rather dourly, Paley concluded that rights to divorce should not be extended, and that 'it ought to satisfy [men and women] to reflect, that when their happiness is sacrificed to the operation of an unrelenting rule, it is sacrificed to the happiness of the community.'[122]

In his manuscripts, Bentham considered a first objection to divorce. This is that if divorce is permitted, then neither husband nor wife will ever see their marriage as permanent. The husband will look around to find a woman better suited to him, and the wife will do exactly the same thing in order to find a better husband. This will bring about a perpetual and mutual insecurity with regard to 'a most precious property'.[123] Paley raised just such an objection to allowing men to divorce their wives at will (but did not envisage the possibility of women divorcing men at will). He argued that if men could so easily be released from a marriage they would be continually seeking new objects of desire. Just because a man once preferred his wife to all other women, it did not follow that he would always do so. Only if a woman could be fully restored to her pre-marriage state might it be possible to entrust the power of divorce to men with less danger of abuse and inconvenience.[124] Paley believed that because all men were by nature fickle, 'new objects of desire would be continually sought after, if men could, at will, be released from their subsisting engagements'. Therefore, indissoluble marriage was necessary in order to impart stability to marriage, and particularly to protect the interests of women.[125]

Hume had similar reservations about divorce and suggested that 'nothing is more dangerous than to unite two Persons so close in all their Interests and Concerns, as Man and Wife, without rendering the Union intire and total'. An insecure husband's selfishness 'being accompanied with more power', is even more dangerous to the stability of the marriage.[126]

Bentham had two responses to all of this. The first was that such fickle behaviour (which he attributed to both men and women) was already seen all too frequently in indissoluble marriages – only, instead of a better husband, say 'lover', and instead of a better wife, say 'lover or mistress'. In fact, he ventured, perhaps the very obstacles that society put in the way of infidelity (which he reported as being easy to evade anyway) only served to provoke desires that would not exist at all 'in a regime of liberty'. Therefore, to the argument that divorce will lead to more separations, Bentham's reply was 'more apparent separations, but fewer real separations'.[127] Here Bentham agreed with Montesquieu, who considered that divorce would make 'men and women more likely to stay in marriage'.[128] It is clear that Bentham did not foresee the huge increase in divorce that followed the liberalization of divorce laws in the twentieth century, although this in itself does not disprove his point that divorce leads to fewer real separations.

His second response to the first of the commonly held 'specious objections' to divorce was that the positive advantage of dissoluble marriage was that each partner, fearing to lose the affection of his or her spouse, would use every means to please the other. If love-making is at present only used as a means to 'gain' the other, he continued, it would then be used to 'keep' the other.[129] Here Bentham's remarks echo those of Montaigne, who had suggested that what had made marriages 'so long honoured and secure in Rome' was the liberty to divorce. 'They loved their wives the better as long as there was the chance of losing them'.[130] In contrast, Paley was less sanguine and believed that 'no lessons of duty, no delicacy of sentiment, will go half as far with the generality of mankind and womankind, as this one intelligible reflection, that they must each make the best of their bargain.'[131]

Despite Bentham's firm riposte to the first objection to divorce, he placed limits on an adulterous woman's right to divorce. His reasons for doing so indicate that to some extent he, like Paley, feared that unrestricted divorce laws would lead to unstable marriages. Thus Bentham's laws would prevent an adulterous wife from divorcing her husband on the basis of her own adulterous behaviour. He believed that an unfaithful wife should not be able to divorce her wronged husband, expanding a terse marginal note, 'Divorce – why not to be allowed the woman', to explain that otherwise an adulterous woman might neglect her husband's interests and be continually looking for a new husband.[132]

He next addressed a second commonly held and specious objection to divorce: if marriages were dissoluble, then each partner would see the relationship as transient and treat the family finances with indifference or neglect. This was obviously poor economy. Paley had raised just such an objection to divorce and thought that 'an earlier termination of the union would produce a separate interest'. A wife, believing the marriage temporary, would naturally try to make financial provision for her future and this would produce 'peculation on one side, and mistrust on the other'.[133] Bentham replied that the very same danger was present in commercial partnerships. But dissoluble marriages, in contrast to commercial partnerships, 'have a cement', meaning love, and this cement is strongest of all and will bind the husband and wife together.[134]

ALTERNATIVES TO DIVORCE: MISTRESSES AND MURDER

Bentham mentioned three alternatives to divorce: irregular relationships, murder and separation. All of these had evident disadvantages. He did not mention wife sale, and he regarded bigamy as a consequence of desertion.

By an irregular relationship Bentham meant either adultery or keeping a mistress. As we saw in Chapter 2, such relationships were problematic because, as he was aware, society regarded irregular relationships as dishonourable, and this unavoidable fact was itself an evil that lasts as long as the relationship lasts.[135]

Bentham, and others too, thought that a lack of divorce laws might be a cause of spouse murder. He argued that if a marriage cannot be dissolved it becomes slavery, and death may come to be seen as the only remedy for an unhappy husband or wife. The greater the suffering the greater would be the desire for this drastic remedy. Therefore, marriage without divorce is an incentive to crime, whereas a dissoluble contract of marriage prevents it.[136] Earlier in the century too, Salmon had argued that unless some formal provision were made for the termination of a marriage by divorce an unhappy couple might conspire against one another's lives.[137] Bentham did not think that 'under the current moral system' in England spouse murders were common, but they were rare in the least legislated nations too. He concluded pessimistically that it was all too likely 'that the unreported cases of murder are more numerous than we think'. Bentham was correct that records of spouse murder in England show it to be a relatively infrequent crime, but whether he was also correct that lack of divorce leads to murder, or that many spouse murders remained undetected, are questions that continue to divide opinion.[138]

Bentham maintained an interest in the laws and customs of other countries, so when his brother Samuel travelled to St Petersburg in 1780 (while Bentham was writing on marriage) he asked Samuel to seek information on spouse murders in Russia. Samuel did so and reported that 'some time ago (says the Duke) the laws of Russia were such that if a wife murdered her husband she was put into a hole in the ground in an erect posture buried up to the arm-pits'. She was left there until eventually she was killed, 'either by the vermin which came about her or some such effect'. The woman was provided with food to prevent her from starving and so could live for between eight and ten days. In contrast, if a husband murdered his wife, he was sent to do penance, which meant paying certain fines to the priests, putting on penitential dress, and saying a certain number of prayers. Samuel reported that the Duke told him that he himself 'has known a man mix in Society without any sense of shame after having killed 3 wives one after the other through jealousy and expiated each crime by such penance'. Samuel concluded his grim report on this terrible punishment by reporting that capital punishments in Russia were now limited to treason alone. But murders were more frequent in Russia than ever. However, 'I must have some other credence than his Highness's word. I will not fail to enquire about the proportion'.[139]

SEPARATION

An unhappy husband and wife, unable to divorce, might try to live apart from one another. In the eighteenth century the problem was how to effect such a separation, because canon law still imposed a duty to cohabit on all married people, a duty regarded as a 'central obligation in matrimony'.[140] By the time Bentham wrote the church courts no longer played an active role in enforcing this duty, but nevertheless the disadvantages of separation, particularly for women, made it a poor substitute for divorce.

As we saw above, unhappy spouses could separate formally by means of an order for divorce *a mensa et thoro* from a church court. This would effectively terminate their duty to cohabit. Some eighteenth-century critics claimed that the church court separation order was a mistaken 'fiction' of canon law and had no basis in either scripture or reason.[141] In fact, very few matrimonial suits of any sort were brought to the church courts in the eighteenth century. Only the Consistory Court in London, known as Doctor's Commons, attracted litigants, and even there the number of cases was not great. Also, by the time Bentham was working on divorce, the great expense involved in bringing a case to Doctor's Commons restricted litigation to the wealthy.[142]

The church courts could make an order for such a divorce on the grounds of misconduct on the part of either spouse, although in reality most petitions were brought by men (possibly because the consequences of separation were so harsh for women). Misconduct was limited to adultery, life-threatening physical cruelty, and, in theory at any rate, sodomy.[143] A decree of divorce *a mensa et thoro* would end the duty to cohabit, but because the marriage itself was not ended remarriage was not possible.[144]

Since the mid-seventeenth century the alternative to divorce *a mensa et thoro*, for those able to afford it, was a separation agreement drawn up by lawyers. This set out the terms under which husband and wife agreed to live apart.

The deed was a contract between a husband and trustees for his wife, and husband and wife made reciprocal promises. The husband promised not use the church courts to compel his wife to cohabit with him, and agreed to pay her an annual allowance, frequently by means of a bond for her separate maintenance. In return the wife agreed to indemnify him against her future debts.[145]

The disadvantage of separating by means of an agreement was similar to that of a separation order from the church court: all the legal consequences of marriage with respect to property and contracts remained in place. A separation agreement also offended against the canon law duty to cohabit, with the result that the agreement was not recognized by the common law or church courts irrespective of any promise a husband made to let his wife live apart from him. This rendered an agreement worthless.[146] Public policy arguments were also advanced against the use of separation agreements. It was said that contracting to live apart would be in contravention of the general policy of the law in 'settling the relations of domestic life', in which the public had an interest in preserving. Also, only Parliament, and not individuals by means of separation agreements, had the power alter the law of marriage.[147]

As we have seen, with the limited exception to the doctrine of coverture provided by the customs of London, any wife separated either by an agreement or by divorce *a mensa et thoro* faced an uncertain future. Any money she earned or property she acquired belonged to her husband, and even if he had agreed to pay her an allowance, he might stop doing so at any time. In that case he would be liable once more for payment of his wife's 'necessaries' – for example, food. But a wife would have to convince tradesmen of this before they would advance her credit, because she was still under coverture and they had no means of redress against her.[148] Her ability to carry on business was compromised too because a married woman could not enter into contracts unless she acted as agent for her husband, and she had no capacity to bring a legal action in her own name. Most cruelly, the husband of a separated wife retained control of their children. They would probably live with him, and he could refuse her permission to see them.[149]

Despite all the potential difficulties, many people did make their own private agreements to live apart when a marriage broke down. By the eighteenth century, even if the church courts would not act to enforce the terms of a separation agreement, the Court of Chancery would. By the 1770s, draft separation deeds appeared in conveyancer's handbooks for practical use.[150]

Bentham had little to say about separation deeds, which brought none of the benefits of either marriage or divorce, but only disadvantages. The major disadvantage was that separation, howsoever effected, offered no possibility of remarriage.[151] However, as we saw in Chapter 5, Bentham's penal code provided help for separated wives. In fact, he was particularly sympathetic to the plight of separated women. Everywhere, he reported, a mistreated wife is allowed to separate from her husband, but only on condition that she does not remarry. The only comfort to her suffering must be that her husband cannot remarry either: 'the outraged wife and her tyrant suffer the same fate, save for a few differences'. The most important 'difference' was that a man, despite being still married, was able to live in an irregular union without serious damage to his reputation, while a woman had no such liberty. He concluded that this 'is the liberty that public opinion grants to the dominant sex and the shame to which it subjects the weaker sex'.[152]

8

Afterword

Bentham wrote extensively on the law of marriage, proposing detailed reform of the existing canon and common law rules. His most radical proposals were for the reform of the divorce laws; here the existing male right to divorce was to be extended to women, and two fault-based grounds for divorce for adultery and desertion introduced. Divorce for incompatibility, which Bentham saw as a liberal reform of harsh laws, was to be by mutual consent. Bentham's most controversial proposal was for short-term marriages.

Bentham did not restrict himself to drafting reformed, codified, utilitarian laws, and also addressed wider questions on the nature of marriage, and on sexual 'non-conformity'. By this he meant relations between men and women either outside marriage or for reasons other than procreation, and homosexual relations too. His earliest work was 'Non-Conformity', written between 1770–4, and then 'Pederasty' in 1785.[1] Underlying all his work on the laws of marriage, and on the relations between men and women outside marriage, was Bentham's keen interest, as a moralist, in improving the position of women.

The greater part of Bentham's manuscripts on marriage and on sexual non-conformity were never published. Neither Dumont nor Bowring included them in their editions of Bentham's writings, possibly fearing legal consequences.[2] Bowring, looking back on the eighteenth century from Victorian England, expressed some personal distaste, confiding that 'I have often heard Mr. Bentham speak of the state of society at that period . . . the elopements of women . . . the irregularities of men . . . '. He decided to 'discard' some subjects from his *Memoir* of Bentham because 'some of the details of penury are so distressing, some of the facts of the profligacy so disgusting, that I think it best to suppress them'. His modern age would 'not . . . tolerate habits and usages which were almost universal seventy or eighty years ago'.[3]

Bowring's disapproval of the eighteenth-century world in which Bentham had lived as a young man reflects a change in sensibility, often referred to as the reformation of manners.[4] As a result of this, Bentham's great moral and legal projects for reforming the private laws regulating sexual relations, particularly the relations between men and women in marriage, have been less known to scholars than his proposals for the reform of public law.

But does Bentham's failure to publish his civil and penal codes, together with the editorial suppression of controversial subjects, mean that his ideas were known only to a few and had no widespread influence? Perhaps not, for the contexts of some contemporary references to Bentham provide brief glimpses of his ideas resonating widely in intellectual life.

Bentham may have intended to circulate his opinions through 'disciples' rather than by publication; for instance, there is evidence that his ideas on birth control were behind those that Francis Place promulgated.[5]

Etienne Dumont was Bentham's friend and editor, but in one instance also acted as a disciple. Between 1818 and 1821 Dumont prepared a Penal Code for the Republic of Geneva, which can be found among his papers in the *Bibliothèque de Genève*. It is evident that Dumont relied on Bentham, and used Bentham's 1790s penal code as the model for his own. Thus Bentham's editorial comments appear on Dumont's manuscripts, and he used Bentham's language and method. The definition of the offence of 'Adulterie', a 'Delit contre la Condition' of marriage, is followed by rules and punishments in Bentham's style.[6] Dumont also discussed an English bill of 1800 proposing to prevent the remarriage of a woman divorced for adultery, and Montesquieu's *Persian Letters*. Dumont discussed the disadvantages of divorce to women, just as Bentham had, and also divorce by mutual consent which he, unlike Bentham did not favour. By preparing a Benthamic code of law Dumont tried, in the event unsuccessfully, to put Bentham's ideas into practice.[7]

Despite Dumont's enthusiasm, Bentham's plans for the codification of his utilitarian laws of marriage may have been less acceptable to his contemporaries than his ideas for the reform of the existing divorce laws. Elie Halevy considered that late eighteenth- and early nineteenth-century opinion in England was particularly unfavourable to Bentham's plans for systematic codification of civil and penal law, and that as a result he had turned for his audience to other lands where he was more likely to receive a favourable reception.[8] In 1811, for example, Bentham wrote to James Madison, offering to draft a code for the United States of America, and he went on to draft codes for Spain, Portugal, Italy and France.[9] In England great opposition to Bentham's suggestions for the codification of property law was expressed by many of the lawyers who contributed to the work of the Real Property Commission in 1828.[10]

Although Bentham's law of marriage was codified, nevertheless his ideas on divorce law reform were talked about and met with approval. Significantly, in 1852 John Stuart Mill, the advocate of women's equality, acknowledged the debt owed to Bentham on the questions of divorce and sexual equality.[11] Was Mill's suggestion of communal living after divorce also an idea he owed to Bentham?

Lastly, Aaron Burr's *Private Diaries* kept to record his life in exile, provide an intimate picture of Bentham as a friend and companion, and also make very apparent that Bentham's radical ideas for reform were widely discussed by his contemporaries. As we have seen, during Burr's exile in England Bentham invited him to visit, and sometimes stay at, Queen Square Place. Evidently a generous friend, Bentham provided Burr with many convivial evenings of supper and conversation. One of Burr's diary entry records 'evening with Bentham; conversed of tattooing, and how to be made useful; of infanticide; of crimes against nature, etc. etc.' On another occasion Burr reported that after 'dinner with Bentham and Koe' he visited Godwin and took tea with Godwin and the children. Then, 'home at 10. Talked an hour with B. and K. To bed at 12.'

Burr's most amusing and pertinent diary entry describes his eight-hour coach journey from London to Oxford to dine with the provost and fellows of one of the colleges. The provost arranged for a young 'fellow' to give Burr a rather chilly three-hour guided tour of the college, and then two other 'plump, hale' fellows joined the party for dinner, and 'all is canonicals'. Conversation turned to Bentham, 'I had rather our friend Bentham should write on legislation than on morals' one of the fellows remarked. Then the conversation settled on 'the single point of divorce, and Hume was quoted . . . [b]y mutual consent divine authority was laid aside, and I made a speech'. Burr indicates that the discussion on religion, morals and American politics then became somewhat heated, but 'we parted with many expressions of courtesy'. He added, 'He [the provost] . . . speaks of Bentham with reverence, and, probably prays for him, I presume he thinks that he will be eternally damned, and I have no doubt he expects to be lolling in Abraham's bosom with great complacency, hearing Bentham sing out for a drop of water.'[12]

Thus Aaron Burr's records of his time in England vividly bring to light Bentham's willingness to talk about his ideas, his connection with Godwin's household, and most importantly show that despite remaining unpublished, Bentham's ideas on marriage and divorce were widely known to and discussed by his contemporaries.

Notes

Notes to Chapter 1: Introduction: Contemporary Contexts

1. Bentham 1996, 11.
2. Bentham 1996, 143.
3 On Bentham as an Enlightenment figure see Rosen 2007 and Burns 1984.
4. Burns 1989, 218.
5. Bentham 1968, 1:241.
6. Schofield 2003 argues that it is necessary to return to Bentham's manuscripts in order to recover the historical Bentham.
7. Prest, Wilfrid 2008, 115, and see 111–18 on Blackstone's lectures.
8. See Doolittle 2001, 24.
9. Bentham 1838, 10:45; see also Lockmiller 1938, 50–1, and Doolittle 1982. For Blackstone's influence on Bentham see Bentham 1977, xxii; Doolittle 2001, 46; Everett 1928, 11; and Sokol 2009; for Bentham's opinion of Blackstone see Bentham 1968, 2:102–3; Prest, Wilfrid 2008, 216; Lieberman 1989, 221, 258–60; and Lobban 1991, 156.
10. Prest, Wilfrid 2008, 150, 217–21.
11. Prest, Wilfred 2009. See Prest, Wilfrid 2008, 219–22; Warden 1938; and Blackstone 1781, xvii.
12. See Warden 1938, xi; Hoeflich 2009; Emerson 2009; Dippel 2009.
13. See Jones 1973, x, xi, and Bentham 1996, xxii.
14. See: Warden 1938, ix; Prest, Wilfred 2009; Doolittle 2001, 85–6; Lockmiller 1938, 156–9; Jones 1973, ix–xi.
15. Wilmot 1822, 2, 3.
16. Bentham 1977, xxi.
17. Bentham 1977, xxii; see Sokol 2009.
18. Doolittle 2001, 50–1, describes the personal animosity towards Blackstone among colleagues at the University aroused by his appointment to the Vinerian chair; see Prest, Wilfrid 2008, 158–62; and Lockmiller 1938, 45–6.
19. Bentham 1838, 10:21.
20. Bentham 1838, 10:38; see Bentham 1968, 1:20n.
21. *Oxford English Dictionary*, 'genius' 3.a.
22. Bentham 1838, 10:27.
23. See Bentham 1838, 10:21, 31, 39; see Dinwiddy 1989, 1–2, on Jeremiah Bentham's ambitions for his son.
24. Bentham 1838, 10:16.
25. Lemmings 1998.

26. Blackstone's 'Introductory Lecture' is reproduced in Lockmiller 1938, Appendix III, 199–229.
27. Lemmings 1998, 215.
28. Lemmings 1998, 221–22.
29. See Lemmings 1998, 253, and Lobban 1991, 47–79.
30. Gray's Inn, Lincoln's Inn, Middle Temple and Inner Temple.
31. See Lemmings 1998, 253, for Lord Eldon's advice on legal training.
32. Lockmiller 1938, Appendix III, 219, 223–4; see Lobban 1991, 6–7, on the common law understood as a system of remedies.
33. Lemmings 1998, 224.
34. Prest, Wilfred 2009; see also Lemmings 1998, 224.
35. Lemmings 1998, 224.
36. Lemmings 1998, 251 n. 153.
37. See Bentham 1977, xix.
38. Bentham 1931, xxxi.
39. See Bentham 1931, xxxi and Bentham 1968, 1:235.
40. See the Burial register 1756 to 1812, ERO D/P209/1/5 Essex Records Office document 70201430, 2.4.1767 Thos Dunckley, accessed at http://linux02.lib.cam.ac.uk/earlscolne/people/Thos_Dunkesle.htm, 29 December 2010.
41. Bentham 1968, 1:190n and 233n; see Bentham 1968, 232–6 and 251–5 for indications of family quarrels about Bentham's proposed marriage; see Lockmiller 1938, 161 n. 45. The Essex Record Office gives Polly's date of baptism as 1 January 1758.
42. Bentham 1968, 1:232–4; see Bentham 1977, xxvi–xxvii.
43. See Vickery 1998, 52.
44. See Vickery 1998, 39–44, and Bentham 1968, 1:252. I am grateful to Penelope Corfield for her comments on arranged marriages.
45. Bentham 1968, 1:235.
46. Bentham 1838, 10:5.
47. Bentham 1968, 1:302–3.
48. See Bentham 1968, 1:xxiv, 99–101, 241n, 252.
49. See Wollstonecraft 2004, 9; the first quotation is from the text and the second is an editorial comment by Janet Todd; Jane Austen's novel *Sense and Sensibility* was published in 1811, but written earlier.
50. Bentham 1968, 1:234–6.
51. See Todd 2000, 415, for indication of Mary Wollstonecraft's dependence on her publisher Joseph Johnson; see also Gordon 2005, 122–3, and Todd 2007, 60–1, for William Godwin's publishing enterprise.
52. See Bentham 1968, 1:185.
53. Bentham 1968, 1:235.
54. Bentham 1968, 1:291n.
55. See Bentham 1968, 1:294–8, 322, 324, 329, 335, 336, 337–9, 344–8, 351–55.
56. Dinwiddy 1989, 5.
57. Dinwiddy 1989, 6.
58. British Library, Bowood Papers, Box 49, fos. 199–200. I am grateful to Catherine Fuller for bringing this to my attention.

59. British Library, Bowood Papers, Box 49, fos. 201–8.
60. British Library, Bowood Papers, Box 49, fo. 198.
61. British Library, Bowood Papers, Box 49, fo. 198.
62. In 1805 Bentham did propose marriage to Caroline, and was refused; see Dinwiddy 1989, 6.
63. Reported in Campos Boralevi 1984, 27–8; see Isenberg 2007, 373–5, for Burr's description of Bentham.
64. See Richardson 1740, Richardson 1985 and Godwin 1970, on arranged and forced marriage.
65. For an overview of earlier mainly French thought see Israel 2001, 82–96.
66. Godwin's rejection of the institution of marriage appears in Godwin 1993, 82–4, 846–54; see Todd 2007, 7–8, and Philp 1986, 182–4.
67. For Shelly's schemes see Todd 2007, 83–4, 90–2.
68. Holmes 1989, 72–8.
69. Bentham credited Paul Whitehead the Poet Laureate of the day with authorship, Bentham 1838, 10:35.
70. Bentham's language echoed *History of Some of the Penitents* 1760, said to be written by Barbara Montague; see also Thompson 2000, xi.
71. Phillips, Teresia Constantia 1750; see Stone 1992, 248; see also Gally 1750, 14–15, for contemporary comment on Phillip's clandestine marriage. Constantia Phillip's creditors could not pursue her for payment of her debts because under the doctrine of coverture a married woman could not own property. Her 'husband' disappeared.
72. Thompson 2000, 1, 14.
73. See Bowring 1838, 10:27.
74. Porter 1982.
75. See Offen 2000, 39–49; see Spencer 1984, 272–316; see *Letter to the Public* 1753 for parliamentary debate.
76. Montesquieu 1989.
77. Fletcher, T. H. 1939, 17–33; Kra 1984, 272–84; for a reference by Bentham see UC xxxii 106.
78. Fletcher, T. H. 1939, 93, points out this theory was not new, but Montesquieu applied it in a systematic manner.
79. UC xxxii 106.
80. Rousseau 1997.
81. Godwin 1970, 89; see also d'Epinay 1787, 2:291 for the story of Cecily.
82. Richardson 1985.
83. See Goldberg 1984, generally for a discussion of Clarissa's influence on European literature.
84. See British Library, *Add.* 29,806 fo. 162; British Library, *Add.* 29,808 fo. 54; British Library, *Add.* 29,809 fo. 437 for Bentham's references to characters and events from Richardson's *Clarissa*. I am grateful to Catherine Fuller for this information.
85. See Eagleton 1982, 4–5. *Pamela* became a play, an opera and a waxwork.
86. See Richardson 1740, and Fielding 1993.
87. Bentham 1968, 2:397.
88. Offen 2000, 33.

89. *Young Lady's Pocket* 1790; Pennington 1761; but see Chesterfield 1786, aimed at young gentlemen; Tague 2001.
90. Goldberg 1984, 24.
91. Gregory, John 1774.
92. Bentham 1968, 1:346–7; Pennington (1761) advises her daughters to adopt the childcare regime made famous by Rousseau: a mother should breast-feed her baby instead of farming it out during infancy; babies should not be swaddled; cold water bathing is good for young children.
93. Wollstonecraft 1985, 26.
94. A woman brings sin and suffering to mankind in the Greek myth Pandora, and in Genesis 3.1–7. See Hesiod 1988, 39; Moller Okin 1979, 16–20, 26; Bock 2002, 2, 9.
95. Authorship has been attributed to Lady Mary Wortley Montagu.
96. Sophia 1739, 23.
97. Sophia 1739, 10; see also Bock 2002, 11.
98. Gentleman 1739, 46, 65.
99. Gregory, John 1774, 19.
100. See UC lxxvii 22; UC lxxvii 156.
101. By 1776 Bentham was already at work on 'Critical Elements of Jurisprudence' which Dumont used for the *Traites* published in 1802, see Bentham 1968, 1:358.
102. UC xxx 49.
103. UC lxxvii 181; UC lxxvi 152.
104. UC xxx 51.
105. UC xxx 50.
106. UC xxx 49.
107. Bentham 1996, 234–58; see Chapter 4.
108. Bentham 1802; 2:202–36. See Bentham 1931, xxxii on Dumont's redaction, and xxxvii–xxxviii on Dumont's aims.
109. Bentham 1996, 237–8, n. 3.
110. Bentham 1802; UC xxxii 114.
111. For John Bowring's suppression of Bentham's writings on sex, and for Francis Place as an editor, see Campos Boralevi 1984, 37, and Campos Boralevi 1983, 138.
112. Bentham 1838, 1:349–58.
113. I am grateful to F. Rosen for bringing my attention to the history of the translations of Bentham's work. See Bentham 1931, xi–li, for a history of the translations, and Bentham 2004, vii–xxi, for the history of Dumont's redaction of Bentham's work and its subsequent translation back into English.
114. See Bentham 1931, xxxi; Blamires 1990, 56; Dinwiddy 1989, 4; Burns 1989; Burns 1984.
115. I am grateful to J. H. Burns and Philip Schofield for bringing this to my attention.
116. Bentham 1968, 2:265–6n.
117. Bentham 1968, 2:388.
118. Bentham 1968, 2:397 and 3:14.
119. Rosen 2007.

Notes to Chapter 2: Sex and Utility

1. The two other categories of motives for human behaviour are 'social', including goodwill and love of reputation, and 'dissocial', including the pleasures and pains of antipathy. See Bentham 1996, 11, and 96–124 on motives, especially 116. See Rosen's Introduction to Bentham 1996, xlix, and xci–xciii on Bentham's psychological hedonism. See also the discussions in: Dinwiddy 1989, 22; Postema 2002, 1:xii; Burns 1989, 211.
2. Plato 1951 said to have been written around 385 BC.
3. Plato 1951, 87; see Price 1989, 15–25, 90–1.
4. UC xxxii 103.
5. UC lxxvi 147.
6. Dinwiddy 1989, 22. See Bentham 1996, 42–59, 103–4, 115–16.
7. See Postema 1986, 147.
8. See Kelly, P. J. 1989, 71. See also Kelly, P. J. 1990, 40–1, 59 and 64 for a brief historical survey of the arguments. See Lobban 1991, 117. On a second related question asking whether Bentham intended the principle of utility to be both a principle of moral obligation as well as the source of reasons for action in any given circumstance, in other words was pleasure a good for Bentham, see Kelly, P. J. 1990, 39–59.
9. UC xxxii 103.
10. See Porter 1982, 4.
11. Hume 2000, 312.
12. See Edmiston 1985, 9 and 10, on Chanderlos de Laclos who considered marriage a violation of nature.
13. Edmiston 1985, 8–13, 96; generally see Spencer 1984, 16–18; for the Encyclopedist's views on women and marriage see Malueg 1984, 259–69.
14. Montesquieu 1989. See also Montesquieu 1964, first published 1721. For discussion see Kra 1984, 272–84.
15. This theory was not new, but Montesquieu applied it in a systematic manner and popularized it. See Fletcher, T. H. 1939, 39.
16. 'Montesquieu distinguished the servitude of 'slaves established for the family' from the servitude 'in which women are held in some countries'. The latter he described as 'domestic servitude proper'. See Montesquieu 1989, 264, and also 254, 270.
17. Bentham 1838, 10:54. See Bentham 1931, 41, 45–6 for Bentham's rejection of climate theory.
18. UC xxxii 124.
19. UC lxxi 91.
20. UC lxxi 91.
21. UC lxxi 90, 91.
22. See UC xxxii 103, UC lxxi 91.
23. UC xxxii 116.
24. See Campos Boralevi 1983, 123, for a survey of Bentham's writings on *Non-Conformity* and *Sexual Eccentricities.*
25. UC lxxi 91.

26. See McLaughlin 1984, 297.
27. Rousseau 1994, 112–13.
28. Rousseau 1994, 111.
29. UC lxxi 92.
30. See Hobbes 1962, 143, and Rousseau 1994.
31. UC lxxi 96.
32. UC lxxi 96.
33. See Pease-Watkin 2002.
34. Burns 1989, 212.
35. Kra 1984, 282.
36. Paley 1785, 167–8.
37. See McLaughlin 1984, 301.
38. Rousseau 1994, 59.
39. UC lxxi 95.
40. UC lxxi 96.
41. See Edmiston 1985, 102, and Diderot 1926, 119–59.
42. UC lxxi 96.
43. UC lxxi 96.
44. See Chapter 6 for details of Bentham's fable.
45. See Montesquieu 1964; Montesquieu 1989; Salmon 1724, 81–108; Smith 1790, part V, V. I. 19; Blackstone 1979, 1:424; and Paley 1785, 260–67.
46. UC lxxi 101.
47. UC lxxi 97.
48. UC lxxxxix 180.
49. Bentham proposed the decriminalization of homosexual activity. See Campos Boralevi 1984, 37–9; see also Campos Boralevi 1983, 123, 133, and Crompton 1993.
50. UC lxxi 97.
51. Shakespeare's play *Measure for Measure* is premised on the moral paradoxes that arise when private morals are regulated by the state. For debates on the merits of statutory regulation of personal conduct in early modern England see Kent 1973, and Sokol and Sokol 2003, 4.
52. UC lxxi 97.
53. UC lxxi 96.
54. Porter 1982, 9, estimates that there were over 10,000 prostitutes on the streets of London alone at the time. See Hill 2001, 110, for a suggestion that the term prostitution was not used publicly until 1822, and Hill 2001, 112, on the numbers of prostitutes. See Probert 2004, 463, for criticism of estimates of the number of prostitutes in eighteenth-century London.
55. Shoemaker 2004, 80.
56. See Hill 2001, 115, and Jackson 1996, 29–30. On Bentham's National Charity Company see Bahmueller 1981, 20–8.
57. See Hitchcock 1997, 71, who finds connections between the reduced age of marriage and increased number of illegitimate births. See also Probert 2005, 249, on the problems of interpreting evidence about irregular marriages.

58. UC lxxxxvi 197. Bentham also mentioned the offence of 'solitary venery', and its 'superior attractiveness'.
59. See Hill 2001, 96, 100, and 94–105 on poor women generally.
60. UC lxxxxvi 197.
61. An illegitimate child was a *filius nullius*, or child of no one, and in canon law had inferior legal status. At common law various legal disabilities attached to illegitimate children. The parents' subsequent marriage would legitimate an illegitimate child in canon law, but not at common law, apart from very limited exceptions. See Baker 2002, 489–90.
62. UC lxxxxvi 197.
63. Infanticide was a term that was to become more familiar in the nineteenth century.
64. UC lxxxxviii 207. Infanticide had become a capital crime for the first time in 1624, an Act that was repealed in 1803. In 1922 the Infanticide Act made infanticide a form of manslaughter. See Jackson 1996, 6–7.
65. UC lxxxxvi 214. See Hill 2001, 113–15. Jackson 1996, 3, indicates that assize court records reveal that an overwhelming majority of those indicted for child murder were unmarried women.
66. UC lxxxxvi 207.
67. UC lxxxxvi 210. I am grateful to Peter Morris for bringing the following details to my attention. Bentham here referred to Dr William Hunter 1718–83, obstetrician and the physician to Queen Charlotte. Hunter's paper 'On the Uncertainty of the Signs of Murder in the Case of Bastard Children' was read posthumously to the Medical Society on 14 July 1783, and it subsequently appeared in *Medical Observations and Inquiries by a Society of Physicians in London* 6 1784, 266–90.
68. UC lxxxxvi 207. In practice, throughout the eighteenth century, grand juries consistently discharged women indicted for child murder, and trial juries would acquit them. See Hill 2001, 114; Jackson 1996, 3. See Campos Boralevi 1984, 13–14 for Bentham on infanticide and abortion.
69. UC lxxxxvi 210.
70. UC lxxxxvi 210. Thomas Coram established London's first Foundling Hospital in 1741. See Wagner, Gillian 2004.
71. Hines 1936.
72. Bahmueller 1981, 104–5.
73. Out-of-work servants frequently resorted to prostitution. See Hill 2001, 109–10.
74. UC cliv 153. For Bentham's planned sotimion see Semple 1993, 290–5.
75. Dingley 1758. See Porter 2000, 373. See Mahood 1990, 29–39, on the opening of Lock Hospitals for sick women and Mahood 1990, 56–9, on the Magdalens and for the comment that reformers saw prostitutes as more sinned against than sinning.
76. UC cli 162.
77. UC cli 163.
78. UC lxxxxvi 197.
79. UC cli 164.
80. UC cli 164. Dram drinking referred mainly to gin drinking, still a problem in the 1790s.
81. Bentham 1931, 385–6; see Hill 2001, on women driven to prostitution by lack of alternative means of subsistence.

82. Bentham 1931, 386, and Bahmueller 1981, 16.
83. See Chapter 7 for details.
84. UC lxxxxvi 197.
85. See Bentham 1931, 221–31.
86. See UC xxxii 116.
87. See Wilkinson 1997, on registered partnership debates.
88. UC xxxii 111.
89. UC xxxii 116.
90. UC xxxii 116.
91. UC cli 162. Compare Bentham's comments with the Dumont redaction's rather obscure discussion of 'engagements, left-handed marriages, and legitimating contracts' in Bentham 1931, 387–93. Bentham 1931, 388–9, also reports Bentham stating marriage for a limited period ought not to be so honourable as permanent marriage.
92. For a biography of Mary Robinson see Byrne 2005.
93. UC xxxii 113.
94. UC xxxii 113.
95. Hickman 2004, 131. Several books have been published in recent years on the careers of courtesans, including Griffin 2002.
96. Probert 2004, 457.
97. Wagner, Peter 1982, 135.
98. See Richardson 1740.
99. But the sprightly Pamela successfully holds out for marriage.
100. UC xxxii 112.
101. UC lxxi 97.
102. UC xxxii 111.
103. UC xxxii 111–12.
104. UC xxxii 111.
105. Paley 1785, 243.
106. Paley 1785, 247.
107. Paley 1785, 248.
108. Paley 1785, 248.
109. UC lxxxxvi 197.
110. *Chesterfield (Earl of) v. Jannsen* 2 Ves. Sen. 125, 28 English Reports 82. See also *Champion v. Pickax* 1737 1 Atk 472, 26 English Reports 301.
111. See *exparte Cottrell in the matter of Evans* 1778 2 Cowp 742, 98 English Reports 1338–9. But see also *Priest v. Parrot* 1751 2 Ves. Sen. 160, 28 English Reports 103.
112. See cases discussed in Probert 2004, 459, including especially *Franco v. Boulton* 1797 3 Ves. Jun. 369, 30 English Reports 1058, where the woman was a prostitute who had already moved in with another protector.
113. See *Beaumont v. Reeve* 1846 8 QB 483, 115 English Reports 958.
114. See Probert 2004, 459.
115. See Wilkinson 1997, 46, 57 n. 46.
116. Outhwaite 1995, gives details of campaigns for repeal of the Act. See Lemmings 1996, on House of Commons debates, and Probert 2002, on interpretation by the courts.

117. Pennant was a naturalist and topographical writer; see Pennant 1790, 91, 92. Anton (1958) has convincingly argued that Pennant misunderstood what he saw. I thank Rebecca Probert for bringing this latter point to my attention. See also Parker 1990, 18.
118. Diderot 1926, 141; see McLaughlin 1984, 303.
119. Like Bentham, Diderot looked for a rational reconciliation of human nature and desires with the need for an ordered society. See McLaughlin 1984, 301.
120. J. H. Burns, in an unpublished paper 2008, examined Bentham's friendship with Jacque-Pierre Brissot 1754–93 that led to an exchange of ideas and literature. Brissot, who was guillotined in 1793, was responsible for nominating Bentham to be an honorary citizen of France in 1792. See Dinwiddy 1989, 8.
121. See Rogers 1984, 44–5.
122. See de Gouges 1989. Presumably de Gouges intended lifelong marriage and marriage for the duration-of-mutual-love to be available as alternatives.
123. UC lxxvi 109.
124. Thomas 1983, 39.
125. UC lxxii 208, and UC lxxi 102.
126. UC xxxii 106.
127. UC lxxxxvi 197.
128. UC lxxi 116, UC lxxi 113.
129. See Lacey 2000, Williford 1975, and the debate in Campos Boralevi 1980, Ball 1980a and Ball 1980b.
130. See, for an example, Whately 1768, 46–8.
131. Pufendorf 1994, 198–200.
132. Paley 1785, 194–5.
133. See Rousseau 2003, 259–308.
134. Blackstone 1979, 1:410, 433.
135. Campos Boralevi 1984, 10–11. Lea Campos Boralevi, however, did not have access to Bentham's manuscripts on marriage.
136. UC lxxvii 184.
137. UC xxxii 112.
138. See Diderot 1966, 226–7.
139. UC xxxii 111.

Notes to Chapter 3: Making a Marriage

1. 26 Geo II, c. 33.
2. These customary marriages had supposedly been popular, although exactly how many there were is a matter of dispute. See Ingram 1987, 132–3; see Parker 1990, 17, 18; Brown 1981, 117–20; and Probert 2005, 249–50.
3. Provided such marriages could be proved; for contemporary comment see Salmon 1724, 180–1, 198–9; *Treatise of Feme Coverts* 1732, 30; *Letter to the Public* 1753, 38–9; 'Letter from a By-Stander' 1753, 17–20; see Probert 2009, 178–82; Brown 1981, 118.
4. Subsequent Acts of Uniformity followed; 1552 (5 & 6 Edw. VI c. 1); in 1553 the Catholic Queen Mary outlawed the *Book of Common Prayer*, and restored the use of the Latin

Breviary and Missal; a new 1559 Act of Uniformity (1 Eliz. 1 c. 2) followed Elizabeth's succession, see MacCulloch 1996.

5. See Ingram 1987, 193; Probert 2009, 108–22.
6. Keane 1995, 76.
7. See Probert 2009, 7, for an explanation of 'clandestine'.
8. See Outhwaite 1995, 26–31; Brown 1981; see Probert 2009, 175–6, on legislation passed 1695–6 to put an end to these practices.
9. Ingram 1987, 134.
10. Phillips, Teresia Constantia 1750; see Stone 1992, 248; see also Gally 1750, 14–15.
11. *Letter to the Public* 1753, 9.
12. Probert 2009, 2–5, argues that in practice Lord Hardwicke's Act did not act as a break with the past.
13. See Outhwaite 1995, 75–97, and Lemmings 1996, 340, for opposition in Parliament.
14. This term includes all nonconformists, Baptists, Congregationalists and Presbyterians, except Quakers. See Probert 2009, 143–51.
15. Roman Catholics, nonconformists and secularists had to wait until the Marriage Act 1836, 6 & 7 Will. IV c. 85.
16. Lieberman 1989, 13–28.
17. Probert 2005, 255.
18. See, for example, 'Letter from a By-Stander' 1753, 16.
19. Blackstone 1979, 1:426.
20. 'Letter from a By-Stander' 1753, 4–5.
21. See Lemmings 1996, 351–2.
22. Blackstone 1979, 1:423, 426.
23. UC lxxii 207.
24. Probert 2005, 254 et passim.
25. See Outhwaite 1995, 101–13; Lemmings 1996; Probert 2002, 143–6; Parker 1990, 40–7.
26. UC lxxi 113.
27. Bentham 1931, 235, a translation of Bentham 1802, 2:231. An unsuccessful bill of 1765 proposed tightening up on banns and preventing English people avoiding the Act by going to Scotland to marry.
28. Waddams 2000, 62; Outhwaite 2006, 104–67. In 1828 Henry Brougham included reform of the church courts in his famous law reform speech to Parliament, which Bentham must have known about. See Hansard, 2nd ser, xviii, 153 (7 February 1828).
29. See UC v 33, and Bentham 1818.
30. UC lxxvi 109.
31. UC lxxvi 109.
32. 20 & 21 Vict. c. 85; see Baker 2002, 496.
33. Phillips, Roderick 1988, 210–26; Cornish and Clark 1989, 374.
34. The Counter-Reformation Tridentine reforms, particularly the decree *Tametsi* of the Council of Trent (1564) regulated marriage in Catholic Europe, see Outhwaite 1995, 5; Carlson 1994, 3.
35. 2 & 3 Edw. c. I; Carlson 1994, 45.
36. Pufendorf 1994, 198–200.

37. Blackstone 1979, 1:421; Salmon 1724, 63; however, Salmon also made many references to the work of the civilian lawyer Henry Swinburne, see, for example, 201.
38. Salmon 1724, A7v–A8r; Bentham UC xxxii 108; Paley 1785, 269.
39. See Chapter 1.
40. For Montesquieu influence on Blackstone see Lieberman 1989, 37; Prest, Wilfrid 2008, 67–8, 163–4.
41. Blackstone 1979, 1:421; see Sokol 2009, 96–7.
42. Salmon 1724, A7v–A8r.
43. Paley 1785, 267; see Chapter 6.
44. Blackstone 1979, 1:14–15. For Blackstone, canon law was 'foreign' law permitted to operate in England by the Common Law, see Sokol 2009, 97.
45. Blackstone 1979, 1:84; see Blackstone 1979, 3 43; Sokol 2009, 98.
46. Edmiston 1985, 103; Diderot 1926, 119–59.
47. Montesquieu 1964; Montesquieu 1989; see Chapter 1.
48. Kra 1984, 282.
49. See Salmon 1724, 214–310.
50. Civil marriages did not take place after 1657; Blackstone 1979, 1:427; Firth and Rait 1911, 2:715–17, 1139; Outhwaite 1995, 11–13; Sokol 2009, 97.
51. House of Commons Sessional Papers, xxviii, 1837–8, 377.
52. But Bowring failed to sign the Report which often indicates disagreement with the findings, so his appointment may have been because he was a Unitarian rather than Bentham's associate.
53. UC xxxii 114. See Bentham 1802, 2:212, and Bentham 1931, 231.
54. UC xxxii 114.
55. UC xxxii 114; see Bentham 1802, 2:225, Bentham 1931, 230, and Chapter 4.
56. UC xxxii 114, 115.
57. UC xxxii 114.
58. See Chapter 7.
59. UC xxxii 114, 115.
60. UC xxxii 114.
61. See Chapter 1.
62. See Chapter 1 for an explanation of harm in a utilitarian scheme of law.
63. UC xxxii 114.
64. UC xxxii 115.
65. UC xxxii 115.
66. Pease-Watkin 2002, 10.
67. UC xxxii 115.
68. UC xxxii 108.
69. Bentham 1931, 232; UC xxxii 116.
70. UC lxxi 113.
71. See UC lxxi 95, Bentham 1802, 2:229, and Bentham 1931, 232.
72. For example, see Godwin 1970, 89, and Rousseau 1997, 279–301; see also d'Epinay 1787, 2:291. See Bentham 1968, 1:302–3.
73. Philogamus 1985, 29.

74. UC lxxi 95.
75. UC lxxi 95.
76. UC lxxi 95.
77. See Chapter 1.
78. See 'Counsellor's Plea for' 1715 and Chapter 7.
79. UC xxxii 124.
80. See Chapter 7.
81. 'Letter from a By-Stander' 1753, 7; Cornish and Clark 1989, 361–2, reflects this interpretation of Lord Hardwicke's Act.
82. Blackstone 1979, 1:425–6.
83. Edmiston 1985, 37.
84. Salmon 1724, 7.
85. Salmon 1724, 7.
86. Salmon 1724, 68; see Keymer 2010, 564, on Salmon's reference to Milton.
87. See Baker 2002, 270.
88. Spring 1993, 50–1; Erikson 1993, 121–2; Goldberg 1984, 51–5.
89. UC xxxii 108. See Bentham 1802, 2:215, and Bentham 1931, 234.
90. UC lxxvii 156. See also Bentham 1931, 218.
91. See Macfarlane 1986, 245–7.
92. See Thomas 1983, 39.
93. UC lxxii 208.
94. See McCabe 1993, 12, on the theory of natural avoidance.
95. UC lxxii 208.
96. UC lxxii 208.
97. UC lxxii 208.
98. Bentham 1931, 216. See Bentham 1802, 2:203.
99. UC lxxii 208.
100. Paley 1785, 160.
101. UC xxxii 102, UC lxxii 208.
102. UC xxxii 106; see Genesis, 18.36.
103. UC xxxii 104.
104. These differ, mostly in order and expression, from the reasons later published by Dumont in Bentham 1802, 2:206 ; see UC lxxii 105 and Bentham 1931, 218.
105. UC lxxii 208.
106. UC lxxii 208.
107. 1 Jac. 1, c. 11. See Cornish and Clark 1989, 360.
108. UC lxxi 106.
109. Montesquieu 1989.
110. Montesquieu 1989, 264–74; see Phillips, Roderick 1988, 165.
111. More 1834, 2 and 103.
112. Paley 1785, 263.
113. Bentham 1838, 1:216; For Bentham's comments on Montesquieu see, for example, UC xxxii 106.
114. UC lxxi 105.

115. UC lxxi 105.
116. UC lxxi 106.
117. UC lxxi 108.
118. UC lxxi 108.
119. UC lxxi 108.

Notes to Chapter 4: The Subordination of Women

1. *Midland Bank Trust Co. v. Green* 1981 3 All England Law Reports 744.
2. The Married Women's Property Act 1870 (33 & 34 Vict.), and Married Women's Property Act 1882 (45 & 46 Vict.); see Baker 2002, 484–8.
3. Law Reform Married Women and Tortfeasors Act 1935 (25 & 26 Geo. V.); the Married Women's Property Act 1882 allowed married women to be sued as a feme sole judgement in some circumstances; see Baker 2002, 488–9; Staves 1990, 2–3; coverture was subject to exceptions; a married woman was liable for her own crimes, unless coerced by her husband; importantly, the customs of London allowed a married woman trader to sue or be sued in the city courts as a feme sole.
4. Blackstone 1979, 1:430 (Bk 1, ch. 15).
5. Blackstone thought legal fictions 'highly beneficial and useful'. Blackstone 1979, 1:430.
6. Stretton 2009, 127, quoting Bentham; see Dinwiddy 1989, 55–6, on legal fictions.
7. Phillips, Teresia Constantia 1750; see Stone 1992, 248; see also Gally 1750, 14–15, for contemporary comment on Phillip's clandestine marriage.
8. Bentham 1968, 2:7–8n, 33–8.
9. Bentham 1968, 2:13, 22, 27, 31–42.
10. Bentham 1968, 2:37.
11. Bentham 1968, 2:73–4.
12. See Bentham 1968, 2:7–10.
13. See generally Baker 2002, 270–1.
14. Statute of Uses (1536) 27 Hen.VIII, c. 10.
15. Stat. 3 & 4 Will. c. 105.
16. Bingham 1816, 161–366; Canning 1820, 15–16.
17. See Ryan 1984, 91–6, for Bentham's reconciliation of the right of private property contrasted with William Godwin's denial of such rights. Also see Bentham 1826, Bentham's review of Humphreys 1826.
18. For the disappointment prevention principle see Kelly, P. J. 1990, 8–9, 79–81.
19. UC xxxii 152, 157.
20. UC xxxii 149.
21. 15 & 16 Geo. 5; UC xxxii 149–55.
22. House of Commons Sessional Papers, x, 1829; see Sokol 1992, for Bentham's involvement with the Real Property Commission.
23. See generally Staves 1990, 27–94.
24. Booth 1985, 94–7.
25. Genesis 2.21–4; Mark 10.6–8; St Paul's Letter to the Ephesians.

26. See Baker 2002, 484.
27. 2 & 3 Edw. c. I; Carlson 1994, 49.
28. See the influential thesis of affective individualism and the family in Stone 1988, 164–8, now much doubted by historians; see Bailey 2003, 4; Fletcher, Anthony 1995, 154–72; Wrightson 1982, 90–2; and Houlbrooke 1984, 102–6.
29. Gregory, John 1774, 4.
30. Whately 1768, 46–8. For parallels see: Filmer 1648; Gouge 1622, 353; *Baron and Feme* 2005, 7.
31. Blackstone 1979, 1:430 (Bk 1, ch. 15).
32. See Chapter 3 on companionate marriage.
33. See Dolan 2008, 2, 4.
34. Dolan 1994, 93, 95; but see Biberman 1999.
35. See Clark 1995, 63–4.
36. Blackstone 1979, 1:410. According to Pufendorf, whom Blackstone cited, natural law supposed an original equality in faculties between men and women which was modified by the laws of state and civil society. See Pufendorf 1994: 199–200; see Hunter 2001: 182–5, and 333 on Pufendorf's pact; see Paley 1785, 279.
37. Stretton 2009, 111–13.
38. Bentham 1838, 5:391–2.
39. Paley 1785, 279.
40. Wollstonecraft 1985, 10; More 1834, 37–40.
41. See Bingham 1816, 161–4 and passim, an infant's contracts were for the most part voidable, but those of a married were with few exceptions absolutely void; Holcombe 1983, 18–36; see Stretton 2009, for an analysis of the descriptions applied by legal writers to coverture.
42. Stretton 2002, 48.
43. See Finn 1996, 714–16; Stretton 1994; Stretton 1999; Stretton 1998; but note Eileen Spring's qualification of the role played by equity in Spring 1993, 117–22.
44. Finn 1996, 717.
45. Finn 1996, especially 705–6. The event she refers to was the theft of a wife's purse, described in court as the husband's property.
46. See Chapter 2.
47. See Bentham 1996, 237–8, Bentham 1802, 2:226, and Bentham 1931, 178.
48. Burns and Hart 1970, xxxxiii.
49. Burns and Hart 1970, xxxiii, Bentham 1838, 1:301.
50. Dumont Archive Catalogue, Ms. Fragment 3787 fo. 6, Letter Jeremy Bentham to J. L. Duval dated Tuesday 20 October 1829.
51. Bentham 1996, 237.
52. Bentham 1996, 237–8, n. 3.
53. Bentham 1996, 238n.
54. Bentham 1996, 237.
55. Bentham 1931, 230–1. Dumont's list of other conditions of marriage gave priority to the principle of equality: both men and women were to be sexually faithful during marriage (although this last was less important for a man than his wife); property was to be enjoyed in common by husband and wife.

56. UC xxxii 114, Bentham 1802, 2:225.
57. UC lxxvi 153.
58. UC lxviii 25, UC lxviii 27, UC lxviii 268; see Gardner, Simon 1990, 7: 'the trust is an "equitable" concept'; see Baker 2002, 309–11, for development of the trust as an interest in land.
59. All kinds of property can be subject to a trust, and trustees' duties allow for all sorts of trust purposes. Trusts can be expressly created or implied by law for the benefit of individuals or groups of individuals. See further Gardner, Simon 1990, 2.
60. UC lxviii 27.
61. UC lxviii 27.
62. See UC lxviii 27, where Bentham explained that trusts can be created to benefit particular groups or classes of peoples connected politically or topographically. This benefit could then be enforced by a court of law.
63. UC lxviii 271.
64. UC lxviii 27.
65. UC lxviii 27; see Baker 2002, 113–15, on the nineteenth-century legislation to fuse law and equity.
66. UC lxviii 28.
67. UC lxviii 271.
68. UC lxviii 237.
69. UC lxviii 271.
70. Bentham 1996, 238.
71. UC lxviii 271.
72. See: Pufendorf 1994, 199–200 n. 36; Blackstone 1979, 1:433; Sokol 2009, 106.
73. See Campos Boralevi 1984, 10–11.
74. See Bentham 1996, 237–8 n. 3.
75. Locke 1997, second treatise, para. 78, 362; para. 83, 365; para 82, 364, quoted in Shanley 1989, 11; see Stretton 2009, 113, for Lord Hardwicke's remarks in 1735 on the need to preserve the peace of families.
76. Bingham 1816, 162.
77. Bingham 1816, 162–3, concludes that if legal equality were allowed to women then they would at once be relieved from the necessity of pleasing men now imposed on them and 'rouse up in [husband's] a dangerous antagonist'.
78. Bingham 1816, 164.
79. Stretton 2009, 120.
80. See Staves 1990, 4; Vickery 1998, 41.
81. See Dolan 2008, 27–8, on the 'persistent dilemma of reconciling spiritual equality and social hierarchy', which is evidence for continuity in gender relations.
82. Stretton 2009, 114; Doggett 1992, 34–6.
83. Stretton 2009, 115.
84. Stretton 2009, 119–21.
85. UC lxxvii 158.
86. UC lxxvii 156.
87. UC xxxii 114.
88. UC xxxii 152.

89. This continues ‘saving for whatever dispositions the law may have allowed to be made to the contrary in the marriage settlement’. UC xxxii 152.
90. UC lxxvii 22.
91. UC xxxii 152.
92. UC lxxi 42.
93. UC lxxi 42.
94. Warnock 1985, vii.
95. Rousseau 2003, 259–308.
96. Bentham 1996, 235–7.
97. Bentham 1838, 1:302, Bentham 1802, 2:6, and Bentham 1931, 96.
98. Kelly, P. J. 1990, 79.
99. Staves 1990, 4.
100. Williford 1975, 169.
101. UC lxxvii 157.
102. UC xxxii 114.
103. See Staves 1990, 30–1.
104. On a wife’s right to seek legal remedies for ill-treatment see Chapter 5.
105. Bentham concluded, UC xxxii 114, that there may be a need to set out examples ‘as used by Sancho Panza to pay for the accusation of rape’.
106. Cornish and Clark 1989, 370–1.
107. Wollstonecraft 2004, 43–5, 48–9.
108. Cornish and Clark 1989, 371.
109. 2 Russ. 1.
110. See Ram 1928, 18.
111. UC lxviii 272.
112. UC lxviii 273.
113. UC lxviii 273.
114. UC lxviii 274.
115. UC lxviii 274.
116. UC lxviii 275.
117. UC lxviii 275.
118. Bingham 1816, 232–65.
119. *Oxenden v. Oxenden* 1705 2 Vern. 493, 23 English Reports 916; *Bennet v. Davies* 1725 2 P. Wms. 316, 24 English Reports 726.
120. See Bingham 1816, 332–41, for a marriage settlement; see Humphreys 1826 and Bentham 1826. See Staves 1990, 131–61, on pin-money.
121. See *Lance v. Norman* 2 Chan. Rep. 77, 21 English Reports 621 where the intended wife entered into a recognizance with her brother to benefit him.
122. *Lady Strathmore v. Bowes* 1789 1 Ves. 22, 30 English Reports 211.
123. Staves 1990, 134–5, 139–47.
124. Staves 1990, 228.
125. Bentham 1838, 5:387.
126. Vickery 1998, 41.
127. Philogamus 1985.

128. Bailey 2003, 88.
129. Erikson 1993, 129–30.
130. Staves 1990, 20.
131. Bentham 1993, 208.
132. The chairman of the Commission was John Scott, Earl of Eldon, the Lord Chancellor from 1801–6, and 1807–27.
133. On the problems in the English bankruptcy system between 1800–25 see Lester 1995, 25–37.
134. Humphreys 1826, 219.
135. Bentham 1838, 111: 299.
136. The Small Debts Act 1846, 9 & 19 Vict. c. 95.
137. Cornish and Clark 1989, 38.

Notes to Chapter 5: 'Offences against domestic conditions'

1. UC lxxi 90; see further Chapter 6.
2. See Bentham 1996, 214–24, for offences against trust.
3. See, for example, UC lxviii 83; see Dinwiddy 1989, 16.
4. See UC lxviii 266, 271.
5. See Baker 2002, 500–11.
6. Dinwiddy 1989, 16, 60.
7. Baker 2002, 510; Dinwiddy 1989, 10–11.
8. See Chapter 4.
9. See Bentham 1996, 255–7.
10. Bentham 1996, 283, and Bentham 1931, xxiv.
11. Bentham 1996, 158–9.
12. Bentham acknowledged the influence of Beccaria 1767 on punishment, and referred to Montesquieu 1989, 91. See Bentham 1996, 166.
13. Bentham 1996, 168.
14. The other two were the rule of severity (the condition of prisoners should not be 'more eligible' than that of the 'poorest class of subjects'), and the rule of economy; see Dinwiddy 1989, 92 and 95, for Foucault's criticisms.
15. Presumably this achieved the desired effect of silencing the offender in much the same manner as placing a cover over a bird's cage silences the bird.
16. See Bentham 1996, 168.
17. UC lxviii 368.
18. See Chapter 3.
19. Shoemaker 2004, 80.
20. Shoemaker 2004, 87, reports that the 1831 Royal Commission reported that the church courts rarely required public penance.
21. Shoemaker 2004, 88–92; public executions ended in 1868.
22. Shoemaker 2004, 88–92.
23. See UC lxviii 350, 352, for the definition of presence banishment.

24. Bentham considered presence banishment especially appropriate as a punishment for a challenge to a duel, see UC lxviii 354; see UC xvi 125 for Bentham on Aaron Burr's duel with Alexander Hamilton.
25. UC lxxi 19.
26. See the case reported in Doggett 1992, 13.
27. UC lxxi 19.
28. Amussen 1994; Foyster 1996; Gowing 1996; Hunt, Margaret 2000.
29. See MacCulloch 1996, 58–9, 420–1, on Cranmer's acceptance of a companionate theory of marriage.
30. 'Homilie of the State' 1968, 245.
31. Doggett 1992, 7–8; Baker 2002, 484 n. 26 on Justice Buller; Kelly, Henry Asgar 1994.
32. Lambarde 1592, 130, and *Lawes Resolutions of Womens Rights* 1632, 128.
33. See Bailey 2003, 138.
34. See Dolan 2008, 52–3; Ingram 1987, 183; and Bailey 2003.
35. Bingham 1816, 264.
36. See Bingham 1816, 264, and Doggett 1992, 11–15, on the history of the right to beat wives.
37. Bailey 2003, 5. For a description of the struggle for power within a household see Kugler 2001.
38. Clark 1995, 63–87; Phillips, Roderick 1991, 97–100; Gowing 1996, 219–20.
39. The writer once practised as a family law solicitor in Woolwich, London. An irate young woman attended an appointment seeking an emergency injunction for domestic violence for the friend she brought with her. She explained that her friend was subject to unacceptable violence whereas 'my husband only hits me when I deserve it'.
40. See Bailey 2003, 8–9, for a summary of optimistic and pessimistic views of marriage presented by historians; see also Amussen 1994, 70–89; Foyster 1996, 214–24; and Shoemaker 1998, 112.
41. Bailey 2003, 39, 35–60.
42. Ingram 1997, 64; Houlbrooke 1984, 117–18.
43. See *Lawes Resolutions of Womens Rights* 1632, 128.
44. *Treatise of Feme Coverts* 1732, 81.
45. Whately 1768, 49.
46. Blackstone 1979, 1:432–3; Bailey 2003, 138.
47. See Hunt, Lynn Avery 1992.
48. Mainardi 2003, 4–5; Hunt, Lynn Avery 1992.
49. UC lxviii 224.
50. Blackstone 1979, 1:432.
51. Blackstone 1979, 1:433; Lord Leigh's Case 2 Keb. 433; 84 English Reports 807; see Coke's comments in *Lord Seymour's Case* 1613 Godb. 215, 72 English Reports 966, although his was a minority opinion; see Kelly, Henry Asgar 1994, 355.
52. Doggett 1992, 11.
53. UC lxviii 224.
54. UC lxviii 224.

55. UC lxviii 224.
56. UC lxviii 240.
57. UC lxxi 107.
58. Quoted in Tadmor 2001, 19.
59. Tadmor 2001, 20.
60. UC lxxi 11, 12, and lxxi 18, 19, 23.
61. UC lxxi 19.
62. UC lxxi 23.
63. Bailey 2003, 113–15; see also Kugler 2001, 201–2.
64. Bentham 1996, 237.
65. UC cliv 152.
66. See UC cliv 152; see Chapter 2.
67. UC cliv 152.
68. Mill et al. 1994, 52–100.
69. See Baker 2002, 528, and Campbell 1984.
70. 25 Edw. III, st. v 1351 c. 2; see Dolan 1994, 21–4.
71. Bentham 1996, 168.
72. 9 Geo. IV. c. 31, s. 2.
73. Kugler 2001, 194–5.
74. UC lxxxxvi 213.
75. UC lxxxxvi 213.
76. See Baron and Feme 2005, 9.
77. See, for example, *Sir Cleave Moore v. Ellis Freman et al.* (1725) Bunb. 205, and 145 English Reports 648. See Doggett 1992, 13.
78. Doggett 1992, 13, for the Countess of Strathmore's Case (1787) *R. v. Bowes* 99 English Reports 696.
79. Bingham 1816, 265; see also 1 Burr. 631 (Earl Ferrers' case).
80. UC lxxi 120.
81. UC lxxi 120.
82. UC lxxi 121.
83. UC lxxi 107.
84. UC lxxi 107.
85. UC lxxi 106 and see Chapter 6 for criminal conversation cases. See Stone 1993, 22–3, and Baker 2002, 456–7.
86. UC lxxi 107.
87. UC lxxi 107.
88. UC lxxi 107.
89. Bailey 2003, 50.
90. Stone 1990, 194–5.
91. UC lxxi 107.
92. See Bailey 2003, 32–5.
93. Bailey 2003, 55–7.
94. UC lxvi 107.

95. UC lxxi 107.
96. UC lxxi 107.
97. UC lxxii 210, and UC lxxi 113. It may be that the manuscripts were once a whole, but for some reason were stored in different boxes.
98. UC lxxii 210.
99. UC lxxii 210.
100. UC lxxii 210.
101. UC lxxi 113.
102. UC lxxi 113. This description of a remote attempt echoes the plot of Richardson's novel *Clarissa*, which Bentham had certainly read. Clarissa was confined and raped by the villainous anti hero, see Richardson 1985.
103. UC lxxi 113.
104. UC lxxii 210.
105. UC lxxii 210.
106. UC lxxii 210.
107. UC lxxii 206.
108. UC lxxii 206.
109. See 1 Hale PC 629; Lowe and Douglas 2007, 112.
110. [1992] 1 AC 599, HL.
111. UC lxxii 208; other justifications for the Ravisher were that the victim had lived with him as his concubine, or that she had previously consented to sexual intercourse with him, or that she was a 'common harlot'.
112. UC xxx 4.
113. UC xxx 4.
114. UC lxviii 240.
115. UC lxviii 241.
116. UC lxviii 244.
117. UC lxviii 247.
118. UC lxviii 248.
119. UC lxviii 224.
120. See the example in Bailey 2003, 64.
121. UC lxviii 223.
122. UC lxviii 219.
123. UC lxviii 220.
124. UC lxviii 226.
125. Bailey 2003, 65–6.
126. UC lxviii 226.
127. UC lxviii 227.

Notes to Chapter 6: Adultery

1. UC lxxi 101.

2. UC lxxi 101; the code is set out in 10 consecutive numbered pages, and is in a finished state as if prepared for publication.
3. See Chapter 1.
4. Etienne Dumont published part of Bentham's proposals for divorce in 1802, but none of his work on adultery. Bentham 1802, 2:212–24.
5. See Outhwaite 2006, 5–6, 7, 60, on divorce *a mensa et thoro;* see Chapter 7 on divorce.
6. Blackstone 1979, 1:429.
7. See Stone 1990, 257, on moral panic, and Binhammer 1996, on the sex panic; Philogamus 1985, 5.
8. Stone 1990, 277; Binhammer 1996, 416–19, adds fears of women's sexuality.
9. 'Lady Strathmore's Claim' 1802.
10. Mainardi 2003, vii.
11. See Ingram 1987, 151–2.
12. Ingram 1987, 249 et passim; Outhwaite 2006, 81, 142.
13. Stone 1993, 22–3; Baker 2002, 456–7.
14. Stone 1990, 238.
15. UC lxxi 96. Bentham probably referred to Lord Grosvenor's action for criminal conversation against the Duke of Cumberland in 1771. Bailey 2003, 165, reports that Grosvenor stopped his subsequent suit in Doctor's Commons against his wife for a separation order in 1772 because she had been deserted by her seducer and left destitute.
16. Gregory, Jeremy 1999, 98; Tosh 1999, 222.
17. Lloyd 2006, 422.
18. Lloyd 2006, 422; Wagner, Peter 1982, 122–4.
19. Sibbit 1800, 4, 8–18, 33–5, supported Lord Auckland's attempts to make adultery a crime; Philogamus 1985, 21–9; *Crim. Con. Actions* c. 1890, 1–4, for descriptions of the terrible punishments imposed on adulterers in past civilizations.
20. *Northanger Abbey* was first published in 1818 but written earlier.
21. Bentham 1838, 10:21, records Bentham's mother and father both forbade the reading of children's stories and histories.
22. UC lxxi 97; Wagner, Peter 1982, 134–6, and Bailey 2003, 142–3.
23. UC lxxi 97; Porter 1982, 16.
24. UC lxxi 90.
25. UC lxxxxvi 84.
26. See UC lxxxxvi 84 which includes the example of 'the negligence of drovers' which must reflect the presence of herds of animals on London's streets.
27. UC lxxxxvi 84.
28. UC lxxxxvi 84.
29. Baker 2002, 129, church court offences were punishable as sins.
30. Shoemaker 2004, 82, 87–8.
31. Phillips, Roderick 1988, 129–30. The Act was repealed with the restoration of the monarchy in 1660.
32. Phillips, Roderick 1988, 413; Stone 1993, 25.
33. Trumbach 1984, 24, for *Conjugium Languens.*
34. *Free Thoughts on Seduction* 1771, 25–30.

35. UC xxx 47.
36. UC xxx 41a–42.
37. UC xxx 44.
38. UC xxx 44, UC xxx 41a, UC xxx 43. Bentham explained that 'These distinctions apply to general not to particular codes.'
39. UC lxxi 91.
40. UC lxxi 91.
41. UC lxxi 91.
42. Bentham 1996, 143–52.
43. UC lxxi 97.
44. UC lxxi 95.
45. UC lxxi 96.
46. UC lxxi 97.
47. Savage 1998, 526.
48. Dinwiddy 1989, 83.
49. UC lxviii 12.
50. UC lxxxxvi 98.
51. UC lxxxxvi 98.
52. UC lxxi 90.
53. UC lxxi 98.
54. UC lxxi 98.
55. UC lxxi 98.
56. UC lxxi 98, Bentham concluded that the explanation of the existence of this kind of property belongs to the civil code; UC lxxi 93.
57. *Everard v. Hopkins* 1614 2 Bulst. 332, 80 English Reports 1164.
58. See Baker 2002, *Winsmore v. Greenbank* 1745 Willes 578, 125 English Reports 1330.
59. UC lxxi 98.
60. UC lxxi 94.
61. Bentham's explanation did not take account of the Roman institution of *patria potestas*, or paternal power, which subordinated children to their father until he died. Most free Romans lived under paternal power which was not slavery, although in practice there was little difference between a son who was under his father's power, and a slave owned by that father. I thank Andrew Lewis for his help with Bentham's references to Roman law. Treggiari 1991, 15–36; Gardner, Jane 1986, 45, 67–77.
62. UC lxxi 98.
63. C.1780, UC lxxi 90.
64. UC lxxi 97, other mischiefs were shame and quarrels.
65. Traer 1980.
66. Mainardi 2003, vii–viii.
67. Mainardi 2003, viii, 1.
68. UC lxxi 100; see Philogamus 1985, 16, for the harsh judgement on women's morals, but see Porter 1982.
69. UC lxxi 93.
70. UC lxxi 93.

71. UC lxxi 94.
72. UC lxxi 93; see Philogamus 1985, 27–8, on modesty in women, 'when Women become lewd, they surpass the Lewdness of men, as I believe the most virtuous Matron will not deny'.
73. UC lxxi 97.
74. UC lxxi 97, Bentham thought the loss of her dower was already punishment enough for an adulterous separated wife.
75. Bailey 2003, 163–4.
76. UC lxxi 98.
77. UC lxxi 93.
78. Tosh 1999, 223; Foyster 1996.
79. Hitchcock and Cohen 1999, 15.
80. UC lxxi 99.
81. Philogamus 1985, 2, 10.
82. See Chapter 7.
83. UC lxxi 97; Thomas 1959.
84. Ashton 2002, 157, on Thomas Carlyle's opinions on Mill's relations with Harriet, and also Ashton 2002, 153.
85. UC lxxxxvi 193.
86. UC lxxxxvi 181.
87. UC lxxi 102.
88. Otherwise he would have suffered no loss.
89. See *Joseph Biscoe v. Robert Gordon* 1794 in A Civilian of Doctor's Commons 1799.
90. UC lxxi 98; in *Free Thoughts on Seduction* 1771, 41, adultery was described as 'robbing [a husband] of the most valuable part of his personal estate'.
91. UC lxxi 98.
92. A Civilian of Doctor's Commons 1799.
93. *Free Thoughts on Seduction* 1771.
94. UC lxxi 98.
95. UC lxxi 97. This argument was frequently made, see *Free Thoughts on Seduction* 1771, 41–2.
96. UC lxxi 97.
97. UC lxxxxvi 194.
98. UC lxxxxvi 193.
99. *Free Thoughts on Seduction* 1771, 16–23.
100. See *Free Thoughts on Seduction* 1771, 30–2.
101. Moore 1814, 9–182; see the criticism of Lord Mansfield in *Free Thoughts on Seduction* 1771, 32–46.
102. Bentham took particular note of cases in which Lord Mansfield appeared as counsel, or sat as Lord Chief Justice, for example, *Worsley v. Worsley* 1781 on which see Rubenhold 2008. As a young man Bentham walked up and down in front of Mansfield's Hampstead house, hoping to catch a glimpse of his hero, see Bentham 1838, 10:46.
103. UC lxxxxvi 193.
104. UC lxxxxvi 193.

105. Truelove 1739, 5.
106. UC lxxxxvi 193.
107. UC lxxi 93. See *Biscoe v. Gordon*, *Duberly v. Gunning* in *New Collection of Trials* 1799 and 1802.
108. UC lxxi 94.
109. UC lxxi 94.
110. Bailey 2003, 165–6.
111. UC lxxi 96; see *Crim. Con. Actions* c. 1890, 89–94.
112. UC lxxi 97.
113. UC lxxi 100. Stone 1993, 26–7.
114. UC lxxi 100. Bentham may have had in mind Shakespeare's *Merry Wives of Windsor* in which Falstaff attempts to seduce Mistress Page, or other later citizen comedies; see Philogamus 1985, 35–6, 39, 'habituate them [married women] to the Love of a decent Retirement; as a Bird may be habituated to love his Cage'.
115. UC lxxi 96.
116. UC lxxi 96.
117. UC lxxi 96.
118. UC lxxi 96.
119. UC lxxi 96
120. UC lxxi 95.
121. UC lxxi 95.
122. Mainardi 2003, 4; Phillips, Roderick 1988, 351–2.
123. Bodanis 2006, Emilié du Châtelet died in childbirth. The father of her child was neither Voltaire nor her husband, although Bentham may well not have known this.
124. See Rubenhold 2008, 213–17, which also mentions Willey Reveley's harrowing report of Sir Richard's purchase of a child slave in Turkey.
125. Rubenhold 2008, 154.
126. *Moorson v. Moorson* (1792), English Reports 162: 1090–1; *Rix v. Rix* (1777) English Reports 162: 1085; *Timings v. Timings* (1792) English Reports 162: 1086–9; *Crewe v. Crewe* 1800 English Reports 162: 1106.
127. Stone 1990, 207–9.
128. UC lxxi 96.
129. UC lxxi 94.
130. UC lxxi 94.
131. UC lxxi 94.
132. UC lxxi 94; Bentham's description accords with the plot of Thomas Middleton's play, A *Chaste Maid in Cheapside*.
133. Joseph Addison's play *Cato* was first performed at Drury Lane Theatre in 1713. Both Whigs and Tories laid claim to the patriotic virtues displayed, but the play was criticized for its love scenes. It was revived in 1764 as *Cato a Tragedy Without the Love Scenes*, see further Freeman 1999, 463, 464.
134. UC lxxi 94. See Gardner, Jane 1986, 82. I thank Andrew Lewis for his information on Cato.
135. UC lxxi 93.
136. UC lxxi 97.

137. UC lxxi 93.
138. UC lxxi 93.
139. UC lxxi 93.
140. UC lxxi 97.
141. UC lxxi 97.
142. UC lxxi 91.
143. UC lxxi 92.
144. UC lxxi 92.
145. UC lxxi 92.
146. For Bentham's fable see UC lxxi 91–2.
147. See Chapter 1 on Bentham as a reader of contemporary fiction.
148. Hobbes 1962, 143; Rousseau 1994.
149. Hobbes 1962, 186.
150. Wolfe 1996, 8.
151. Locke 1960, Second Treatise, 309.
152. Locke 1960, Second Treatise, 311.
153. Locke 1960, Second Treatise, 314.
154. Paley 1785, 262. Paley here considers polygamy.
155. Westminster School Archive, A 1913/1/1 & 2, vol. 2; Bentham's list also included four volumes of Handel's solos and Sonatas, and a slate. I am grateful to F. Rosen for telling me about the existence of Bentham's school books.
156. This was published anonymously in 1774 as *The White Bull, an Oriental History from an Ancient Syrian Manuscript*; see Bentham's letter to his brother Samuel reporting the book's publication in June 1774 in Bentham 1968, 1:185; see Voltaire 2008. See UC lxxxxvi 70 for Bentham's reference to Voltaire's tale.
157. Voltaire 2008, 279.
158. See Campos Boralevi 1984, 44–52, for Bentham's neo-Malthusianism.
159. UC lxxi 93.
160. UC lxxi 93.
161. UC lxxi 101. The code is set out in consecutive numbered pages and in a finished state ready for publication.
162. UC lxxi 101.
163. UC lxxi 101.
164. Twining 1985, 31–2.
165. UC lxxi 101.
166. UC lxxi 101, 102; see Chapter 7.
167. UC lxxi 101.
168. See Chapter 7.
169. Phillips, Roderick 1988, 302–3; see Mainardi 2003.
170. UC lxxi 101.
171. UC lxxi 101.
172. UC lxxi 101.
173. Stone 1990, 197–8.
174. UC lxxi 101–2.
175. UC lxxi 102.

176. UC lxxi 102.
177. UC lxxxxvi 193.
178. Aliens also retained legal disabilities as did villeins, at least in theory, see Baker 2002; Magna Carta had prohibited lords from arranging a ward's marriage if the marriage would 'disparage' his status, for example, with someone diseased in mind or body. In practice few cases were ever brought, Bean 1968, 13, 14.
179. UC lxxi 102.
180. UC lxxi 102.
181. UC lxxi 102.
182. UC lxxi 102.
183. Baker 2002, 491–2.
184. Bailey 2003, 170.
185. Pederson 2000, 88; Helmholz 1987, 145–56.
186. UC lxxi 102.

Notes to Chapter 7: Divorce and Separation

1. Pevsner and Cherry 1977, 79; Britton and Wedlake 1808.
2. Sir Lionel died in 1793 and his wife in 1814.
3. The Parish Guide.
4. Stone 1993, 12.
5. Phillips, Roderick 1988, 36–9, 40–94; MacCulloch 1996, 58–9, 420–1.
6. See Stone 1990, 301; Phillips, Roderick 1988, 131–3.
7. 20 & 21 Vict. 1857 c. 85, ss. 27, 33, 54; the jurisdiction of the church courts over marriage was abolished and replaced with a new Court for Divorce and Matrimonial Causes. A husband could divorce his wife on the grounds of her adultery, while a wife could divorce her husband on the grounds of his adultery when combined with incest, bigamy, rape, sodomy, bestiality, cruelty or desertion for two years.
8. Suits for divorce from bed and board and annulment remained low, see Horstman 1985, 4.
9. Diramentary impediments were a lack of capacity to consent to a marriage: insanity, lack of required age, or that force had been used compel the marriage. Impotency, or marriage within the prohibited degrees also allowed the court to find the marriage void, see Baker 2002, 491–2.
10. For the traditional view about the pre-Reformation Catholic church courts see Blackstone 1979, 1:429; Pollock and Maitland 1968, 2:393; McGregor 1957, 4; and more recently Cornish and Clark 1989, 375. See Sheehan 1996, 84, 85; Ingram 1987, 146, 171–9; and Phillips, Roderick 1988, 9, who doubt the traditional view.
11. Stone 1990, 192, and Phillips, Roderick 1991, 3.
12. See Macqueen 1842, 551–61.
13. Wolfram 1985, 160. In 1798 a House of Lords Standing Order regularized the situation by requiring a successful King's Bench, or other a common law court, verdict for criminal conversation as a preliminary to petitioning Parliament.
14. Macqueen 1842, 488.

15. See Macqueen 1842, 578–80, 582, 583.
16. Baker 2002, 495; Anderson 1984, 412–14; Wolfram 1985, 159; Jordan 1997.
17. On publicity see Stone 1990, 248–51, on the cost of parliamentary divorce see Anderson 1984, 436.
18. Phillips, Roderick 1991, 66.
19. See Horstman 1985, 20–2, for details of Jane Addison's petition brought on the grounds of her husband's adultery with his sister-in-law, see Wolfram 1985, 162; Macqueen 1842, 476–7, 594–8.
20. All were in the nineteenth century, Horstman 1985, 23, and Phillips, Roderick 1991, 66.
21. 'Husband and Wife: Criminal' 1919, 576.
22. Stone 1990, 326–8.
23. See Leathley 1916, 106; McGregor 1957, 19.
24. UC xxxii 111.
25. See Anderson 1984, 412, 414 et passim.
26. UC xxxii 111.
27. See Stone 1990, 350–1, on the English reaction to the French Revolution, and see 273; Binhammer 1996; Anderson 1984, 423–7, on the hostility (or otherwise) to divorce displayed by successive Lord Chancellors.
28. UC xxxii 111.
29. Bentham 1996, 11, 96–124.
30. UC xxxii 103.
31. UC xxxii 124.
32. UC xxxii 108.
33. UC xxxii 109.
34. UC xxxii 108.
35. UC xxxii 108.
36. UC xxxii 108.
37. UC xxxii 108.
38. UC xxxii 108. See the distinction made between slavery and drudgery in Locke 1997, 2:352.
39. UC xxxii 108.
40. UC xxxii 111.
41. UC xxxii 111.
42. UC xxxii 111.
43. UC xxxii 109.
44. See the discussion in Phillips, Roderick 1991, 56–8.
45. See Phillips, Roderick 1988, 175–85; Spencer 1984, 33–46.
46. See Bentham 1802, 2:224, Bentham 1931, 229, and Spencer 1984, 229; in Bentham 1802, 2:224 Dumont comments on the number of Parisian divorces which dates this part of Bentham's work to after 1792. Alternatively Dumont himself may have inserted these figures.
47. Phillips, Roderick 1988, 210–18.
48. Paley 1785, 269; Salmon 1724, 153; *Cases of Polygamy, Concubinage* 1732; Wolseley 1673, 111; see Phillips, Roderick 1988, 210–18, on secular theories of marriage.
49. 6 & 7 Will. IV 1836, c. 85.

50. See Phillips, Roderick 1988, 97, on Filmer 1680.
51. Phillips, Roderick 1988, 18–20; see *Cases of Polygamy, Concubinage* 1732, 67 et passim, for the much-reported story of Barnadino Ochino who left his religious order in Italy in 1547, and travelled to Geneva where he married. He next published his thoughts on the benefits to mankind of polygamy and divorce.
52. See *The Doctrine and Discipline of Divorce* (1643 and 1644), *The Judgement of Martin Bucer* (1644), *Tetrachordon* (1645) and *Colasterion* (1645), which are collected in Milton 1820.
53. Milton 1820, *Tetrachordon*, 232, 126; Virgil 1991, viii:485–8.
54. Genesis 2.18.
55. Milton translated Martin Bucer as *The Judgement of Martin Bucer, Concerning Divorce* 1664. Bucer, who influenced the drafting of Thomas Cranmer's Prayer Book marriage service, placed companionship as the first and not third purpose of marriage; Genesis 11.18; Gloucester 1910, 252–8; Carlson 1994, 45; Sokol and Sokol 2003, 74–81; see Bray 1994, cxxv–cxxvii, 247–79, for Martin Bucer's influence in England on the drafting of the abortive *Refomatio Legum Ecclesicarum* (1553) which would have allowed divorce and remarriage for men and women for adultery, desertion or criminal ill-treatment.
56. Stone 1988, 164–8, on the growth of affective individualism and companionate marriage.
57. Milton went on to cite scriptural authority for divorce on several grounds, see Milton 1820, 139; see also 17, 20, 23, 37 and generally; see Locke 1997, Two Treatises on Government, 2:6, 385.
58. Stone 1990, 17, 348; Keymer 2010, 563.
59. For example, UC xxxii 108.
60. See. Keymer 2010, 563, on Salmon's knowledge of Milton; Salmon 1724, 160–1.
61. .UC xxxii 111; Dolan (2008) argues Milton did not extend his radical proposals for divorce to women, but see Biberman 1999.
62. UC xxxii 108.
63. UC xxxii 108.
64. UC xxxii 108.
65. UC xxxii 108.
66. See Godwin 1993, 3:82–4, 453–4, 846–54; Philp 1986, 182–4; see Todd 2007, 84, 102, 106, for Shelley quoting his father-in-law and Milton on marriage; see Keymer 2010; see Bruder 1997, 94–6, on Godwin's failure to address radical feminism.
67. UC xxxii 108.
68. UC xxxii 108.
69. UC xxxii 108.
70. UC xxxii 108.
71. UC xxxii 108. The length of time needed will vary with the probability of more pregnancies and more births.
72. UC xxxii 108.
73. UC xxxii 110.
74. UC xxxii 110.

75. Bailey 2003, 24; Gowing 1996, 128; see Bingham 1816, 258, on the Court of Chancery's refusal to intervene to protect a wife's separate property if her husband obtained a divorce *a mensa et thoro*. Dick. 321. 806.
76. Stone 1990, 326–8; Phillips, Roderick 1988, 230.
77. Horstman 1985, 20; see *Cases of Polygamy, Concubinage* 1732, 67, for sixteenth-century arguments for divorce. See Wolseley 1732, 117, for the claim that a wife's adultery dissolved or nullified the marriage bond, and see. Blackstone 1979, 1:428.
78. On the double standard see Thomas 1959, and Gowing 1996, 3.
79. Mainardi 2003, 7.
80. Reported in Mainardi 2003, 8.
81. Phillips, Roderick 1988, 413.
82. See Paley 1785, 275; but see Salmon 1724, 161, who described the 'great Absurdity' of refusing remarriage to those divorced 'even for Adultery'.
83. See Castamore 1700.
84. Macqueen 1842, 482–3.
85. See Brougham quoted in Macqueen 1842, 480–3, 485, see *Cases of Polygamy, Concubinage* 1732, 67, and Wolseley 1732, 117.
86. UC lxxi 101, 102.
87. UC lxxi 102.
88. UC lxxi 102.
89. UC lxxi 103.
90. Cases of necessity are accepted, added Bentham mysteriously, UC lxxi 103.
91. Foreman 1998, 100–1.
92. A Civilian of Doctor's Commons 1799.
93. UC lxxi 103.
94. UC lxxi 101
95. UC lxxi 101.
96. UC lxxi 101.
97. UC lxxi 101.
98. Paley 1785, 192.
99. UC lxxi 102–3.
100. UC lxxi 108.
101. UC lxxi 108.
102. UC lxxi 108.
103. UC lxxi 108; Phillips, Roderick 1988, 233–4.
104. UC lxxi 108.
105. See Stone 1993, 5–6; see Bailey 2003, 37, 171–8.
106. Bailey 2003, 36.
107. UC lxxi 108; this provision applied to a deserted husband too who was able to take over the management his wife's property during the continuance of the marriage.
108. Locke 1997, 2:383, 385; see Salmon 1724, 111.
109. UC xxxii 108.
110. Hume 1987, Essay 19: Of Polygamy and Divorces, 6.

111. Paley 1785, 268.
112. See Mill and Mill 1970, 81, 86.
113. Bentham 1931, 228.
114. Stone 1990, 340.
115. UC lxxi 95.
116. UC lxxi 95.
117. Bentham 1968, 1:98–102.
118. UC xxxii 109.
119. Part of UC xxxii 109 was published in Bentham 1802, 2:217–22, and Bentham 1931, 225–8, corresponding to Paley 1785, 267–81.
120. Paley 1785, 271.
121. Paley 1785, 271. See also Salmon 1724, 112, who thought that 'Besides, when women are thus left to the Humour or Inconstancy of the Men, it is not difficult to imagine, what Influence and ill Effects this may have, in Relation to the Children'.
122. Paley 1785, 273.
123. UC xxxii 109; see Salmon 1724, 112.
124. Paley 1785, 271.
125. Paley 1785, 270.
126. Hume 1987, Essay 19: Of Polygamy and Divorces, 7.
127. UC xxxii 109.
128. See Phillips, Roderick 1988, 171. Montesquieu 1964, Letter 116.
129. UC xxxii 110.
130. Quoted in Phillips, Roderick 1988, 38–9.
131. Paley 1785, 270.
132. UC xxi 93.
133. Paley 1785, 269–70.
134. UC xxxii 110.
135. UC xxxii 109.
136. UC xxxii 109.
137. See Salmon 1724, 161–2, on remarriage after divorce for adultery; Dolan 2008, 84–6, 87–93.
138. UC xxxii 109; Phillips, Roderick 1988, 306–10; Dolan 2008, 68, recounts that roughly half the women murdered in the United Kingdom and America are killed by husbands or boyfriends; 4 per cent of male victims of homicide are killed by wives or girl friends.
139. Bentham 1968, 2:395.
140. Cornish and Clark 1989, 374.
141. *Cases of Polygamy, Concubinage* 1732, 131; see Sokol and Sokol 2003, 144, on Cranmer.
142. Outhwaite 2006, 102–3.
143. Baker 2002, 493, lists sodomy as a ground, but by the late eighteenth century very few cases of sodomy were heard in the church courts. See Stone 1990, 193.
144. Helmholz 1974, 101, on the court as mediator.
145. See Doggett 1992, 18–21, and Bailey 2003, 66.
146. Stone 1993, 5.
147. Bingham 1816, 174–6, and Carlson 1994, 397.
148. Bingham 1816, 174.

149. Helmholz 1974, 101, and Stone 1990, 3, 170. On divorce *a mensa et thoro* generally see Phillips, Roderick 1988, 13–15.
150. Stone 1990, 150–56.
151. Bentham 1931, 229.
152. UC xxxii 111.

Notes to Chapter 8: Afterword

1. See generally Crompton 1993; Campos Boralevi 1984, 37–39; and Campos Boralevi 1983. See generally Dabhoiwala 2010.
2. An edition of Bentham's writings on sex is planned for the Collected Works.
3. Bentham 1838, 10:24.
4. Ingram 1996.
5. See Campos Boralevi 1984, 69, and Hines 1936, 275.
6. Dumont included 'Instruction pour les juges', and an 'Exposition'.
7. *Bibliothèque de Genève*, Dumont Mss. Collection, Box 43, Code Penal pour la Republic de Genève, 1821; on divorce see folder 19, fo. 81–5.
8. Halevy 1928, 76, 79.
9. See Sullivan 2007, 22–3, and 28–32 on the eventual rejection of Bentham's ideas for codification in America where codes were 'too radical, even for American codifiers, most of whom did not want to give up the common law'. See Bentham 1998.
10. Sugden 1826 and Sokol 1992.
11. See Mill 1924, 88; Mill et al. 1994, xii–xiv, 28–31; and Campos Boralevi 1984, 24.
12. Burr 1903.

Bibliography

Amussen, Susan Dwyer. 'Violence and Domestic Violence in Early Modern England.' *Journal of Women's History* 6 (1994): 69–89.

Anderson, Stuart. 'Legislative Divorce – Law for the Aristocracy?' *Law, Economy and Society, 1750–1914: Essays in the History of English Law*. Ed. G. R. Rubin and David Sugarman. Abingdon: Professional Books, 1984. 412–44.

Anton, A. E. 'Handfasting in Scotland.' *The Scottish Historical Review* 37 (1958): 89–102.

Ashton, Rosemary. *Thomas and Jane Carlyle: Portrait of a Marriage*. London: Chatto and Windus, 2002.

Bahmueller, Charles F. *The National Charity Company; Jeremy Bentham's Silent Revolution*. Berkeley: University of California Press, 1981.

Bailey, Joanne. *Unquiet Lives: Marriage and Marriage Breakdown in England, 1660–1800*. Cambridge: Cambridge University Press, 2003.

Baker, J. H. *An Introduction to English Legal History*. London: Butterworths, 2002.

Ball, Terence. 'Bentham No Feminist: A Reply to Boralevi.' *Bentham Newsletter* 4 (1980a): 47–8.

—. 'Was Bentham a Feminist.' *Bentham Newsletter* 4 (1980b) www.ucl.ac.uk/Bentham-Project/journal/newsletter/Newsletter_04, accessed 10 January 2009: 25–32.

Baron and Feme: A Treatise of Law and Equity Concerning Husbands and Wives. Facs. of 1700, in *The Early Modern Englishwoman*, vol. 3. Ed. Lynne A Greenberg. London: Ashgate, 2005.

Bean, J. M. W. *The Decline of English Feudalism*. Manchester: Manchester University Press, 1968.

Beccaria, Cesare. *Essay on Crimes and Punishments*. London, 1767.

Bentham, Jeremy. *Traites de Legislation Civile et Penale*. Ed. Etienne Dumont. Paris, 1802.

—. *Church-of-Englandism and Its Catechism Examined*. London: Effingham Wilson, 1818.

—. 'Bentham on Humphreys' Property Code.' *Westminster Review* 6 (1826): 446–507.

—. *The Theory of Legislation*. Ed. C. K. Ogden, trans. Richard Hildreth from the French of Etienne Dumont. New York: Kegan Paul Trench, Trubner & Co., 1931.

—. *Works*. Ed. John Bowring. 11 vols. Edinburgh: William Tait, 1838–43.

—. *The Correspondence of Jeremy Bentham*. 10 vols. London and Oxford: Athlone Press and Clarendon Press, 1968–. *Collected Works of Jeremy Bentham*.

—. *A Comment on the Commentaries and a Fragment on Government*. Ed. J. H. Burns and H. L. A. Hart. London: Athlone Press, 1977.
—. 'Indications Respecting Lord Eldon.' *Official Aptitude Maximised Expense Minimised*. Ed. Philip Schofield. Oxford: Oxford University Press, 1993. 203–89. *The Collected Works of Jeremy Bentham*.
—. *An Introduction to the Principles of Morals and Legislation*. Intro. F. Rosen. Oxford: Clarendon Press, 1996. *The Collected Works of Jeremy Bentham*.
—. *'Legislator of the World': Writings on Codification, Law and Education*. Ed. Philip Schofield and Jonathan Harris. Oxford: Clarendon Press, 1998.
—. *The Theory of Legislation*. Trans. from the French of Etienne Dumont by Richard Hildreth, intro. James E. Crimmins. Bristol: Thoemns Continuum, 2004.
Biberman, Matthew. 'Milton, Marriage, and a Woman's Right to Divorce.' *Studies in English Literature, 1500–1900* 39 (1999): 131–53.
Bingham, Peregrine. *The Law of Infancy and Coverture*. London: J. Butterworth & Son, 1816.
Binhammer, Katherine. 'The Sex Panic of the 1790s.' *Journal of the History of Sexuality* 6 (1996): 409–34.
Blackstone, William. *Reports of Cases Determined in the Several Courts of Westminster Hall 1746–1779*. London, 1781.
—. *Commentaries on the Laws of England: A Facsimile of the First Edition of 1765–69*. 4 vols. Chicago: University of Chicago Press, 1979.
Blamires, Cyprian. 'Etienne Dumont: Genevan Apostle of Utility.' *Utilitas: A Journal of Utilitarian Studies* 2 (1990): 55–70.
Bock, Gisela. *Women in European History*. Oxford: Blackwell, 2002.
Bodanis, David. *Passionate Minds: The Great Enlightenment Love Affair*. London: Little, Brown, 2006.
Booth, George Earl of Warrington. 'Considerations upon the Institution of Marriage.' *Marriage, Sex and the Family in England 1660–1800*. Facs. London, 1739. Ed. Randolph Trumbach; London: Garland Publishing,1985.
Campos Boralevi, Lea. 'In Defence of a Myth.' *Bentham Newsletter* 4 (1980) www.ucl.ac.uk/BenthamProject/journal/newsletter/Newsletter_04, accessed 10 January 2009: 33–46.
—. 'Jeremy Bentham's Writings on Sexual Non-Conformity: Utilitarianism, Neo-Malthusianism, and Sexual Liberty.' *Topoi. An International Review of Philosophy* 2 (1983): 123–48.
—. *Bentham and the Oppressed*. Berlin: Walter de Gruyter, 1984.
Boucè, Paul-Gabriel, ed. *Sexuality in Eighteenth-Century Britain*. Manchester: Manchester University Press, 1982.
Bray, Gerald, ed. *Documents of the English Reformation*. Cambridge: James Clark, 1994.

Britton, John, and Edward Wedlake. *The Beauties of England and Wales*. London, 1808.
Brown, Roger Lee. 'The Rise and Fall of the Fleet Marriages.' *Marriage and Society: Studies in the Social History of Marriage*. Ed. R. B. Outhwaite. London: Europa Publications, 1981. 117–36.
Bruder, Helen P. *William Blake and the Daughters of Albion*. Basingstoke and London: Macmillan Press, 1997.
Burns, J. H. 'From Radical Enlightenment to Philosophic Radicalism.' *Bentham Newsletter* 8 (1984) www.ucl.ac.uk/Bentham-Project/publications/journals/newsletter_8, accessed 31 January 2011: 4–11.
—. 'Utilitarianism and Reform: Social Theory and Social Change, 1750–1800.' *Utilitas: A Journal of Utilitarian Studies* 1 (1989): 211–55.
Burns, J. H., and H. L. A. Hart, eds. *Jeremy Bentham, An Introduction to the Principles of Morals and Legislation*. London: Methuen, 1970.
Burr, Aaron. *The Private Journal of Aaron Burr*. '250 copies for private distribution', NYPL copy 227 scanned at www.archive.org/stream/privatejournalof01burr2/privatejournalof01burr2_jvu.txt. 2 vols. Rochester, NY: Genesee Press, 1903.
Byrne, Paula. *Perdita: The Life of Mary Robinson*. London: Harper Perennial, 2005.
Campbell, Ruth. 'Sentence of Death by Burning for Women.' *The Journal of Legal History* 5 (1984): 44–54.
Canning, Thomas. *Observations Occasioned by a Case Lately Submitted to Counsel Respecting the Question, How Far a Contingent or Reversionary Interest of Husband and Wife in Her Right, in Personal Estate, is Assignable, in Deed or in Law, during the Coverture*. London, 1820.
Carlson, Eric Joseph. *Marriage and the English Reformation*. Oxford: Blackwell, 1994.
The Cases of Polygamy, Concubinage, Adultery, Divorce, &c. London, 1732.
Castamore, pseud. *Conjugium Languens, or the Natural, Civil, and Religious Mischiefs Arising from Conjugal Infidelity and Impunity*. London, 1700.
Chesterfield, Lord. *Principles of Politeness, and of Knowing the World*. Portsmouth, NH, 1786.
A Civilian of Doctor's Commons. *A New Collection of Trials for Adultery: Or General History of Modern Gallantry and Divorces*. London, 1799.
Clark, Anna. *The Struggle for the Breeches: Gender and the Making of the British Working Class*. London: Rivers Oram Press, 1995.
Cornish, W. R., and G. de N. Clark. *Law and Society in England 1750–1950*. London: Sweet & Maxwell, 1989.
'The Counsellor's Plea for the Divorce of Sir G. D. and Mrs. F.' London, 1715.
Crim. Con. Actions and Trials and Other Legal Proceedings Relating to Marriage before the Passing of the Present Divorce Act. London, c. 1890.

Crompton, Louis. 'Jeremy Bentham's Essay on Pederasty.' *Jeremy Bentham Critical Assessments*. Ed. Bikhu Parekh. London: Routledge, 1993. 258–62.

Dabhoiwala, Faramerz. 'Lust and Liberty.' *Past and Present* 207 (2010): 89–179.

de Gouges, Olympe. *The Rights of Woman*. Trans. Val Stevenson. London: Pythia Press, 1989.

Diderot, Denis. *Rameau's Nephew and Other Works*. Trans. Wilfred Jackson. London: Chapman and Hall, 1926.

—. *Rameau's Nephew and D'Alembert's Dream*. Trans. Leonard Tancock. Harmondsworth: Penguin Books, 1966.

Dingley, Robert. *Proposals for Establishing a Public Place of Reception for Penitent Prostitutes*. London, 1758.

Dinwiddy, John. *Bentham*. Oxford: Oxford University Press, 1989.

Dippel, Horst. 'Blackstone in Germany.' *Blackstone and His Commentaries*. Ed. Wilfrid Prest. Oxford: Hart Publishing, 2009. 199–214.

Doggett, Maeve E. *Marriage, Wife-Beating and the Law in Victorian England*. London: George Weidenfeld and Nicolson, 1992.

Dolan, Frances. *Dangerous Familiars: Representations of Domestic Crime in England 1550–1700*. Ithaca and London: Cornell University Press, 1994.

—. *Marriage and Violence: The Early Modern Legacy*. Philadelphia: University of Pennsylvania Press, 2008.

Doolittle, Ian. 'Jeremy Bentham and Blackstone's Lectures.' *Bentham Newsletter* 6 (1982) www.ucl.ac.uk/BenthamProject/journal/newsletter/Newsletter 06, accessed 10 January 2009: 23–5.

—. *William Blackstone: A Biography*. Haslemere: Ian Doolittle, 2001.

Eagleton, Terry. *The Rape of Clarissa: Writers, Sexuality and Class Struggle in Samuel Richardson*. Oxford: Basil Blackwell, 1982.

Edmiston, William. *Diderot and the Family*. Saratoga: Anma Libri, 1985.

Emerson, John. 'Did Blackstone Get the Gallic Shrug.' *Blackstone and His Commentaries*. Ed. Wilfrid Prest. Oxford: Hart Publishing, 2009. 185–98.

d'Epinay, Madame. *The Conversations of Emily*. 2 vols. London: J. Marshall and Co., 1787.

Erikson, Amy Louise. *Women and Property in Early Modern England*. London and New York: Routledge, 1993.

Everett, Charles Warren, ed. *Bentham's Comment on the Commentaries*. Oxford: Oxford University Press, 1928.

Fielding, Henry. *Joseph Andrews and Shamela*. Oxford: Oxford University Press, 1993.

Filmer, Robert. *The Necessity of the Absolute Power of All Kings*. London, 1648.

—. *Patriacha*. London, 1680.

Finn, Margot. 'Women, Consumption and Coverture in England, c. 1760–1860.' *The Historical Journal* 39 (1996): 703–22.

Firth, C. H., and R. S. Rait, eds. *Acts and Ordinances of the Interregnum 1642–1660*. 3 vols. London: His Majesty's Stationery Office, 1911.
Fletcher, Anthony. *Gender, Sex, and Subordination in England, 1500–1800*. New Haven, CT: Yale University Press, 1995.
Fletcher, T. H. *Montesquieu and English Politics (1750–1800)*. London: Edward Arnold and Co., 1939.
Foreman, Amanda. *Georgiana Duchess of Devonshire*. London: Harper Collins Publishers, 1998.
Foyster, Elizabeth. 'Male Honour, Social Control and Wife Beating in Late Stuart England.' *Transactions of the Royal Historical Society* 6 (1996): 214–24.
Free Thoughts on Seduction, Adultery and Divorce by a Civilian. London, 1771.
Freeman, Lisa A. 'What's Love Got to Do with Addison's "Cato"?' *Studies in English Literature, 1500–1900* 39 (1999) http://www.jstor.org/stable/1556215, accessed 20 January 2011: 463–82.
Gally, Henry. *Considerations upon Clandestine Marriages*. London, 1750.
Gardner, Jane. *Women in Roman Law and Society*. London: Croom Helm, 1986.
Gardner, Simon. *An Introduction to the Law of Trusts*. Oxford: Oxford University Press, 1990.
Gentleman, pseud. *Man Superior to Woman, or a Vindication of Man's Natural Right of Sovereign Authority over the Woman: Containing a Plain Confutation of the Fallacious Arguments of Sophia, in Her Late Treatise Entitled 'Woman not inferior to man'*. London, 1739.
Gloucester, Edgar C. S. *The First and Second Prayer Books of King Edward the Sixth*. London: J. M. Dent, 1910.
Godwin, William. *Caleb Williams*. Oxford: Oxford University Press, 1970.
—. *Political and Philosophical Writing of William Godwin*. Vol. 3. Ed. Mark Philp. London: Pickering & Chatto, 1993.
Goldberg, Rita. *Sex and Enlightenment: Women in Richardson and Diderot*. Cambridge: Cambridge University Press, 1984.
Gordon, Lyndall. *Mary Wollstonecraft: A New Genus*. London: Little, Brown, 2005.
Gouge, William. *Of Domesticall Duties*. London, 1622.
Gowing, Laura. *Domestic Dangers: Women, Words, and Sex in Early Modern London*. Oxford: Clarendon Press, 1996.
Gregory, Jeremy. 'Homo Religiosus: Masculinity and Religion in the Long Eighteenth Century.' *English Masculinities*. Ed. Tim Hitchcock and Michele Cohen. London: Addison Wesley Longman, 1999. 85–110.
Gregory, John. *A Father's Legacy to His Daughters*. London, 1774.
Griffin, Susan. *The Book of the Courtesans*. London: Pan Macmillan, 2002.
Halevy, Elie. *The Growth of English Radicalism*. Trans. Mary Morris. London: Faber and Faber, 1928.

Helmholz, R. H. *Marriage Litigation in Medieval England*. Cambridge: Cambridge University Press, 1974.

—. *Canon Law and the Law of England*. London: Hambledon Press, 1987.

Hesiod. *Theogony and Works and Days*. Oxford: Oxford University Press, 1988.

Hickman, Katie. *Courtesans*. London: Harper Perennial, 2004.

Hill, Bridget. *Women Alone: Spinsters in England 1660–1850*. New Haven and London: Yale University Press, 2001.

Hines, Jeremy E. 'Jeremy Bentham and the Genesis of Neo-Malthusianism.' *Economic History* 3 (1936): 267–76.

A History of Some of the Penitents in the Magdelen-House, as Supposed to be Related by Themselves. London, 1760.

Hitchcock, Tim. '"Unlawfully begotten on her body": Illegitimacy and the Parish Poor in St. Luke's Chelsea.' *Chronicling Poverty: The Voices and Strategies of the English Poor, 1640–1840*. Ed. Tim Hitchcock, Pamela Sharpe and Peter King. Basingstoke: MacMillan Press, 1997. 70–86.

Hitchcock, Tim, and Michele Cohen. 'Introduction.' *English Masculinities 1660–1800*. London: Longman, 1999. 1–22.

Hobbes, Thomas. *Leviathan*. Ed. John Plamenatz, first published 1651. London: Collins, 1962.

Hoeflich, Michael. 'American Blackstones.' *Blackstone and His Commentaries*. Ed. Wilfrid Prest. Oxford: Hart Publishing, 2009. 171–84.

Holcombe, Lee. *Wives and Property: Reform of the Married Women's Property Law in Nineteenth-Century England*. Oxford: Martin Robinson, 1983.

Holdsworth, Sir William. *A History of English Law*. 14 vols. London: Methuen, 1952–.

Holmes, Richard. *Coleridge: Early Visions*. London: Hodder & Stoughton, 1989.

'An Homilie of the State of Matrimonie.' *Certaine Sermons or Homilies*. Facs. 1623. Ed. Mary Ellen Rickey and Thomas B. Stroup. Gainsville: Scholars' Facsimiles and Reprints, 1968. 239–48.

Horstman, Allen. *Victorian Divorce*. London and Sydney: Croom Helm, 1985.

Houlbrooke, R. A. *The English Family 1450–1700*. London: Longman, 1984.

Hume, David. *Essays Moral and Political*. 2 vols. Edinburgh, 1742.

—. *A Treatise of Human Nature*. Ed. David Fate Norton and Mary J. Norton. Oxford: Oxford University Press, 2000.

Humphreys, James. *Observations on the Actual State of the English Laws of Real Property with the Outlines of a Code*. London: John Murray, 1826.

Hunt, Lynn Avery. *The Family Romance of the French Revolution*. London: Routledge, 1992.

Hunt, Margaret. 'Wives and Marital "Rights" in the Court of Exchequer in the Early Eighteenth Century.' *Londinopolis*. Ed. Paul Griffiths and Mark S. J. Jenner. Manchester: Manchester University Press, 2000. 107–29.

Hunter, Ian. *Rival Enlightenments: Civil and Metaphysical Philosophy in Early Modern Germany*. Cambridge: Cambridge University Press, 2001.

'Husband and Wife: Criminal Conversation: Right of Wife to Sue.' *Harvard Law Review* 32 (1919): 576.

Ingram, Martin. *Church Courts, Sex and Marriage in England, 1570–1640*. Cambridge: Cambridge University Press, 1987.

—. 'Reformation of Manners in Early Modern England.' *The Experience of Authority in Early Modern England*. Ed. P. Griffiths, A. Fox and S. Hindle. Basingstoke: Macmillan, 1996. 47–88.

—. 'Judicial Folklore in England Illustrated by Rough Music.' *Communities and Courts in Britain 1150–1900*. Ed. Christopher Brooks and Michael Lobban. London: Hambledon Press, 1997. 61–82.

Isenberg, Nancy. *Fallen Founder: The Life of Aaron Burr*. New York: Viking, 2007.

Israel, Jonathan I. *Radical Enlightenment: Philosophy and the Making of Modernity 1650–1750*. Oxford: Oxford University Press, 2001.

Jackson, Mark. *New-Born Child Murder, Women, Illegitimacy and the Courts in Eighteenth Century England*. Manchester: Manchester University Press, 1996.

Jones, Gareth. *The Sovereignty of the Law*. Toronto: University of Toronto Press, 1973.

Jordan, Elaine. 'Criminal Conversation: Mary Wollstonecraft's *The Wrongs of Woman*.' *Women's Writing* 4 (2) (1997): 221–34.

Keane, John. *Tom Paine: A Political Life*. London: Bloomsbury, 1995.

Kelly, Henry Asgar. '"Rule of Thumb" and the Folklaw of the Husband's Stick.' *Journal of Legal Education* 44 (1994): 341–65.

Kelly, P. J. 'Utilitarianism and Distributive Justice: The Civil Law and the Foundations of Bentham's Economic Thought.' *Utilitas: A Journal of Utilitarian Studies* (1989): 62–81.

—. *Utilitarianism and Distributive Justice: Jeremy Bentham and the Civil Law*. Oxford: Clarendon Press, 1990.

Kent, Joan. 'Attitudes of Members of the House of Commons to Regulation of Personal Conduct.' *University of London Bulletin of the Institute of Historical Research* 46 (1973): 41–71.

Keymer, Thomas. 'Wollstonecraft and Milton on Divorce.' *Notes and Queries* 17 (2010): 563–5.

Kra, Pauline. 'Montesquieu and Women.' *French Women in the Age of Enlightenment*. Ed. Samia I. Spencer. Bloomington: Indiana University Press, 1984. 272–84.

Kugler, Anne. 'Constructing Wifely Identity: Prescription and Practice in the Life of Lady Sarah Cowper.' *Journal of British Studies* 40 (2001): 291–323.

Lacey, Nicola. 'Bentham as a Proto-Feminist? or An Ahistorical Fantasy on Anarchical Fallacies.' *Current Legal Problems 1998: Legal Theory at the End of the Millennium*. Ed. Michael Freeman. Oxford: Oxford University Press, 2000. 421–66.

'Lady Strathmore's Claim against Her Husband, Andrew Robinson Stoney Bowes, for Cruelty.' *A New Collection of Trials for Adultery: Or, General History of Modern Gallantry and Divorces*. 2 vols. Vol. 2 dated 1802, author R. Gill. London, 1799. n.p.

Lambarde, William. *Eirenarcha: Or of the Office of the Justices of Peace*. London, 1592.

The Lawes Resolution of Womens Rights: Or, the Lawes Provision for Women. London, 1632.

Leathley, Samuel Arthur. *The History of Marriage and Divorce*. London: John Long, 1916.

Lemmings, David. 'Marriage and the Law in the Eighteenth Century: Lord Hardwicke's Marriage Act of 1753.' *The Historical Journal* 39 (1996): 339–60.

—. 'Blackstone and Law Reform by Education: Preparation for the Bar and Lawyerly Culture in Eighteenth Century England.' *Law and History Review* 16 (1998): 211–55.

Lester, V. Markham. *Victorian Insolvency, Bankruptcy, Imprisonment for Debt and Company Winding Up*. Oxford: Oxford: Clarendon Press, 1995.

'A Letter from a By-Stander Containing Remarks and Objections to the Bill Now Depending in Parliament.' London, 1753.

Letter to the Public: Containing the Substance of What Hath Been Offered in the Late DEBATES upon the Subject of the Act of Parliament, for the Better Preventing of Clandestine Marriages. London, 1753.

Lieberman, David. *The Province of Legislation Determined Legal Theory in Eighteenth Century Britain*. Cambridge: Cambridge University Press, 1989.

Lloyd, Sarah. 'Amour in the Shrubbery: Reading the Detail of English Adultery Trial Publications of the 1780s.' *Eighteenth-Century Studies* 4 (2006): 421–42.

Lobban, Michael. *The English Common Law and English Jurisprudence 1760–1850*. Oxford: Clarendon Press, 1991.

Locke, John. *Two Treatises of Government*. New York: Cambridge University Press, 1960.

—. *Works*. Facs. London, 1794. 9 vols. London: Routledge/Thoemmes Press, 1997.

Lockmiller, David. *Sir William Blackstone*. Chapel Hill: University of North Carolina Press, 1938.

Lowe, Nigel, and Gillian Douglas. *Bromley's Family Law*. 10th ed. Oxford: Oxford University Press, 2007.

McCabe, Richard. *Incest, Drama and Nature's Law 1550–1700*. Cambridge: Cambridge University Press, 1993.

MacCulloch, Diarmaid. *Thomas Cranmer: A Life*. New Haven: Yale University Press, 1996.

Macfarlane, Alan. *Marriage and Love in England: Modes of Reproduction 1300–1840*. Oxford: Basil Blackwell, 1986.

McGregor, O. R. *Divorce in England*. London: William Heinemann, 1957.

McLaughlin, Blandine L. 'Diderot and Women.' *French Women and the Age of Enlightenment*. Ed. Samia I. Spencer. Bloomington: Indiana University Press, 1984.

Macqueen, John. *A Practical Treatise on the Appellate Jurisdiction of the House of Lords and Privy Council Together with the Practice on Parliamentary Divorce*. London: A. Maxwell & Son, 1842.

Mahood, Linda. *Prostitution in the Nineteenth Century*. London: Routledge, 1990.

Mainardi, Patricia. *Husbands, Wives, and Lovers*. New Haven and London: Yale University Press, 2003.

Malueg, Sarah Ellen Precious. 'Women and the Encyclopedie.' *French Women and the Age of Enlightenment*. Ed. Samia I. Spencer. Bloomington: Indiana University Press, 1984. 259–69.

Mill, John Stuart. *Autobiography*. Oxford: Oxford University Press, 1924.

Mill, John Stuart, and Harriet Taylor Mill. *Essays on Sexual Equality*. Ed. A. S. Rossi. Chicago: University of Chicago Press, 1970.

Mill, John Stuart, Harriet Taylor Mill and Helen Taylor. *Sexual Equality: Writings by John Stuart Mill, Harriet Taylor Mill, and Helen Taylor*. Ed. Ann P. Robson and John M. Robson. Toronto: University of Toronto Press, 1994.

Milton, John. *The Doctrine and Discipline of Divorce: In Two Books: Also the Judgement of Martin Bucer; Tetrachordon; and an Abridgement of Colasterion*. London: Sherwood, Neely, & Jones, 1820.

Montesquieu. *The Persian Letters*. First pub. 1721. Indianapolis: Bobbs-Merrill Company, 1964.

—. *The Spirit of the Laws*. Ed. Anne M. Cohler, Basia C. Miller and Harold S. Stone. Cambridge: Cambridge University Press, 1989.

Moore, A. *The Annals of Gallantry: Or, The Conjugal monitor: Being a Collection of Curious and Important Trials for Divorces, and Actions of Crim. Con. during the Present Reign*. 3 vols. London, 1814.

More, Hannah. *Strictures on the Modern System of Female Education*. London: Thomas Tegg and Son, 1834.

A New Collection of Trials for Adultery: Or, General History of Modern Gallantry and Divorces by a Civilian of Doctor's Commons. 2 vols. London, 1799 and 1802.

Offen, Karen. *European Feminisms 1700–1950, A Political History*. Stanford, CA: Stanford University Press, 2000.

Okin, Susan Moller. *Women in Western Political Thought*. Princeton: Princeton University Press, 1979.

Outhwaite, R. B. *Clandestine Marriage in England, 1500–1850*. London: Hambledon Press, 1995.

—. *The Rise and Fall of the English Ecclesiastical Courts, 1500–1860*. Cambridge: Cambridge University Press, 2006.

Paley. *The Principles of Moral and Political Philosophy*. London, 1785.

Parker, Stephen. *Informal Marriage, Cohabitation and the Law, 1750–1989*. Basingstoke and London: Macmillan Press, 1990.

Pease-Watkin, Catherine. 'Jeremy and Samuel Bentham – The Private and the Public.' *Journal of Bentham Studies* 5 (2002) www.ucl.ac.uk/Bentham-Project/journal/jnl_2002.htm, accessed 19 May 2008.

Pederson, Frederick. *Marriage Disputes in Medieval England*. London: Hambledon, 2000.

Pennant, Thomas. *Tour in Scotland*. 2nd ed. London, 1790.

Pennington, Lady Sarah. *An Unfortunate Mother's Advice to Her Absent Daughters*. London, 1761.

Pevsner, Nikolaus, and Bridget Cherry. *Herfordshire*. Harmondsworth: Penguin Books, 1977.

Phillips, Roderick. *Putting Asunder: A History of Divorce in Western Society*. Cambridge: Cambridge University Press, 1988.

—. *Untying the Knot: A Short History of Divorce*. Cambridge: Cambridge University Press, 1991.

Phillips, Teresia Constantia. *An Apology for the Conduct of Teresia Constantia Phillips*. London, 1750.

Philogamus. *The Present State of Matrimony: Or the Real Causes of Conjugal Infidelity and Unhappy Marriages*. Facs. London, 1739, series *Marriage, Sex and the Family in England 1660–1800*. Ed. Randolph Trumbach. New York: Garland Publishing, 1985.

Philp, Mark. *Godwin's Political Justice*. London: Duckworth, 1986.

Plato. *The Symposium*. Ed. Robert Baldick, G. A. Jones and Betty Radice. Harmondsworth: Penguin Books, 1951.

Pollock, Sir Frederick, and F. W. Maitland. *The History of English Law before the Reign of Edward 1*. 2 vols. Cambridge: Cambridge University Press, 1968.

Porter, Roy. 'Mixed Feelings: The Enlightenment and Sexuality in Eighteenth Century Britain.' *Sexuality in Eighteenth-Century Britain*. Ed. Paul-Gabriel Boucè. Manchester: Manchester University Press, 1982. 1–27.

—. *Enlightenment: Britain and the Creation of the Modern World*. London: Penguin Books, 2000.

Postema, Gerald J. *Bentham and the Common Law Tradition*. Oxford: Oxford University Press, 1986.

—. ed. *Bentham: Moral, Political and Legal Philosophy*. 2 vols. Aldershot: Ashgate, 2002.

Prest, Wilfred. 'Sir William Blackstone 1723–1780.' *Oxford Dictionary of National Biog raphy*. Ed. H. C. G. Matthew and Brian Harrison. Oxford: Oxford University Press, 2009. http://0-www.oxforddnb.com.catalogue.ulrls.lon.ac.uk/view/article/2536, accessed 28 January 2011.

Prest, Wilfrid. *William Blackstone: Law and Letters in the Eighteenth Century*. Oxford: Oxford University Press, 2008.

Price, A. W. *Love and Friendship in Plato and Aristotle*. Oxford: Clarendon Press, 1989.

Probert, Rebecca. 'The Judicial Interpretation of Lord Hardwicke's Act 1753.' *The Journal of Legal History* 23 (2002): 129–51.

—. 'Sutton v Mishcon de Reya and Gawar & co. – Cohabitation Contracts and Swedish Sex Slaves.' *Family Law Quarterly* 16 (2004): 453–64.

—. 'The Impact of the Marriage Act of 1753: Was it Really "A Most Cruel Law for the Fair Sex"?' *Eighteenth Century Studies* 38 (2005): 247–62.

—. *Marriage Law and Practice in the Long Eighteenth Century: A Reassessment*. Cambridge: Cambridge University Press, 2009.

Pufendorf, Samuel. *The Political Writings*. Ed. Craig L. Carr, trans. Michael J. Seidler. Oxford: Oxford University Press, 1994.

Ram, James. *Observations on the Natural Right of a Father to the Custody of His Children, and to Direct Their Education, His Forfeiture of His Right and the Jurisdiction of the Court of Chancery to Control It*. London: Maxwell, 1928.

Richardson, Samuel. *Pamela, or Virtue Rewarded*. London, 1740.

—. *Clarissa, or, the History of a Young Lady*. London: Penguin Books, 1985.

Rogers, Adrienne. 'Women and the Law.' *French Women in the Age of Enlightenment*. Ed. Samia I. Spencer. Bloomington: Indiana University Press, 1984. 33–48.

Rosen, Frederick. 'Jeremy Bentham, 1748–1832.' *Oxford Dictionary of National Biography*. Ed. H. C. G. Matthew and Brian Harrison. Oxford: Oxford University Press, 2007. http://0-www.oxforddnb.com.catalogue.ulrls.lon.ac.uk/view/article/2153, accessed 28 January 2011.

Rousseau, Jean-Jacques. *Discourse on Inequality*. Trans. Franklin Philip. Oxford: Oxford University Press, 1994.

—. *Emile or Treatise on Education*. Trans. William H. Payne. Amherst: Prometheus Books, 2003.

—. *Julie or the New Heloise*. Trans. Philip Stewart and Jean Vache. Hanover: University Press of New England, 1997.

Rubenhold, Hallie. *Lady Worsley's Whim: An Eighteenth-Century Tale of Sex, Scandal and Divorce*. London: Chatto and Windus, 2008.

Ryan, Alan. *Property and Political Theory*. Oxford: Basil Blackwell, 1984.

Salmon, T. *A Critical Essay Concerning Marriage*. First published anonymously by 'A Gentleman'. London, 1724.

Savage, Gail. 'Erotic Stories and Public Decency: Newspaper Reporting of Divorce Proceedings in England.' *The Historical Journal* 41 (1998): 511–28.

Schofield, Philip. 'Jeremy Bentham, the Principle of Utility, and Legal Positivism.' *Current Legal Problems* 56 (2003): 1–39.

Semple, Janet. *Bentham's Prison: A Study of the Panopticon Penitentiary*. Oxford: Clarendon Press, 1993.

Shanley, Mary Lyndon. *Feminism, Marriage, and the Law in Victorian England, 1850–1895*. Princeton: Princeton University Press, 1989.

Sheehan, Michael. *Marriage, Family and Law in Medieval Europe: Collected Studies*. Toronto: University of Toronto Press, 1996.

Shoemaker, Robert B. *Gender in English Society, 1650–1850: The Emergence of Separate Spheres?* London: Longman, 1998.

—. *The London Mob: Violence and Disorder in Eighteenth Century England*. London: Hambledon and London, 2004.

Sibbit, Adam. *Thoughts on the frequency of Divorces in Modern Times*. London, 1800.

Smith, Adam. *The Theory of Moral Sentiments*. First published 1759, transcribed at www.econlib.org/Library/Smith/smMS1.html. Edinburgh and London, 1790.

Sokol, B. J., and Mary Sokol. *Shakespeare, Law and Marriage*. Cambridge: Cambridge University Press, 2003.

Sokol, Mary. 'Jeremy Bentham and the Real Property Commission of 1828.' *Utilitas: A Journal of Utilitarian Studies* 4 (1992): 225–45.

—. 'Blackstone and Bentham on the Law of Marriage.' *Blackstone and His Commentaries*. Ed. Wilfrid Prest. Oxford and Portland, OR: Hart Publishing, 2009. 91–110.

Sophia. *Woman Not Inferior to Man*. London, 1739.

Spencer, Samia I., ed. *French Women and the Age of Enlightenment*. Bloomington: Indiana University Press, 1984.

Spring, Eileen. *Law, Land, & Family: Aristocratic Inheritance in England, 1300 to 1800*. Chapel Hill: University of North Carolina Press, 1993.

Staves, Susan. *Married Women's Separate Property in England, 1660–1833*. Cambridge, MA: Harvard University Press, 1990.

Stone, Lawrence. *The Family, Sex and Marriage in England 1500–1800*. Harmondsworth: Penguin Books, 1988.

—. *Road to Divorce: England 1530–1987*. Oxford: Oxford University Press, 1990.

—. *Uncertain Unions Marriage in England 1660–1753*. Oxford: Oxford University Press, 1992.

—. *Broken Lives*. Oxford: Oxford University Press, 1993.

Stretton, Tim. 'Women, Custom and Equity in the Court of Requests.' *Women, Crime and the Courts in Early Modern England*. Ed. Jenny Kermode and Garthine Walker. London: UCL Press, 1994. 170–89.

—. *Women Waging War in Elizabethan England*. Cambridge: Cambridge University Press, 1998.

—. 'Widows at Law in Tudor and Stuart England.' *Widowhood in Medieval and Early Modern Europe*. Ed. Lydan Warner and Sandra Cavello. Harlow: Longman, 1999. 193–208.

—. 'Women, Property and Law.' *Early Modern Women's Writing*. Ed. Anita Pacheo. Oxford: Blackwell, 2002. 40–57.
—. 'Coverture and Unity of Person in Blackstone's Commentaries.' *Blackstone and His Commentaries: Biography, Law, History*. Ed. Wilfrid Prest. Oxford and Portland: Hart Publishing, 2009. 111–27.
Sugden, E. *A Letter to James Humphreys Esq., on His Repeal the Law of Real Property and Substitute a New Code*. London: J. and W. T. Clarke, 1826.
Sullivan, Kathleen S. *Constitutional Context*. Baltimore: Johns Hopkins University Press, 2007.
Tadmor, Naomi. *Family and Friends in Eighteenth-Century England*. Cambridge: Cambridge University Press, 2001.
Tague, Ingrid H. 'Love, Honor, and Obedience: Fashionable Women and the Discourse of Marriage in the Early Eighteenth Century.' *Journal of British Studies* 40 (2001): 76–106.
Thomas, Keith. 'The Double Standard.' *Journal of the History of Ideas* 20 (1959): 195–216.
—. *Man and the Natural World: Changing Attitudes in England 1500–1800*. London: Allen Lane, 1983.
Thompson, Lynda M. *The 'Scandalous Memorists' Constantia Philips, Laetitia Pilkington and the Shame of 'publick fame'*. Manchester: Manchester University Press, 2000.
Todd, Janet. *Mary Wollstonecraft: A Revolutionary Life*. London: Weidenfeld and Nicolson, 2000.
—. *Death and the Maidens: Fanny Wollstonecraft and the Shelley Circle*. London: Profile Books, 2007.
Tosh, John. 'The Old Adam and the New Man: Emerging Themes in the History of English Masculinities, 1750–1850.' *English Masculinities 1660–1800*. Ed. Tim Hitchcock and Michele Cohen. London: Addison Wesley Longman Limited, 1999. 217–38.
Traer, James F. *Marriage and the Family in Eighteenth-Century France*. Ithaca: Cornell University Press, 1980.
A Treatise of Feme Coverts: Or, the Lady's Law. London, 1732.
Treggiari, Susan. *Roman Marriage*. Oxford: Oxford University Press, 1991.
Truelove, Francis, pseud. *The Comforts of Matrimony; Exemplified in the Memorable Case and Trial, Lately Had upon an Action Brought by Theo-s [Theophilus] C-r [Cibber], against S-r [Sloper], Esq., for Criminal Conversation with the Plaintiff's Wife*. 6th ed. London, 1739.
Trumbach, Randolph, ed. *Marriage, Sex and the Family in England 1660–1800*. New York: Garland Publishing, 1984.

Twining, William. *Theories of Evidence: Bentham and Wigmore*. London: Weidenfeld and Nicolson, 1985.
Vickery, Amanda. *The Gentleman's Daughter: Women's Lives in Georgian England*. New Haven: Yale University Press, 1998.
Virgil. *The Aeneid*. Trans. David West. London: Penguin Books, 1991.
Voltaire. *Candide and Other Stories*. Trans. Roger Pearson. Oxford: Oxford University Press, 2008.
Waddams, S. M. 'English Matrimonial Law on the Eve of Reform 1828–57.' *The Journal of Legal History* 21 (2000): 54–82.
Wagner, Gillian. *Thomas Coram, Gent*. Woodbridge: Boydell Press, 2004.
Wagner, Peter. 'The Pornographer in the Courtroom.' *Sexuality in Eighteenth-Century Britain*. Ed. Paul-Gabriel Boucè. Manchester: Manchester University Press, 1982. 120–40.
Warden, Lewis C. *The Life of Blackstone*. Charlottesville: Michie Company, 1938.
Warnock, Mary, ed. *Mary Wollstonecraft, A Vindication of the Rights of Women, and John Stuart Mill, The Subjection of Women*. London: J. M. Dent, Everyman's Library, 1985.
Watson, Alan. *The Making of the Civil Law*. Cambridge, MA: Harvard University Press, 1981.
Whately, William. *Directions for Married Persons*. First published 1619. Bristol, 1768.
Wilkinson, Helen. *The Proposal: Giving Marriage Back to the People*. London: Demos, 1997. *Demos Project Report*.
Williford, Miriam. 'Bentham on the Rights of Women.' *Journal of the History of Ideas* 36 (1975): 167–76.
Wilmot, John Eardley. *An Abridgement of Blackstone . . . for the Use and Advancement of Female Education*. London, 1822.
Wolfe, Jonathan. *An Introduction to Political Philosophy*. Oxford: Oxford University Press, 1996.
Wolfram, Sybil. 'Divorce in England 1700–1857.' *Oxford Journal of Legal Studies* 5 (1985): 155–86.
Wollstonecraft, Mary. *A Vindication of the Rights of Woman*. First published 1792. London: J. M. Dent, 1985.
—. *The Collected Letters*. Ed. Janet Todd. London: Penguin Books, 2004.
Wolseley, Sir Charles. *The Case of Divorce and Re-Marriage Thereupon Discussed*. London, 1673.
Wrightson, Keith. *English Society, 1580–1680*. New Brunswick, NJ: Rutgers University Press, 1982.
The Young Lady's Pocket Library, or Parental Monitor. London, 1790.

INDEX

www.ingramcontent.com/pod-product-compliance
Ingram Content Group UK Ltd.
Pitfield, Milton Keynes, MK11 3LW, UK
UKHW020817290926
15470UKWH00003B/1204

9 781441 132932